How to Select & Use
OUTDOOR EQUIPMENT

Barclay Kruse & The REI Staff

Executive Editor: Rick Bailey
Editorial Director: Theodore DiSante
Art Director: Don Burton
Book Design: Kathleen Koopman

NOTICE: The information contained in this book is true and complete to the best of our knowledge. All recommendations are made without any guarantees on the part of the authors or HPBooks. The authors and HPBooks disclaim all liability incurred in connection with the use of this information.

Published by HPBooks, P.O. Box 5367, Tucson, AZ 85703   602/888-2150
ISBN: O-89586-210-7   Library of Congress Catalog No. 82-84141
©1983 Fisher Publishing, Inc. Printed in USA

Introduction

This book is unique in a couple of ways. First, it covers a complete range of outdoor equipment. You'll find chapters on clothing, footwear, sleeping bags, tents, food and cooking equipment, snowshoes and cross-country skis, mountaineering gear, bicycles, canoes and kayaks, and a variety of outdoor accessories, such as compasses, maps and binoculars.

This approach makes sense because most outdoor enthusiasts participate in more than one activity. And, much of the available equipment is suited for use in different sports. For example, the summer hiker may turn to cross-country skiing or snowshoeing in the winter. Mountaineers may also enjoy an occasional canoe trip. Whenever possible, consider the practicality and economics of buying equipment that you can use in several activities.

Second, this book isn't the product of one mind. It's based on the accumulated knowledge and experience of the staff of Recreational Equipment, Inc. (REI). Too often, outdoor books reflect the prejudice and limited experience of a single author. By pooling the knowledge of REI's buyers, sales staff and safety experts, we've been able to cover the field more completely than ever before.

WHY THIS BOOK IS USEFUL

More outdoor equipment is available now than ever. Although this means that you can find equipment for nearly any purpose, the wide selection can be bewildering. There are hundreds of styles and brands of coats, packs, tents and shoes, for example. Finding the right one for your needs takes knowledge and experience.

This book supplies both. We give you the necessary facts to ask the right questions, make telling comparisons, and finally, make the most intelligent purchases.

For the most part, we're impartial. After all, everyone has different requirements, and what's best for one person might not work for another. No two people have the same intended uses, esthetic preferences or budgets. Our main goal is to help you make the best buys for *your* specific needs.

But in a few cases, opinions are necessary. We point out certain designs or construction methods that are substandard. And we'll tell you when a perfectly good piece of equipment would be dangerous when used in the wrong situation. Our well-chosen opinions help you steer clear of misguided buys.

The equipment you purchase is important because it can affect the quality of your outdoor experience. Used properly, a well-designed tent lets you sleep peacefully through a rainy night. The alternative, a wet sleep, does little to enhance your outdoor enjoyment. Clothing and boots should be chosen carefully to fit well and be able to meet the conditions you expect to face.

If you want to save money, this book will help. In fact, if we can guide you to just one intelligent buying decision, the book will pay for itself.

Though it can be a mistake to go over budget, it can be equally disastrous to buy inexpensive, poorly constructed equipment. If boots wear out too soon, you'll have to buy another pair. And, in some cases, your safety is jeopardized by improper equipment. Most outdoor hazards revolve around the weather. So when it comes to buying clothing, sleeping bags and tents—all items that can protect you from cold and wet conditions—choose equipment that will stand up to the *worst* weather you'll face. Cutting corners on quality costs more in the long run.

THE CHALLENGE OF THE 1980s

Outdoor enthusiasts of the 1980s face unique challenges. Nearly every outdoor activity, from mountaineering to family camping, is enjoyed by more people than it was a decade ago. This has spawned interest in *low-impact* outdoor use. People recognize that resources are finite. Therefore, our challenge is to protect the environment, leaving it as close to its natural state as possible. This helps ensure its survival for future generations.

Much of today's equipment is designed with this ethic in mind. Indeed, thanks to modern technology, protecting the environment is much easier than it used to be. In an effort to protect scarce, slow-growing vegetation, government regulations require cooking with stoves. But, thanks to small, light backpacking stoves and convenient freeze-dried food, it's easier than ever before.

With this book, you have the information to make the best all-around purchasing decisions. The outdoor world has much to offer. Properly selected equipment helps you enjoy the outdoors and protect it so others may enjoy it too.

Outdoor Clothing

Outdoor clothing can be used in many activities. For example, wool knickers provide warmth and freedom of movement for hikers, climbers and cross-country skiers.

All outdoor activities—whether bird watching, canoeing, cycling or hiking—require appropriate clothing. Therefore, it's important to decide exactly what activities your clothing is for. A garment's design and materials are important.

In this chapter we discuss the different fabrics used in outdoor clothing. Many of the fabrics are also used in equipment discussed in subsequent chapters. You'll learn about the concept called *layering,* and how to select clothing for each layer. It's important to understand both the makeup and proper use of clothing. When you make the right selection, the clothing will last a long time and do its job well.

Any time you go shopping for outdoor equipment it helps to ask yourself a few questions to clarify exactly what your needs are. Here are some suggestions to help you buy the right kind of clothing:

1) What do you want the clothing to do? Keep you dry? Absorb or wick away perspiration? Protect you from the sun? Protect against abrasions? Keep you warm? These are just a few of the things you may want your clothing to do. Of course, some clothing can fulfill more than one function. It's always easier to find a good buy if you know exactly what you want clothing to do.

2) In what kind of activity are you going to be using the clothing? A vigorous one such as hiking or cross-country skiing? Or a more passive one like watching an outdoor sporting event or walking around the city in the winter?

3) Does your clothing need specific features such as extra pockets or zippers? Do you need special sizing?

4) How much money are you willing to spend?

Three factors determine the best function for an item of outdoor clothing—the materials used, its design and the quality of workmanship. We discuss what to look for in each of these areas.

Fabrics

All fabrics begin with a yarn that's woven or knitted into cloth. The six materials used most for outdoor fabrics are wool, cotton, silk, nylon, polyester and polypropylene. Wool, cotton and silk are natural fibers; the others are man-made.

YARN

Yarn is made by either *spinning* or *throwing*. Spinning is the process that converts short fibers into a long, continuous one. Wool and cotton are two examples of spun fibers. Throwing is used with fibers that naturally have a long, continuous fiber, such as silk and man-made fibers. The fibers are twisted together to make a yarn of the required thickness.

The weight of the yarn is specified by a term called *denier*—the weight in grams of a single strand of yarn 9000 meters long. Fabric made from a high-denier yarn will usually be stronger and more resistant to abrasion than fabric made from thinner yarn. Small-denier yarn can be more tightly woven, and it usually has a smoother finish.

WEAVING AND KNITTING

Weaving interlaces two sets of yarn, placed at right angles to each other. The two parts of a woven fabric are called the *warp* and *fill.* Warp consists of the parallel strands held taut on the loom. Fill is the yarn woven between warp strands. Parkas, pants and shirts are examples of clothing made from woven fabrics.

Thread count is a measure of the number of strands of yarn per inch. It's a commonly used measure representing the tightness of a weave. Thread count is represented by two numbers—the number of threads in the warp and the number in the fill—for example, 160x90. Higher numbers indicate a tighter weave.

Knitting is a different process, using only one strand of yarn. Each row of yarn is looped through an adjacent row. Sweaters, hats, mittens, socks and underwear are examples of

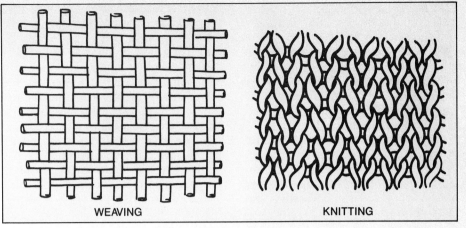

Clothing is either woven or knitted. Weaving interlaces two sets of yarn placed at right angles to each other. In knitted clothing, each row of yarn is knitted through an adjacent row.

knitted clothing. There are variations, too, in the tightness of knitted fabrics. A tightly knitted fabric will be more wind- and abrasion-resistant.

WOOL

No fabric is more closely associated with the outdoor world than wool. Traditionally, its name is synonymous with cold weather and rugged conditions, a reputation well-deserved. Although many man-made fabrics are now found in outdoor clothing, wool is still among the most versatile and durable fabrics you can buy.

Wool fibers have a natural *crimp,* or bend, that produces bulk without additional weight, thus trapping a great amount of air between fibers. Wool won't lose its crimp when wet, and it can absorb as much as 30% of its own weight in water without feeling damp to your touch.

Unless otherwise specified, wool comes from the fleece of sheep. Wool from other animals usually goes by another name. For example, angora is made from rabbit or goat hair. Alpaca is from the South American llama.

Wool fabric is available in a wide range of weights. Catalogs and retailers usually classify wool fabric by its weight in ounces per square yard.

Worsted And Woolen Yarn—Two different kinds of fabric are made from wool—*worsteds* and *woolens.* The difference stems from the yarn used to make the fabric. Worsted yarns are combed and brushed to remove short fibers while the remaining long fibers are arranged in a parallel fashion. This gives worsted yarns a nearly uniform diameter. They are usually used in

woven fabrics and lightweight sweaters. Worsted fabrics can be tightly woven, and as a result, are wind- and abrasion-resistant.

Woolen yarns aren't combed and brushed to the same extent as worsteds, so they are bulkier and less uniform. Woolen yarn is often knitted into sweaters, mittens and hats. Because it is usually bulky, woolen clothing is very warm.

Wool/Nylon Blends—Wool yarns are often blended with nylon threads to produce a stronger, less-expensive fabric. The garment's label should tell you whether it is 100% wool or a blend of wool and nylon. The most common wool/nylon blend is 85% wool/15% nylon.

Virgin vs. Reprocessed Wool—Virgin wool is yarn that has never been used before. Reprocessed wool is recycled from waste cuttings of wool that has already been spun and woven into fabrics.

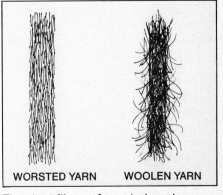

WORSTED YARN   WOOLEN YARN

The short fibers of worsted wool yarn are removed. This isn't done to woolen yarns, so they're bulkier and less uniform.

COTTON

Cotton fibers are the protective covering of the seeds of the cotton plant. The fibers are spun and woven into fabric. Cotton fabric is lightweight, comfortable and relatively inexpensive, but not as durable as either wool or man-made fibers such as nylon or polyester.

Cotton readily absorbs moisture. Depending on your situation, this can be either a blessing or a curse. Cotton T-shirts are popular in warm weather because they absorb perspiration and then allow it to evaporate, cooling your body. But if cotton gets wet in cold weather, it loses almost all of its insulating ability. This can lead to a dangerous lowering of your body temperature—a condition called *hypothermia*.

Cotton Blends—Like wool, cotton is frequently blended with other fibers. The most common combination is 65/35 cloth, an intimate blend of 65% polyester and 35% cotton. *Intimate* means that the two fibers are spun together into a single strand of yarn, the polyester for strength and the cotton for comfort. The combination yarn is spun into cloths of varying thread counts.

60/40 cloth is a cotton/nylon blend with a different construction method. It's not an intimate blend. Instead, nylon yarn (60%) is used as the warp, and cotton (40%) is used as the fill. In this case, nylon provides strength. When wet, the cotton swells, closing gaps between threads.

SILK

Silk is the thinnest, strongest and most comfortable of all natural fibers. It is frequently used in socks, glove liners, underwear and hats.

Silk fibers are *trilobal*—meaning three-sided—a configuration that gives it a distinctive sheen. It's also slippery, making it useful in socks. Silk inner socks help the sock layers slide against each other a bit, protecting your feet from direct rubbing and reducing the incidence of blisters.

Silk is a poor conductor of heat, so it's a good insulator for cold-weather underwear, gloves and hats.

Silk requires special care. You should wash it by hand and protect it from damage caused by perspiration, sunlight and chemicals. Be sure to follow the washing and handling instructions that come with your silk items.

NYLON

Nylon was one of the first man-made fibers to be produced and is still the most widely used fabric in outdoor equipment. It's lightweight, durable and abrasion-resistant. It can be coated easily, which accounts for its wide use in rainwear. In addition, it's relatively inexpensive to make.

Nylon is a petroleum-based product. To make it, solid nylon chips are melted and the liquid forced through microscopic holes, forming filaments. These filaments are then twisted together into yarn. The size and weight of the yarn (denier) are determined by the number and size of filaments.

The yarn is then woven into fabric. The tightness of the weave, measured in thread count (threads per inch), determines how resistant the nylon will be to insulation leakage and wind.

Because nylon threads are slippery, the yarn in woven fabrics has a tendency to slide around and separate, causing the fabric to unravel. Manufacturers overcome this problem by slightly melting edges of the cut fabric. Individual threads melt together and do not unravel.

Nylon deteriorates slowly when exposed to long doses of ultraviolet radiation. This is of little concern in clothing, which usually isn't exposed to the sun continuously. It's more important for tents. These may stand in the sun for long periods of time, over the course of many years, and sometimes at high altitudes, where there's more ultraviolet radiation.

Nylon used in insulated parkas and sleeping bags is sometimes *calendered*.

Taffeta cloth is the most commonly used nylon for outdoor clothing. It's naturally windproof and can be coated to become waterproof.

The nylon is drawn through heated metal rollers that soften and flatten each thread. This is done to close pores so goose down and other insulation can't escape.

There are many different kinds of nylon. Following are some of the most common nylon fabrics used in outdoor clothing and equipment.

Taffeta—This is a general-purpose, lightweight cloth used in many different types of clothing, rainwear and tents. It's shiny and smooth.

Ripstop—The fabric has a special weave pattern that gives it extra tear strength for very little additional weight. It has a heavy thread about every 1/4 inch. These form reinforcing lines that stop rips from spreading. You can recognize ripstop by its characteristic "checkerboard" pattern. It's used in some clothing but finds its greatest application in tents.

Cordura—The yarn of this fabric is spun in a stream of fast-moving air, a process called *air bulking*. This gives the fabric a rough look, desirable in packs, gaiters and soft luggage. Because Cordura fabric is woven from high-denier yarn, it's very rugged and abrasion-resistant.

Taslan—It is air-bulked like Cordura, but the threads used in weaving the Taslan fabric are much thinner. Also, the texturing produced by air bulking is smoother than that of Cordura. Taslan is used in outer garments in which abrasion resistance is needed and a rugged look is desirable.

Antron—This is woven from a special trilobal yarn that produces a distinctive sheen. The fabric is used for fashion outdoor wear such as ski parkas.

The special reinforcing weave of ripstop nylon gives it extra strength with very little extra weight.

Tricot—It is a knitted, not woven, nylon fabric. Tricot is most commonly used as an inner lining on Gore-Tex garments, which are explained on page 16. Because Tricot is knitted, moisture easily passes through gaps between threads. Tricot is also used as a lining in some footwear.

POLYESTER

Polyester is another pretroleum-based, man-made fiber. Unlike nylon, however, polyester won't deteriorate in sunlight. Fibers are smooth and absorb little water, meaning that polyester maintains its shape even when wet.

It's often used for blending with natural fibers to add strength and wrinkle-resistance. Polyester's newest use in outdoor clothing is in *pile* garments, in which fibers are looped and tied onto a heavy base fabric, then cut and brushed to produce an insulating *nap*. Because polyester doesn't absorb water, pile jackets and pants insulate even when wet. They are also amazingly light.

POLYPROPYLENE

This man-made, petroleum-based fabric has long been used in carpets and marine ropes. Now it's becoming increasingly popular in outdoor clothing primarily as an inner layer, such as in underwear and socks.

Polypropylene, the lightest of all textile fibers, doesn't absorb water. When knitted into a porous fabric, it becomes an excellent transport layer that passes perspiration away from your skin.

Polypropylene is easy to maintain. It's machine-washable and, because it absorbs virtually no water, is nearly dry when it comes out of the washing machine. Usually, all you have to do is give it a quick wringing and line dry.

Workmanship & Quality

When buying any item of clothing, it pays to spend some time closely investigating the workmanship that went into it. High-quality construction may cost a little more, but it can pay off in increased durability and versatility.

You don't have to be a sewing expert to evaluate quality. Common sense and good eyes are all you need.

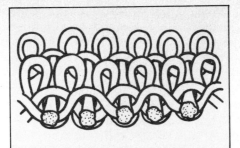

Polyester pile clothing is made by looping and tying polyester fibers into a base fabric, as shown. The loops are then cut and brushed to produce an insulating *nap.*

For example:

1) Buttons should be stitched on with enough sturdy thread to hold through repeated buttonings and unbuttonings.

2) Stress points—such as at pockets corners and the ends of zippers—should be *bar-tacked.* Stitching is run back and forth a few times to reinforce the sewn area and prevent tearing.

3) All seams should have even stitching.

You'll find two kinds of seams in outdoor clothing. The simpler is the *serged* seam, in which the two ends of fabric are stitched and overcast. Much stronger is the *felled* seam, in which the edges of the fabric are overlapped, interlocked and double-stitched through all layers. The felled seam is used on rugged outdoor garments in places that endure a lot of abrasion.

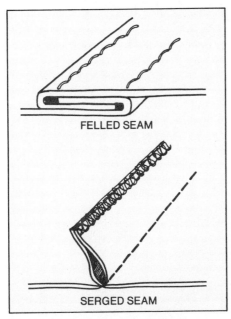

FELLED SEAM

SERGED SEAM

These are the two most common seams in outdoor clothing. Typically, the felled seam is more durable.

Layering

Outdoor clothing does three basic things—transports perspiration away from your skin; keeps you warm; and protects you from wet weather, wind and abrasion. *Layering* is a way to dress that ensures your clothing does all three while giving you maximum comfort and versatility. Understanding layering is simplest when you break outdoor clothing into three categories, each one corresponding to one of the tasks your clothing should accomplish.

The *inner,* or transport layer, lies next to your skin. Clothing such as underwear, long underwear, T-shirts and socks comprise the inner layer. The *secondary,* or middle, layer of clothing is designed to keep you warm and absorb moisture from the inner layer. This category includes shirts, sweaters and pants. The *outer* layer is designed to protect you from the elements. Rain parkas and pants, ponchos, insulated and uninsulated parkas, and gaiters are examples of outer-layer clothing.

LAYERING IN PRACTICE

It's better to wear several thin layers than one heavy one. This greatly increases the versatility of your clothing. If you have two wool shirts, you can decide to wear one, two or none. As conditions change during the day and the temperature rises or falls, you can remove or put on shirts to meet the changing conditions. If all you have is a heavily insulated parka, you would either have it on or off. The first might be too warm, the second too cold.

Here's an example of how layering works in practice: Setting off on a day hike, in the chill of morning, you might wear a T-shirt, a wool shirt and a wool sweater. As the trail becomes steeper and your body warms to the task, you stop for a moment and take off the sweater, putting it in your pack.

Later, as the trail climbs onto a sunny hillside, you first unbutton the wool shirt, and eventually take it off, continuing to hike in a cotton T-shirt.

Reaching the high point of the trail in the early afternoon, you stop for a rest and lunch break. Clouds roll in and a brisk wind picks up. The air is becoming chilly, so you take off your damp cotton T-shirt, replace it with a polypropylene long-underwear top, and put the wool shirt and sweater back on.

Just as you're getting ready to hike back down the trail, it begins to rain. You get out your rain parka. But because you'll be hiking, you know that wearing both a wool shirt and sweater will be too warm. So, you take off the sweater, pack it away, and hike in the wool shirt and rain parka.

In the cooler, cloudier afternoon, you don't want your inner layer of clothing to get soaked with perspiration. But because the open weave of the polypropylene underwear allows your perspiration to pass through to the wool-shirt secondary layer, the inner layer stays dry.

As you can see, with some simple clothing adjustments you can meet a wide variety of conditions. You often don't need to wear all three layers at the same time. Only when it started to rain in the afternoon did you need an outer-layer parka. And, by having several thin layers rather than one heavy one, you were able to manage your body temperature so you didn't get too hot or cold.

Multiple layers also insulate better than a single layer of the same thickness. More dead air is trapped between individual layers than can be trapped by a single layer. In addition, the air is trapped in small, confined areas. Because the air is held still, it can be warmed and become a good insulator.

Layering works for all outdoor activities, from hiking and mountain climbing to canoeing, from cross-country skiing to chopping wood.

The Inner Layer

As mentioned, the inner layer is what you wear next to your skin. The layer's main function is warmth and comfort. Underwear should keep your skin dry. This is best done with clothing that either absorbs perspiration or transports it to the secondary layer. Your choice is determined largely by the outside temperature and your degree of physical activity.

Insulated or long underwear keeps you warm. It does this by trapping a layer of still air between your skin and the secondary layer of clothing. When that air is held still, your body heat warms it.

UNDERWEAR

In warm weather, it's not essential that your skin stay dry. In fact, underwear that's lightly damp from perspiration can provide some pleasant cooling. Of course, when an undershirt or shorts become very wet, they can be uncomfortable, and you'll probably prefer to change into something dry.

In warm weather, it's hard to beat cotton. It absorbs perspiration and is very comfortable. Cotton T-shirts and underwear are staples of warm-weather outdoor activities. They won't chafe or bind, and their breathing ability keeps you from getting too hot and clammy.

Cotton may be a good choice for warm weather, but it's lousy for cold-weather activities. If you stop strenuous activity, even to take a short rest, your perspiration-dampened underwear can quickly drop your body temperature to dangerous levels. Anytime the air temperature is below your body temperature, you lose heat to the surroundings. Because water is an excellent heat conductor, wet clothing accelerates the heat loss.

The most important function of cold-weather underwear is to keep you warm and dry. Underwear can keep you dry by creating a non-absorbent layer of fabric that allows perspiration to pass through to the secondary layer, where it can be absorbed.

Wool Underwear—This is a good choice for active sports. It provides excellent insulation and absorbs up to 33% of its own weight in water before it begins to feel wet.

Dual-Layer Underwear—Most people can wear wool, but some find it unpleasantly itchy. A good alternative is to buy dual-layer underwear made with wool on the outside for warmth, and cotton on the inside, next to the skin, for comfort. Dual-layer underwear is excellent if you won't be perspiring heavily. But if you do, the cotton inner layer gets wet quickly, with all the resulting liabilities of cotton underwear. Dual-layer underwear is therefore most ideal for leisurely activity.

You can increase the versatility of your clothing by wearing several thin layers rather than one or two heavy ones. As weather conditions or your activities change, you can remove or put on shirts, a sweater, coat or hat.

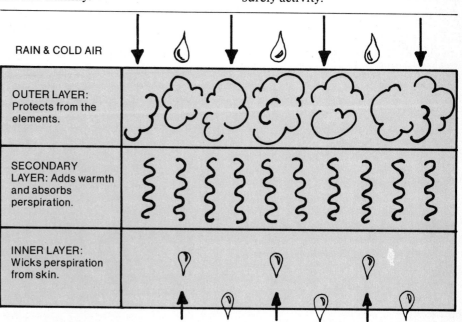

RAIN & COLD AIR

OUTER LAYER: Protects from the elements.

SECONDARY LAYER: Adds warmth and absorbs perspiration.

INNER LAYER: Wicks perspiration from skin.

This diagram shows the function of each clothing layer in a three-part layering system. Remember, depending on the weather and your activity, you might not wear all three layers all the time.

Polypropylene Underwear—Using polypropylene in underwear is a major development. It's a man-made fiber that is very light, stretchy and non-absorbent to water. Because polypropylene underwear has an open weave, it allows perspiration to pass freely through the porous fabric to be absorbed by the secondary layer.

Polypropylene underwear insulates best when worn under another layer of clothing. It is widely used by people participating in strenuous outdoor sports, such as cross-country skiing, hiking and mountaineering. These athletes speak of the ultimate combination—polypropylene underwear to transport perspiration away from the skin, and an outer layer of wool to absorb moisture and provide good insulation.

Wool and polypropylene turtleneck shirts are an ideal inner layer for cold-weather activities.

SOCKS

Socks do two things. They provide insulation to keep your feet warm in cold weather, and they also pad your feet to prevent blisters and soreness. With the wide range of outdoor footwear—from running shoes to hiking and mountaineering boots—it's difficult to tell you exactly which socks work best. Instead, we supply information that applies to all kinds of outdoor sports.

How many pairs of socks should you wear? It largely depends on how rough the activity will be on your feet. Most hikers and mountain climbers wear at least two pairs of socks to absorb some of the rubbing and pounding their feet endure. The socks rub against each other, reducing friction and protecting feet from blisters. For casual and less strenuous activities, one pair of well-chosen socks is usually adequate.

When choosing socks for active sports, make sure they fit *perfectly*. Anytime your socks wrinkle or bunch, you may get blisters. Bunching can also inhibit blood circulation to part of your foot. When buying a second or third pair of socks to go over your inner pair, make sure they are sized slightly bigger to fit well.

To keep your feet properly cushioned, socks should be resilient and retain their original shape. For your feet to be warm, dry and comfortable, perspiration must be able to pass through the first layer, away from your feet.

Everyone seems to have slightly different feet and therefore different sock preferences. You may have to experiment to find out how many pairs of socks to wear, of what type, and in what combination.

Wool Socks—Wool socks are resilient, and the crimped fibers trap a lot of still air. Wool maintains much of its insulating value when it gets wet. Also, perspiration passes through into the outer sock layer or into your boot.

Wool/Nylon Blend Socks—Depending on the quality of the wool used, pure-wool socks may not stand up to abrasion. To avoid the potential problem, most manufacturers make socks of wool/nylon blends. The nylon thread is usually twisted together with the wool yarn.

The most common wool/nylon blend in socks is 85% wool and 15% nylon. These percentages give the improved performance offered by nylon and preserve the great characteristics of wool.

Polypropylene Socks—Polypropylene and *olefin*—which is a type of polypropylene—are non-absorbent fibers most often used in inner or liner socks. The thin inner socks pass perspiration to the outer sock layers. They also reduce friction that can lead to blisters.

Cotton Socks—Cotton is comfortable for warm weather. It's primarily used for running and racket sports. For these, cotton is adequate.

The Secondary Layer

This layer provides added insulation, absorbs perspiration passed through the underwear, and gives some protection from the elements. Shirts, sweaters and pants are the staples of secondary-layer clothing.

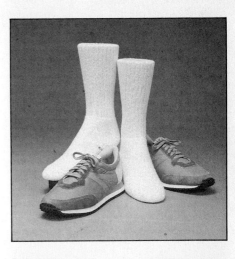

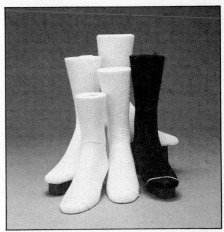

Choose socks according to your intended activity. Cotton socks (top) are very comfortable for warm-weather activities such as running or tennis, or simply for leisure wear. Light wool blend and polypropylene socks (center) work best as liner socks, wicking perspiration away from your feet. Heavier wool and wool-blend socks (bottom) function well as an outer layer, absorbing perspiration and protecting your feet from blisters and bruising shocks.

SHIRTS

Shirts are one of the most valuable parts of an outdoor wardrobe. You can adapt them to either winter or summer, hot weather or cold. Because they are easy to put on and take off, they are practical for all sorts of activities. You can open buttons, roll up sleeves, and adapt them in other ways. When choosing shirts to meet your outdoor needs, consider these factors—warmth, ventilation, sizing and protection.

Outdoor shirts fit best when they are cut large in the armpits and shoulders. This permits a full range of movement and is more comfortable if you'll be carrying a pack. Shirts with long tails are easier to keep tucked in. And, if you need your shirts to provide protection from insects, the sun, or abrasion, be sure you buy long sleeves.

Shirt pockets with flaps, closed with either a button or snap, are very handy. The flap saves you the annoyance of dropping things from your pockets every time you bend over.

Cotton Shirts—These come in a wide variety of styles, adaptable to everything from hot summer weather to the light chill of spring and fall. Only in wet weather and winter cold are cotton shirts inadequate.

Cotton-flannel, chamois and canvas have the widest application to outdoor sports. They are made from heavy, sturdy fabric and provide warmth and durability for mild conditions.

Flannel and chamois are *napped,* meaning that the fabric is brushed to raise a downy finish. This provides extra warmth and comfort. In general, flannel is napped on one side only,

chamois on both. Chamois shirts are usually made from a heavier-weight fabric than flannels.

Canvas shirts are made from an even heavier fabric. It has a tightly twisted yarn and tight weave to give a relatively rugged finish not unlike canvas awnings or sailcloth. Canvas is highly abrasion-resistant—perfect for rugged sports like rock climbing.

Wool Shirts—Cotton shirts have their place in outdoor activities in mild conditions. But if you are going to be facing cold and wet weather, wool shirts are best.

Wool fabric is available in varying weights, so it is easy to find a wool shirt to meet nearly any condition. Shirts made of heavyweight wool fabric may look almost like jackets and, in fact, are frequently called *shirt-jackets.*

Middleweight and lightweight wool shirts are ideal when worn as one of several layers, or by themselves in comfortably cool conditions. The natural crimp in the wool fibers gives wool shirts extra insulating value that can provide insulation when wet.

Some wool shirts are 100% wool; others are blends of wool and nylon, such as 85% wool/15% nylon. Check the shirt's label to find the fabric content.

Wool garments vary greatly in their washing requirements. Some are machine-washable; others must be washed by hand. Washing wool incorrectly can diminish its quality, so be sure to read the label for recommended directions.

SWEATERS

Sweaters are knitted to provide

bulk and excellent insulation. When looking over different sweaters, consider four things—type and weight of yarn used, tightness of knit and design.

Sweater Design—Most important are the collar and sleeves. The most popular collars are turtleneck, crew neck, shawl and V-neck.

Turtlenecks are warmest, with crew, shawl and V-neck collars offering more ventilation around the neck. Choose the collar design that best suits your activity.

Two of the most common sleeve designs are *set-in* and *raglan.* Set-in sleeves are attached to the main body of the sweater at the end of the shoulder. They are recognizable by the seam running along the top of the shoulder. Raglan sleeves are attached to the main body by a slanting seam running from armpit to neck. Raglan sleeves may fit a wider variety of body shapes. But other than these differences, either the raglan or set-in style is satisfactory.

Cotton Sweaters—These are best used for around-town, for casual wear or as a component in layered clothing. They are comfortable and provide some insulation when dry. But cotton sweaters absorb water, and when wet they lose most of their insulating value.

Wool Sweaters—Wool sweaters provide excellent insulation, even when wet. Because wool is so warm, carefully choose your wool sweater with layering in mind. A big bulky sweater will keep you very warm, but for outdoor use, it's usually best to use several lighter layers. Carefully compare the tightness of the knit, too. A tightly

Both flannel (left) and chamois (center) cotton shirts are brushed to raise an insulating nap. They are soft, comfortable and ideal for leisure wear in chilly weather, or as a component in layered clothing. Canvas shirts (right) are made of tightly woven, twisted cotton yarn. They're ideal for rugged outdoor activities.

Base collar selection on comfort, style and the other clothes you'll be wearing. The crew collar (left) works well in cold weather. The V-neck (center) allows more ventilation around your neck. The shawl collar (right) can be buttoned or unbuttoned for easy temperature control. These ragg wool sweaters have a distinctive salt-and-pepper, mottled look. Like many wool sweaters, they are actually a blend of 85% wool and 15% nylon.

knit sweater is more resistant to wind and abrasion and slightly warmer than a loosely woven sweater of the same yarn weight.

You'll see many different kinds of wool sweaters in outdoor catalogs and on clothing racks of outdoor suppliers. Here's a summary of the most common types:

Shetland Wool Sweaters are made from a very fine, soft wool. They are noted for their comfort. Shetland wool is also used in shirts.

Ragg Wool Sweaters have a distinctive "salt-and-pepper" mottled appearance. Originally, ragg wool was made by mixing sheep's wool with goat hair. Now, ragg sweaters are made with natural and dyed wool yarns to give its distinctive color. Ragg wool is also commonly used in hats, gloves and mittens.

Oiled Wool means that the natural lanolin oils of wool have been either left in or put back into the yarn after the wool was first washed. The lanolin helps to repel water, so oiled-wool yarn won't absorb much moisture. This doesn't mean that the sweater

will be waterproof, however, because water can leak through gaps in the knitting. But it does mean that an oiled wool sweater can be easily wrung out and dried, an important feature if you're outdoors a lot in wet climates.

It's important *never* to dry-clean an oiled-wool sweater. It's also best to wash one as infrequently as possible. Everytime it is washed, a little more oil is lost.

Dri-Wool is a trade name of a process that artificially duplicates oiled wool. The yarn is impregnated with a lanolin-type substance before knitting. Like oiled wool, it won't repel heavy rain.

PILE SWEATERS AND JACKETS

Pile fabrics were developed in the 1960s as a substitute for the wool clothing that was used by North Sea fishermen. Since then, pile has become very popular because it is light and maintains loft when wet. In addition, pile garments are ideal for strenuous outdoor activities. The fabric allows excellent ventilation.

Pile fabrics are most often made from polyester. The fibers are crimped into loops that are knitted into a base fabric. The loops are then cut to provide the insulating nap. Because polyester absorbs virtually no water, the fabric won't soak up water and lose its loft. When wet, pile clothing can be wrung out and dried quickly.

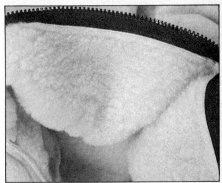

This inside view of a polyester-pile jacket shows the fibers that have been looped, cut and brushed to form the insulating nap.

Pile is not wind- or water-resistant. In rainy, windy conditions, you'll need to wear an outer shell that is water- and windproof.

Over time, the outer surface of pile clothing begins to collect small "polyester balls." This is called *pilling*. It happens because the fibers are so strong that they tend to stretch and clump together, instead of breaking off. Pilling doesn't affect the garment's function, only its looks.

Pile is used in jackets, sweaters (both pullover and cardigan types), pants and vests. All pile garments are machine-washable.

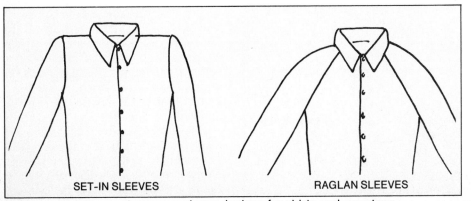

SET-IN SLEEVES   RAGLAN SLEEVES

These are the two most common sleeve designs for shirts and sweaters.

A pile jacket is ideal for cold weather. It's breathable, warm and won't lose loft when wet. In windy weather, though, you should wear a wind shell because the porous weave of pile allows wind to penetrate.

FLEECE GARMENTS

Fleece fabrics are made of 100% polyester fabric brushed on both sides to produce a fuzziness that traps air, much like the loops of traditional pile fabric. Fleece is less porous than pile, which makes it more windproof, but it doesn't ventilate as well as pile. This makes pile a better choice for active sports in which you generate a lot of body heat that needs to escape. Fleece is ideal for less strenuous activities such as rafting or beachcombing on chilly days.

Fleece is used in jackets, sweaters, vests and pants.

PANTS

The right pair of pants offers both warmth and protection from the sun, insects, brush and stinging plants. Any pair of pants will have to endure lots of rubbing and abrasion. To make sure you are purchasing a well-constructed pair, inspect the seams, buttons and zippers, using the guidelines discussed earlier in this chapter.

Because you'll probably want to carry small items in your pockets, make sure that there is enough pocket room.

Cotton Pants—Lightweight cotton pants are adequate for casual wear and hiking along easy trails. If you're going to be walking through brush, scraping against rocks, or doing a lot of kneeling, canvas or denim cotton pants such as jeans are the sturdiest choices. Cotton readily soaks up water and offers little insulation, so cotton pants aren't good for cold, wet conditions.

It's common to see cotton/polyester blends used in pants designed for active sports, such as hiking and rock climbing. Also, you'll find some so-called climbing pants with double knees and seat. Even if you're not a rock climber, such pants are great for rugged activities.

Wool Pants—These are recommended anytime you may face cold, wet weather. Wool is also effective for winter outings because snow brushes off and doesn't soak into the fabric.

Just as with shirts, you'll find wool pants in different weights. Heavyweight fabric is best in cold conditions. Lightweight wool pants are more versatile. You can use them for hiking in the spring and fall, in the occasional chilly weather of mountain summers, and in combination with long underwear for cold, wet weather.

Wool pants—especially those made with heavyweight fabrics—are heavier than cotton pants. Make sure you have a good-fitting belt or suspenders. Some hikers find suspenders more comfortable than belts when they are carrying a pack.

KNICKERS

Long pant legs can get in the way in mountain climbing, skiing and other active sports. Knicker legs, however, stop just below the knee. Because they provide increased freedom of movement, knickers are preferred by many hikers, climbers and cross-country skiers.

In addition, knickers are versatile. On hot days you can wear them with short socks, with leg closures left open. Some hikers will even roll up their knickers and push down their socks. In cold weather, the heavy, long wool socks normally used with knickers will keep you very warm.

Cotton-corduroy knickers are best in mild weather. Wool works best in cold, wet weather, and anytime in the winter.

Knickers must fit properly to work well. The bottom should be just below the knee and be cut full enough to allow complete movement when you bend your leg.

Most knickers have adjustable Velcro closures at the cuff. These let you open the cuff for ventilation or close it for warmth.

SHORTS

Shorts are usually made from warm-weather fabrics—lightweight cotton, denim, canvas and cotton/polyester blends—because the objective is to keep cool. Many summer hikers carry a pair in their packs in readiness for warm temperatures. But don't rely on shorts alone. You should also have a pair of long pants in case the weather suddenly turns bad.

Heavyweight-cotton trail shorts are available for rugged hiking. They have double seats, extra pockets for storage and full-cut legs to reduce binding. You can hike in gym or rugby-type shorts, too.

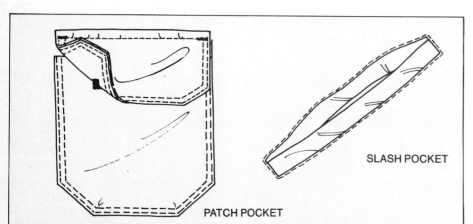

SLASH POCKET

PATCH POCKET

Pants typically have either of these two pocket designs.

Canvas, double-seat shorts are designed for rugged usage.

The Outer Layer

The function of the outer layer is to add any extra insulation you need to keep you warm and protect you from the environment. Ideally, outer garments are wind- and waterproof. In this section, we discuss insulated parkas, uninsulated shells, rainwear, headgear, gloves and mittens.

INSULATION

Insulated parkas keep you warm by preventing both *conductive* and *convective* heat loss. Conduction is the transfer of heat from molecule to molecule. If the outside air is cooler than your body temperature, you'll get cold. The best way to stop conductive heat loss is to reduce the amount of skin in direct contact with the air and put a layer of still air next to your skin. An insulated parka does both. It has a filling that traps a layer of air and holds it still, so your body heat can warm it.

Convection is heat transfer through air movement. If the outside air is moving, as on a windy day, cooling is increased. A windproof layer of material significantly reduces convective heat loss. Most insulated parkas have an outer-shell layer of nylon or other windproof material.

Many different kinds of insulation materials are used, but all are designed to do the same thing. Insulation is made of fibers that trap air molecules, holding them still. The more fibers there are in a filling, and the more surface area those fibers present, the more air can be trapped.

Until recently it was assumed that the amount of warmth provided by an insulating material was directly proportional to its thickness only. More accurately, the amount of insulation provided is also proportional to the *surface area* the fibers present.

Parkas insulate by using either natural down or synthetic fibers.

Down—This is the soft, fluffy underfeathers of geese and ducks. Each down *plumule* has thousands of long, hairy filaments that interlock and produce tiny air pockets. Without question, down offers the best warmth-to-weight ratio of any insulation.

Down clothing is light, making it ideal for hikers and others who want to save weight.

Down clothing is compressible. You can pack it into a smaller space than any of its synthetic counterparts. It is resilient, so if properly cared for it should last for years. In fact, down insulation usually outlasts the outer-shell material.

Down clothing is comfortable to wear. It's breathable and has a soft feel. Even though the feel of a filling doesn't have a direct effect on insulating value, it does increase the comfort and pleasure of wearing a down-filled garment.

It's most important to keep down insulation *dry*. If it gets wet, it loses almost all of its insulating value because the fibers absorb water and collapse. This doesn't mean that down clothing is unsuitable for rugged outdoor use. In some parts of the country rain is rare, even in winter. And if the rain does come, you can use good rain gear to protect your down clothing.

The best down comes from mature geese that have lived in a cool climate. Their down has longer filaments than down from mature ducks. But, geese are usually raised for food, not feathers, and the tastiest geese are young, tender ones. The result is that few geese are allowed to live to full maturity, and the differences between availa-

This close-up photo of a down plumule shows the thousands of filaments that interlock to create tiny air pockets that trap air and hold it still. When the air is still, your body heat can warm it.

ble goose and duck down begin to disappear.

When shopping for a down-filled parka, don't spend too much time worrying about what kind of down it's filled with. You can be certain that reputable manufacturers use quality down.

Instead, consider the down's *lofting ability*—its ability to fluff up and fill space. This is represented by *filling power,* a value you'll often see in catalog descriptions of down clothing. The filling power of down is measured by placing an ounce of down in a cylinder. A slightly weighted piston is allowed to sink until it comes to rest on the lofted down. The volume occupied by the compressed down is then measured.

Not all garments are filled with down of high filling power. There's considerable variation in the price of down garments, and one of the reasons for this is that some manufacturers use down of a filling power less than about 550 cubic inches. Typically, the lower the filling power of the down used, the less expensive the clothing. But, it will have less insulation value.

If the parka's label says that it has down filling, Federal Trade Commission (FTC) regulations say that the fill must contain at least 80% down. Furthermore, if the label lists the filling from a specific source, such as geese, 90% of that 80% must be from the named source.

Man-Made Insulation—Man-made, also called *synthetic,* insulation is widely used in insulated parkas. Most of the man-made fillings go by trade names, such as PolarGuard, Hollofill, Quallofil and Thinsulate.

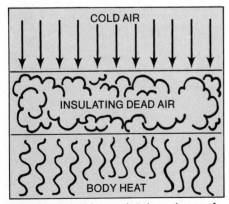
COLD AIR

INSULATING DEAD AIR

BODY HEAT

Insulated clothing maintains a layer of dead air next to your skin so you don't lose heat through conduction.

Hollofil (left) is a polyester insulator with a tubular structure. Quallofil (center) has cross bars that create air shafts in the interior of each fiber. This gives it resilience, helping it to loft fully. Thinsulate (right) has millions of microscopic fibers in a small area. Because the fibers are so tiny, they can trap more air with less bulk than other man-made insulations. Hollofil and Quallofil photos courtesy of DuPont. Thinsulate photo courtesy of 3M.

Most man-made fillings are produced in sheets, called *batts*. This way, if you tear the outside of your parka, the insulation won't spill out.

Compared to down, man-made fillings absorb virtually no water, maintaining close to 85% of their original loft when wet. They dry out quickly, too.

There are price differences among man-made insulations, but all are less expensive than down. On the other hand, all man-made insulations are somewhat heavier than down. And most can't be compressed into as compact a space. An important exception is Thinsulate, which offers as much insulating value as the other man-made fillings but with significantly less bulk.

When first introduced, Thinsulate seemed to contradict prevailing opinion about how insulation works. Thinsulate has less bulk, yet it seems to insulate as well as other, thicker insulations. Thinsulate is unique among man-made fillings in that it has millions of microscopic fibers that are much smaller than other man-made fibers. These tiny fibers are able to trap more air.

Another man-made filling offering some unique features is Quallofil. Its fibers are hollow, with cross bars dividing the center of the fibers into four parts. This makes a stiffer, more resilient fiber—one that lofts effectively. Quallofil has a soft feel and is comparable to down in weight.

INSULATED PARKAS

Insulated parkas come in a wide variety of styles. When choosing a parka, look at more than just filling. Also consider the *amount* of insulation it has, its construction, shell material, hood, zippers and closures. Because a parka is a heat container, all of these features play a part in its effectiveness.

Insulation—Pick the insulation value appropriate for your intended use. A heavily insulated parka will be uncomfortable unless you are planning to be in extremely cold weather. If you are using your parka as part of a layering system, remember that it will usually be worn over other insulating layers—shirts and sweaters.

The amount of filling in down and most synthetic insulated parkas is usually given in ounces. The lightest down parkas may have 6 ounces of down, and the heaviest as much as 18 ounces. The warmest parkas with man-made insulation may have as much as 25 ounces of filling. The style of the parka also affects how much insulation it needs.

A heavily insulated parka is the appropriate choice for winter wear. But you don't necessarily need the warmest parka available. Buy according to the uses you have in mind. This parka has sewn-through seams, raglan sleeves and a detachable hood. A storm flap covers the zipper for extra warmth.

Thinsulate is measured differently. Its manufacturers rate it by the *weight per square meter* of insulation. According to company literature, 100 grams of Thinsulate are equal to about 8 ounces of down.

It's impossible to offer specific guidelines on how warm your parka needs to be for certain activities or weather conditions. Everyone has a different comfort zone. You'll need to buy your parka based on intended use, recommendations and personal experience. Also consider the other layers you'll be wearing.

Parka Construction—Almost all insulated garments are sewn through with horizontal stitching. Though this type of construction is not recommended for sleeping bags, it's a sound method for garments because parkas are usually worn over other layers.

The box-construction system frequently used in sleeping bags would be too bulky and expensive if used in clothing. Expedition parkas, which must be very warm, are often constructed of two sewn-through layers, one inside the other, with seams offset to eliminate cold spots. For a complete discussion of different down-construction methods, see Chapter 3. It's all about sleeping bags.

The Outer Shell—It should be rugged and windproof. Outer shells of insulated parkas are rarely made of coated fabrics, although some are laminated with Gore-Tex, a waterproof, breathable fabric described later in this chapter.

Most outer shells are made from nylon, usually taffeta, taslan or antron. Also common are cotton/polyester or cotton/nylon blends. 65/35 cloth, a polyester/cotton blend, is the most frequently used blend.

The Hood—It's likely you'll want a hood with your insulated coat. Some hoods are attached; others can be removed by means of snaps or buttons. The hood should be cut large enough to fit over a hat, and it should protrude in front of your face a bit to shield you from wind, snow and rain.

Zippers—Nylon zippers are preferable to metal since they won't rust and they work better at low temperatures. Toothed zippers are the strongest, but coil zippers are smoother and are self-repairing if they get off track. An insulated storm flap that snaps or attaches with Velcro over the zipper line protects against heat loss.

Closures—No matter how well insulated a coat is, it won't keep you warm if openings can't be closed off. Look for snug closures at the wrist, with either elastic or knitted sleeves, Velcro or snap closures. More heat can escape out your collar than anywhere else, so make sure the fit is snug there.

SHELL PARKAS

Uninsulated shells are used primarily as the outer layer for protection against wind and rain. Most offer some additional insulation by helping to keep in the heat trapped by your inner layers.

The lightest and simplest outer shell is the wind shirt, made of tightly woven material, usually nylon. It provides some wind protection.

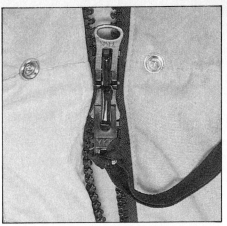

A nylon two-way zipper slides easily in all temperatures and can be opened from the top or bottom to vent away heat and adjust your body temperature.

Parkas should have tight wrist closures to prevent heat from escaping. These close with a gusset and Velcro. Others may have elastic, snaps or knitted sleeves.

More protection is given by full-shell parkas, often called *mountain* or *wilderness* parkas. They are usually made of 65/35 polyester/cotton cloth, and some have linings of taffeta, ripstop nylon, wool or pile. Most shells have been treated with a water-repellent material. The weave of the material and the water-repellent treatment might delay leakage, but in a soaking rain additional rain gear is necessary.

It's important that an uninsulated parka have tight closures and a good zipper. Cuffs may be closed with elastic, buttons, snaps or more commonly, Velcro. Gusseted sleeves have a pleat so they can be opened wide to

put on gloves or mittens, and then closed down tight to keep a good seal.

INSULATED VESTS

Vests filled with either man-made insulation, down, or made of pile or fleece are valuable as a secondary layer. In mild weather, a vest can also function as an outer layer. Insulated vests are usually made with sewn-through seams.

Vests provide insulation where you need it most—over your torso. Because they don't have sleeves, there's no restriction of body movement, which is great for active sports or outdoor work. Some vests are closed with snaps. Others close with zippers.

These wilderness parkas are made of 65/35 cloth, cut to fit over down or wool clothing. Notice the pockets with Velcro-closed flaps, the storm flap over the zipper and the attached hood. All are desirable features in a shell parka.

Vests are fine as an outer insulation layer in cool weather, but they're most effective as a secondary layer under a parka when the weather is cold.

FABRICS FOR RAINWEAR

All of the natural and man-made fabrics mentioned have some natural water resistance. But none is completely waterproof. If it rains long or hard enough, water is either absorbed into the fiber or passes through gaps between threads. Therefore, fabrics must be treated to increase their water resistance.

Treated Polyester/Cotton—Polyester/cotton blends are treated with a waterproofing that's absorbed into the fibers. This treatment cuts down on leakage by preventing the fibers from absorbing water, but the fabric is not completely waterproof. Water can still leak through spaces between threads. Cotton and cotton-blend fabrics retain some breathability after being treated for water. Stormshed is one brand of coated polyester/cotton that is highly water-resistant.

Coated Nylon—Nylon threads will not absorb waterproofing treatments, so nylon has to be coated. Most often polyurethane is used. The coating is spread on the fabric with metal blades and cured with heat. One to five layers are applied, depending on the fabric's intended use. Fewer layers are applied to clothing than on fabrics used in tents and tarps. Fabrics woven of low-denier yarn accept the polyurethane coating better than coarser, high-denier fabrics.

Unless the seams have been sealed at the factory, you'll have to manually apply liquid seam sealer. All rainwear can leak through needle holes along seams. One manufacturer, Helly-Hansen, offers what they call MicroWeld seams. The seams are first

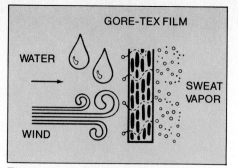

The tiny pores in Gore-Tex film allow vapor to escape yet prevent liquid drops from entering.

sewn, and then the fabric is electronically fused to form a permanent watertight seal that obviates seam sealer.

The biggest problem with coated fabric used in clothing is that it doesn't allow perspiration to pass through. Given no place to escape, the water vapor condenses on the inside of the garment, eventually getting you wet if you are exercising heavily. If you wear coated rainwear for an active sport such as bicycling, you'll become very uncomfortable.

Gore-Tex—This fabric was developed to work better than non-breathable coated fabrics. Gore-Tex is not a fabric. It's a Teflon-based film called *PTFE*—short for polytetraflouroethylene—that is laminated to a man-made fabric. The thin PTFE film is 82% air, with nine billion holes per square inch! These pores are only 0.000008 inch in diameter, too small to allow liquid through, but large enough for water vapor to escape. The result is a fabric that is both breathable and waterproof!

As in coated fabrics, needle holes along seams allow water to leak through. Therefore, most Gore-Tex garments have factory-sealed seams. A special adhesive Gore-Tex tape is mechanically bonded to the seams by heat and pressure.

Gore-Tex garments come in either two- or three-layer forms. In two-layer, the Gore-Tex is laminated to the inside of the fabric, and a separate lining, usually of nylon taffeta, is added to the inside to protect the Gore-Tex membrane. In the three-layer method, the Gore-Tex membrane is bonded between two layers of fabric. Usually the outer layer is taffeta and the inside is knitted tricot. There's no need for an extra lining. Two-layer Gore-Tex has a slightly softer feel but is slightly less abrasion-resistant than the three-layer type.

RAINWEAR

Ponchos, parkas and anoraks are the most popular kinds of upper-body rainwear. All three can be combined with rain pants.

You'll find all common styles in coated-nylon and Gore-Tex laminated fabric. Whether you choose a Gore-Tex laminated fabric or a coated one depends on your intended use and budget. Coated rainwear is less expensive than Gore-Tex, but the breathability of Gore-Tex offers some real advantages for those who need rainwear for active sports.

Some rainwear is made of plastic, but we don't recommend it. It won't stand up under stress, as it tears easily. In addition, it's usually uncomfortable to wear.

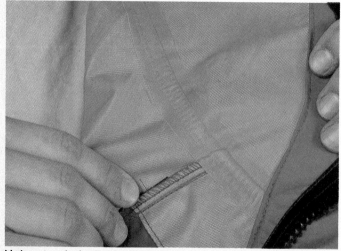

Unless sealed, all rainwear will leak at needle holes along seams. This photo shows the seam of a Gore-Tex jacket sealed with Gore-Tex tape.

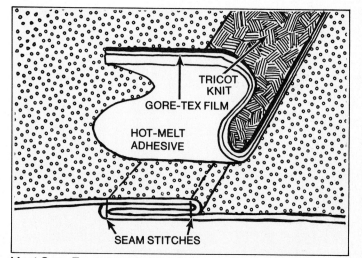

Most Gore-Tex garments have factory-sealed seams to prevent leakage through needle holes. Special Gore-Tex tape is bonded to seams with heat and pressure.

This coated-nylon poncho has a drawstring hood and side snaps that can be used to form sleeves. Because it's an extra-long model, you can adjust it to cover a frame pack when hiking in the rain.

Adding rain pants to a waterproof parka gives you added protection from windy or wet conditions you may encounter when cycling, hiking through wet brush, sailing or mountaineering.

When shopping for rainwear, look for the signs of good workmanship we've already mentioned. Rainwear should have a roomy fit so you can wear other layers underneath.

Poncho—This is essentially a waterproof tarp with a hole in the middle for your head. Typically, a poncho is made of coated nylon. Because it fits loosely, condensation problems are minimal.

A poncho is light and inexpensive and can be used as an emergency tarp shelter. Some hikers like a large poncho because it can be lifted up and draped over a backpack for hiking in the rain.

Parkas—The parka is the most popular choice in upper-body rainwear. It can be a simple unlined shell or an elaborate waterproof version of the mountain parka, with large pockets, a hood, drawstrings and gusseted sleeves.

Zippers should have a flap that snaps over to prevent wind and rain from blowing through. Make sure that pockets have Velcro flaps to keep them from filling with water. A snug-fitting hood allows for full visibility and head movement.

Velcro or snap openings at the cuffs allow you to adjust the parka to fit snugly over gloves. Some parkas have waist drawstrings to help keep out cold air and underarm zippers to provide extra ventilation for active sports.

Anoraks—Anoraks are pullover parkas. Doing away with the zipper cuts a bit of the weight and cost, and eliminates the problem of a stuck or broken zipper. In addition, anoraks

An underarm zipper provides extra ventilation for active sports.

The anorak looks like a cross between a waterproof parka and a sweater.

are more resistant to wind and rain because there's no zipper seam in front. They are ideal if you'll be in wind-blown rain or snow.

Though the pullover design makes the anorak more stormproof, it causes some slight inconveniences. You have to pull the anorak over your head, which can be a problem in a crowded space or if you're wearing a pack.

Rain Pants, Chaps & Overalls—Adding rain pants to a parka, poncho or anorak gives you much greater protection from the weather, especially wind-blown rain or snow. They are a necessity for sailors and fishermen. In addition, many hikers use them when facing very wet weather.

The simplest form of rain pants are chaps. These are long tubes inserted over each leg and tied to your belt. This makes them less expensive than full-fit rain pants. The crotch is left open, offering added ventilation.

Full-fit rain pants come all the way up to the waist and are tied with a drawstring or secured with elastic or snaps. They offer added protection to your crotch and hips.

Overalls are fitted to cover up to mid-chest and are secured by suspender straps over the shoulder. Overalls are most popular with sailors, fishermen, and others who face blowing rain and spray.

Some pants and overalls have zippers running up the side of the legs. This lets you pull the pants on over boots. Extra patches of cloth in the seat and knees will increase the life of the pants.

Gaiters can protect the bottoms of your pants from brush, burrs, snow and water.

GAITERS

Gaiters are ankle coverings that fit over the bottom of your pants and boot tops to keep snow or water from leaking into your boots. Gaiters are used primarily by skiers, snowshoers, mountaineers and hikers. They are usually made of coated or uncoated nylon, or Gore-Tex laminated fabric.

Ankle gaiters cover just the bottom of your pants. They are usually a simple tube with an elastic band on the top and an attachment of some sort on the bottom—usually a strap running under the boot, or a hook that latches into the laces. Ankle gaiters are adequate for spring snowshoeing or cross-country skiing, when you're unlikely to encounter deep, soft snow. They are also useful for hikers who want to keep small rocks from getting into their boots.

Full-length, knee-high gaiters are a big help for any winter mountaineering, skiing, snowshoeing or hiking through deep, wet brush. They have a zipper, Velcro or lace closure running the entire length to make them easy to put on and take off. Typically, they attach to boots with a boot strap and lace hook.

Some gaiters are sized, usually according to shoe size.

HEADWEAR

Your head is usually the warmest part of your body because it has the greatest blood supply. Therefore, covering your head is essential to maintaining comfortable body warmth. It's estimated that you can lose 30% to 40% of body heat from your head. Outdoor experts know they can shiver with cold—even when

wearing an insulated coat—if their heads are unprotected. After putting on a hat, your shivers may stop almost immediately.

Hats are used for more than insulation. They also offer protection from insects, the sun and high brush. And, a water-soaked bandana can be used to cool you off in hot weather.

Headbands—This is the simplest piece of headwear, covering only the ears. Headbands are useful for active sports like hiking and skiing, in which you need warm ears.

Watch Caps—Knit watch caps, also called *stocking* caps, cover the top of your head. They're usually warm enough for all but the coldest conditions. Wool, wool blends and acrylic fibers are used, with wool being warmest.

Knit caps have poor wind resistance, so if the wind is very strong, wear your parka hood over the cap.

Balaclavas—The balaclava is designed for extreme cold. It's a knitted hat that can be unrolled to protect your neck and the sides of your face. Balaclavas are made of acrylic, wool, silk and polyester pile.

A balaclava offers protection from extreme wind and cold. For more moderate conditions, roll it up and wear it like a watch cap.

Rain Hats—The ultimate rain protection is probably provided by a well-designed parka hood. But many people prefer to wear a waterproof hat with a brim because it doesn't interfere with side vision as a hood may.

A *sou'wester*, the traditional broad-brimmed fisherman's hat made of waterproof-coated fabric, offers excellent protection. So does the crusher hat made of Gore-Tex. A crusher can be folded up and stuffed in your pocket. The Gore-Tex laminated fabric makes the crusher breathable for use in strenuous activity.

These Gore-Tex hats are waterproof and breathable. The hat at the left is also insulated with Thinsulate and pile for extra warmth.

GLOVES AND MITTENS

These are a must if you venture into the wilderness, in winter or summer. Heat loss from the fingers is high because they have a large surface area compared to their small volume. Winter hikers and mountaineers use gloves as standard equipment. Summer hikers need them as emergency equipment, even if unused most of the season.

Mittens are warmer than gloves because your fingers are together. Wear mittens alone or with liners of silk, polypropylene, wool or Lurex—a reflective, "space-type" material. Using liners with mittens enables you to remove your mittens to handle a camera or other small item without exposing your skin to air.

Outer mittens and gloves are made of wool, pile, nylon or leather. Leather gloves are best when you need to protect your hands from abrasion, such as in skiing and rock climbing.

Overmitts, insulated with down, man-made filling or polyester pile, are designed for extremely cold conditions. Use them over gloves or mittens.

Use insulated overmitts like these over liner gloves in extremely cold weather.

Footwear

2

You'll be able to find dozens of different kinds of outdoor footwear, ranging from jogging shoes to sturdy, insulated mountaineering boots. The best way to buy exactly what you need is to carefully consider how you'll be using the footwear. Buy the shoes or boots with the necessary features.

To help you consider the wide range of outdoor footwear, we've divided the selection into five categories—athletic shoes, leisure shoes, hiking boots, backpacking boots and mountaineering boots.

ATHLETIC SHOES

Outdoor athletic shoes include running and court shoes. Both styles are primarily designed to cushion your foot and provide lateral support and stability as you move.

Court Shoes—These are made to provide side support and stability for the quick starts and stops of tennis, basketball and other court games. They are usually heavier than running shoes. You need to buy shoes that absorb shocks and are built to stand up to the considerable abuse you'll put them through.

Running Shoes—Runners are confronted with an incredible number of different shoe styles and designs. Selecting the right running shoe can be difficult. As the technology of running shoes continues to improve, the decision may become even more complicated!

Each runner has individual needs, based on body build, leg structure, mileage and terrain. For example, if you run primarily on asphalt, you'll need to find shoes that cushion rear- and fore-foot impact. If you enter races, shoe weight becomes a big consideration. And, if you are an everyday runner, sole durability is important. You need to decide which features are most important to you.

Because the range of products is so extensive, we strongly suggest you do some research before investing in a

Here are some of the materials and tools used for making footwear. Each boot or shoe is molded over a plastic or wooden *last* that gives the upper its shape. Because lasts differ in shape, various manufacturers' footwear of the same size may fit differently.

good pair of running shoes. First, see the box on page 20 about running shoes. Second, your community may have a store that specializes in running shoes, and store personnel should be able to offer additional advice. Third, there are many up-to-date books and magazine articles covering shoe selection.

Running footwear is also bought by non-runners. If you want to use running shoes for light trail hiking over smooth, flat terrain, choose from the heavier models available.

Non-athletes, too, are finding running shoes a good choice for leisure wear. The same features that make them ideal for miles of jogging—ab-

STEPPING THROUGH THE RUNNING-SHOE MAZE

There's an overwhelming variety of running shoes available. Deciding which to buy is one of the most difficult and important athletic choices you'll make. Every runner is different, and feet are as unique as fingerprints. This is why there's so much variation among running-shoe designs. And that also makes it difficult, if not impossible, for us to tell you what kind of shoe to buy. Our best advice is to buy your shoes at a running-supply shop, outdoor store or sporting-goods shop that is experienced in fitting and selling running shoes.

The clerk should fit you carefully and ask lots of questions such as:

"How many miles do you run?"
"On what kind of terrain do you run?"
"Have you suffered any injuries?"
"What kind of shoes are you wearing now?"
"Are they comfortable?"

So that you know some of the things to look for, here's a summary of the design characteristics of running shoes:

THE LAST

Shoes are constructed around a wooden or plastic mold called a *last*. Most feet are slightly curved, so manufacturers build most running shoes on a curved last. However, approximately one-third of the population has a straighter-than-average foot shape. These people should buy a shoe built over a straight last.

To find which shape fits best, go to a knowledgeable dealer and try on several different kinds of shoes. After closely examining your foot and asking questions about your running style, the salesperson should be able to prescribe the proper shoe.

THE SOLE

As in hiking boots, running shoes have an outer sole, a midsole and an inner sole. The soles should be flexible and cushion your feet, yet still be tough enough to withstand repeated shocks. The best running shoes are both flexible and sturdy.

The sole pattern affects both shock absorption and traction. Traction is rarely a problem on firm, dry, level surfaces. But, if you do a lot of running on other terrains—wet, hilly or perhaps muddy ground—you may want to buy a shoe that has a pronounced waffle-like tread.

THE HEEL

Most running shoes have slightly flared heels to give your foot a good foundation when it lands. The *heel counter* is the cup made of rigid material that encloses your heel. Well-designed heels and heel counters support your foot under stress and reduce *pronation*—the rotation of the foot toward the *inside* upon impact—and *supination*—the *outside* rotation of the foot at impact.

WEIGHT

Unless you compete, don't worry too much about buying a light shoe. It's more important to find one that fits and offers the design features you need. Even if you do race, training shoes with a few extra ounces won't make much difference.

MATERIALS & WORKMANSHIP

Nearly all running shoes have nylon uppers. Nylon is light, dries quickly and doesn't need breaking in. Closely examine the stitching and workmanship to make sure your shoe is well-made.

BREAKING-IN

It's a good idea to buy new shoes before your old ones are completely worn out. This way you can shift over to the new ones gradually, wearing your new shoes for a few miles at first and slowly increasing your mileage.

---

sorption, support, light weight—make running shoes comfortable for everyday wear, too.

The popularity of running footwear has influenced the design of leisure shoes and light hiking boots as well. There's a strong trend toward models with lightweight leather or fabric uppers and cushioned soles.

LEISURE SHOES

Leisure shoes are designed for comfort and style. They are light enough to be worn all day long, at work, around town, for traveling or on easy trails. Most have leather uppers, but an increasing number are made with a combination fabric and leather upper. Many leisure shoes come with cushioned rubber soles in an effort to match the comfort of running shoes. Examples of leisure shoes include oxfords, handsewn moccasins and lightweight walking shoes made of fabric uppers.

HIKING BOOTS

Hiking boots have lightweight

Most running shoes have nylon and leather uppers and flexible, yet sturdy, soles.

An increasing number of leisure shoes are being made with fabric and leather uppers. This shoe, made with Gore-Tex laminated nylon, is also suitable for walking on light trails.

Lightweight hiking boots offer more support than leisure shoes, but still maintain many of the running-shoe features you'll find in lighter shoes. They're perfect for trail hiking with a light pack.

uppers of either leather or a combination of leather and fabric. Their soles are flexible, making break-in time very short. These boots are most suitable for trail hiking over easy terrain, with light packs in either wet or dry weather.

Worth repeating here is the trend toward lightweight boots with fabric uppers. In the past, many hikers purchased boots too heavy for their needs. The extra weight caused unnecessary fatigue. Now, the prevailing attitude among boot experts is that it's best to buy the lightest boot that meets the conditions you'll face.

BACKPACKING BOOTS

Backpacking boots have medium-weight uppers and semi-flexible lugged soles. They are ruggedly built for sustained, difficult backpacking on rough terrain with a medium to heavy pack. The added weight of a pack necessitates wearing boots that give good ankle support. Uppers are cut higher and the leather is treated to make it stiffer than leather used in hiking boots. This treatment also gives the uppers better abrasion resistance and waterproofing—a useful feature if you hike rough trails.

MOUNTAINEERING BOOTS

Mountaineering boots have medium- to heavyweight uppers that give your ankle the support you need to carry a heavy pack or hike on very rough terrain.

They have the most rigid of all boot soles. The stiff sole provides a solid platform for climbers standing on small toe holds. It is also necessary for attaching *crampons,* traction devices used in ice climbing.

There's a variety of mountaineering boots, each type designed for a specific kind of climbing. Rock-climbing boots with lightweight uppers and very flexible soles are exceptions to some of the previous statements. They are meant for just one purpose—toeing, edging and jamming on steep, technically difficult rock. See page 97.

At the other end of the spectrum are insulated mountain boots. These have an outer shell of lightweight, strong, waterproof plastic. Inside the shell are leather inner boots, insulated to provide warmth in very cold weather.

In between are boots designed for general mountaineering with semi-

A leather-upper backpacking boot provides the support and traction necessary for rugged hiking with a pack. Leather provides more ankle support than fabric, and the lug soles grab on steep trails. A leather mountaineering boot has deep soles, extra midsoles for stiffness and a heavyweight upper.

A plastic-shell mountaineering boot is insulated to provide warmth in the most extreme cold and wind. Boots of this type have been used on Alaskan and Himalayan mountaineering expeditions.

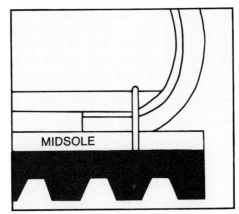

Midsoles are usually made of leather or hard rubber.

stiff soles and one-piece leather uppers offering good ankle support. Due to their versatility, these boots are the choice of most mountaineers.

SOLE CONSTRUCTION

In this book, *sole* refers not just to the outer sole, but also to the midsoles, the steel shank and the insole. The way in which these four are connected to the uppers is called the *construction method.*

Outer Soles—Manufacturers generally match a shoe's sole with its intended use. Deep-lugged soles, such as Vibram Montagnas, are used on mountaineering and backpacking boots. They are designed for travel over rugged terrain where personal

safety and security are primary considerations. Unless you'll encounter such conditions, it's better to choose a lighter sole. Deep-lugged soles are thicker, so they are harder to flex and take longer to break in.

Shallow-lugged soles, used on hiking boots and a few sturdy leisure shoes, are designed for level or gently

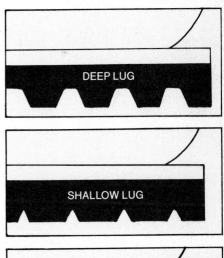

These are the three types of soles found on outdoor footwear: The deep-lugged sole is found on mountaineering boots. The shallow-lugged sole is designed for trail walking. Textured soles are used on walking and running shoes.

sloping trails. The sole is thinner, with the lugs cut less deeply, so it will flex more easily than a deep-lugged sole.

Non-lugged, or textured, soles are used primarily on leisure and athletic shoes. They are very light and flexible, making them suitable for city walking and light hiking over gentle terrain.

Midsoles—These are made of leather and/or rubber and are sandwiched between the outer sole and the insole. They provide extra stiffness to give a solid platform for mountaineering and to protect your foot from sharp objects. Backpacking and mountaineering boots generally have one rubber and two leather midsoles. Hiking boots normally have just a rubber midsole, which provides adequate stiffness and protection for trail hiking.

Many light hiking boots and leisure shoes have midsoles or heel wedges of *blown* or *foam* rubber. These provide a cushioned sole and are very comfortable if you won't be hiking rough trails.

Steel Shank—Most boots and some shoes have a steel shank between the midsoles and the insole. The shank assures that the sole flexes at the proper point—the ball of your foot. A half-length shank is used for hiking, backpacking and general-purpose mountaineering boots. Full-length shanks are used only in technical mountaineering boots needing completely rigid soles. Plastic mountaineering boots don't need shanks because their soles are inherently rigid.

Insoles—The insole comes in direct contact with your stockinged foot. An insole should breathe, absorb moisture and be durable. Most boots and shoes have leather insoles, which provide a fine environment for your foot. Insoles are made of full-grain or split leather, both described later.

Over time, salts from perspiration can make leather brittle. However, the synthetic material called *Texon* is not subject to such deterioration. It's used for the insole in some lightweight hiking boots and leisure shoes. It's not used in heavier boots because it loses this useful characteristic when cut thickly.

THE CONSTRUCTION METHOD—CONNECTING SOLES TO THE UPPER

In outdoor footwear, there are six common methods used to attach the outer sole, midsoles and the insole to the upper. Boot and shoe manufacturers choose the construction method that gives a shoe or boot the features they want—a combination of appropriate strength, stiffness and flexibility.

Norwegian Welt—This is the strongest and most durable construction method. It is used for boots intended for heavy-duty hiking, backpacking and mountaineering. Two rows of stitching attach the upper to the soles. The first row, a horizontal stitch, fastens the upper to the insole. The second row is a vertical stitch that fastens the upper to the midsole. Polyester thread is used because it won't rot when wet.

You can recognize the Norwegian welt from the outside by the two rows of stitching visible along the edge where the upper connects to the midsoles. Only boots manufactured in Europe have Norwegian welts. American bootmakers don't have the equipment to do it.

If your boots are made with a Norwegian welt, you can replace the outer sole and midsoles when they wear out.

Goodyear Welt—It takes its name from Charles Goodyear Jr., son of the discoverer of rubber vulcanization. It was the younger Goodyear who invented the machine used in sewing footwear with a Goodyear welt.

Goodyear welts are used in lightweight hiking boots needing flexibility. It's not appropriate for mountaineering and backpacking boots because it's not strong enough for extremely rugged uses.

The Goodyear welt also has two rows of stitching. The first is an interior horizontal stitch that fastens the upper to both a strip of leather and the insole. This strip, running around the perimeter of the boot's upper, is then attached to the midsole(s) with a vertical stitch.

From the outside, you'll be able to see only one line of stitching. The second is hidden by the strip of leather running around the edge of the boot. Because the upper is not a direct part of the midsole as in the Norwegian welt, the Goodyear welt produces a more flexible sole. The outer sole and midsoles are replaceable.

Inside-Fastened—This type is also

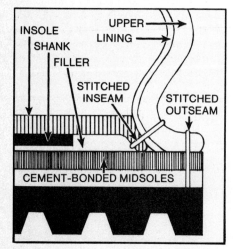

In the Norwegian welt, the upper is attached to the sole by two lines of stitching. It's the stiffest and most durable construction method.

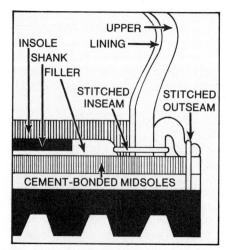

The Goodyear welt produces a more flexible sole than the Norwegian welt. The upper is attached to the soles through a strip of leather stitched around the perimeter of the upper.

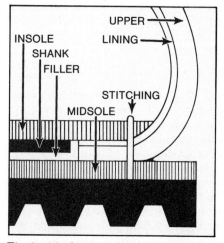

The inside-fastened method yields flexible soles. The upper is rolled between the midsole and insole and is connected with one or two rows of stitching.

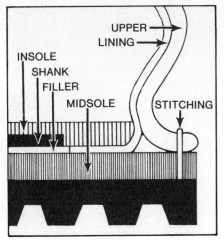

You'll find the outside-stitchdown method used on leisure shoes and a few light hiking boots. It produces a very flexible sole.

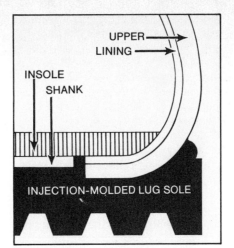

In injection-molding, molten rubber takes the place of stitching. It's widely used for waterproof boots.

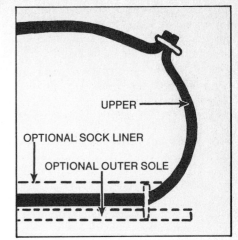

Moccasin construction is used in lightweight leisure shoes.

called *Littleway* and *McKay.* Because it is very flexible, the inside-fastened construction method is used in lightweight hiking boots. The upper is rolled in between the insole and the midsole. Then, one or two rows of stitching—visible only from inside—connect all three layers.

It's a durable system because the stitching is not exposed to abrasion outside the boot. Because there is no outside line of stitching, the sole can be cut very close to the upper. This is especially desirable for rock-climbing shoes. Boots made with the inside-fastened method are easy to resole.

Outside-Stitchdown—The outside-stitchdown method is used primarily in lightweight hiking boots and leisure shoes. It is too flexible for rugged use. In this method, the upper is rolled out and stitched vertically to the midsole with a single or double row of stitching. From the outside it looks similar to the Norwegian welt.

A disadvantage of this method is that if the stitching abrades and breaks, the shoe's upper separates from the sole, allowing water and dirt to get in the boot. Outer soles are replaceable.

Injection-Molded Welt—This method is widely used for insulated, waterproof footwear. Molten rubber takes the place of stitching, a process called *injection-molding.*

In inexpensive boots, the lugged soles may be molded directly to the upper. Better-quality boots, however, are made with the midsole molded to the upper. Then, the lugged sole is cemented to the midsole. This method is superior because it allows

you to replace the lugged outer sole. The injection-molded system allows easy flex and provides maximum protection from water.

Moccasin Construction—This is used in lightweight leisure shoes. The upper is a single piece of leather that is laid down on the sole, stitched on the inside, and then drawn up around the side of the foot. A *vamp plug* is then sewn in the middle, over the top of the foot.

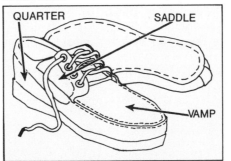

Here are the basic parts of a shoe.

This waterproof boot has an injection-molded sole. The upper is a combination of rubber and leather. Low-cut footwear of this design is also available.

THE UPPER

The uppers of outdoor footwear are made from leather, fabric, a combination of leather and fabric, or a combination of rubber and leather. Each has uses for which it is specifically suited.

The front half of the upper is called the *vamp,* the back half the *quarter.* In leisure shoes, a piece of leather is often sewn across the top of the shoe. It contains eyelets for lacing and is called the *saddle.*

Fabric And Fabric/Leather Uppers—Fabric uppers are usually made with nylon or canvas. They are lightweight and comfortable. Most high-quality fabric hiking boots have uppers laminated with a Gore-Tex film, described in Chapter 1.

Shoes and boots with fabric uppers provide less support than leather, so they are best suited for walking and hiking on level or gently sloping trails when you have a light pack or no pack at all. The stitching leaves the seams exposed, so it's best to confine their use to trails in which there's little danger of abrasion.

Seams should be double-stitched where fabric is stitched to leather. Leather and fabric have a different density, so the thread tension of a single stitch could cut the fabric. With a double stitch, the tension isn't concentrated on one thread.

Leather And Rubber Uppers—Boots with rubber on the bottom half of the upper and leather on the top are used by fishermen, canoeists and hunters who must walk through wet and marshy terrain. The rubber provides complete waterproofing, with the leather adding breathability and support. In strenuous activities, though, your feet are likely to sweat in rubber boots. Some leather/rubber boots have insulation for activities in very cold weather.

Leather Uppers—Leather is the most widely used material in boots designed for rugged use. It stands up to all kinds of abuse and is remarkably durable. When properly constructed and cared for, a boot with a leather upper will last for years. Over time, it should conform to the shape of your foot. Leather even offers some insulation because almost 60% of its volume is trapped air space.

The best mountaineering, backpacking and hiking boots feature *one-piece uppers,* in which the vamp and quarter are cut from a single piece of leather. One-piece boots are the most expensive to produce because the manufacturer can't get as many pieces from a single hide as with two- and three-piece uppers. But for some purposes, the expense is worthwhile. The absence of seams and overlapping pieces eliminates seam abrasion and reduces the chance of water leaking through.

A two-piece upper, however, doesn't mean the boot is poorly constructed. Two-piece uppers give you a less-expensive option, if maximum durability and waterproofing are not your prime concerns.

When examining a two-piece upper, make sure that the overlapping seam wraps toward the back, to minimize the effects of abrasion. Seams should be stitched with several rows. If the stitching is recessed, a two-piece upper can be nearly as sturdy as a one-piece upper.

Cuffs—Mountaineering, backpacking and hiking boots should have a padded cuff, sometimes called a *scree collar,* stitched to the ankle of the boot. The cuff forms a seal, keeping out rocks, twigs and dirt. It also pads your ankle a bit, protecting it from getting bruised as you hike up, down or across steep hills.

Cuffs may be stitched to the inside of the upper or to the top of the boot. Internal cuffs are best because they are not subject to external wear and tear.

Backstays—The backstay is a protective piece of leather stitched over the backseam. It's a feature of all uppers, whether one- or two-piece.

Narrow backstays are less subject to damage from abrasion than wide backstays. Because the edges of a wide backstay reach around the sides of the boot, they can catch on brush and rocks.

If a backstay is damaged, it is nearly impossible to repair. In the original construction, the backstay is stitched to the upper before the heel counter

and lining are inserted. To repair it, the shoemaker would have to stitch all the way through the heel counter and lining—through the entire boot. This would produce interior seams that could lead to blisters.

Lining—Most boots and some leisure shoes have a lining—either a full lining, a quarter lining covering the back half of the boot, or a heel lining protecting just the heel area. The design and materials used in the lining greatly affect foot comfort. Materials should be breathable and absorbent enough to wick perspiration away from your feet.

These qualities are found in leather and some synthetic materials. Mountaineering and backpacking boots are usually lined with smooth leather. Hiking boots can be lined with leather or a synthetic material called *Cambrelle.* This lightweight nylon fabric is absorbent, abrasion-resistant and rot-resistant. *Tricot,* a synthetic with similar properties, is used in some leisure and athletic shoes.

Some inadequate synthetics used inside of shoes include linings made of polyurethane and foot beds of plastic. Avoid these.

No matter what the heel lining is made of, it should be seamless. Interior seams are subject to much wear. If they cause excess rubbing, heel blisters result.

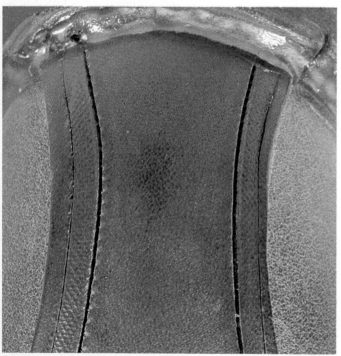

A narrow backstay, pictured here, is subject to less abrasion because seams don't reach around to the side of the boot.

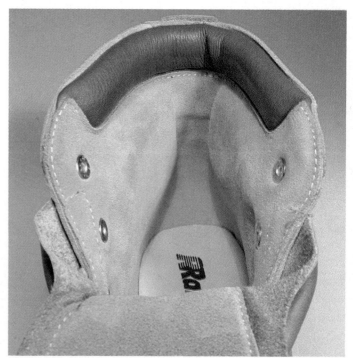

A boot should have a seamless heel lining to reduce the incidence of heel blisters. A padded, internal cuff also contributes to hiking comfort.

The gusseted tongue provides good waterproofing because it has an unbroken leather barrier. It's most often used on backpacking and mountaineering boots.

The overlapping tongue isn't as waterproof as the bellows, but if the two sides substantially overlap, as shown here, it's a good design for all but the wettest conditions. Many top-quality boots feature it.

Tongue—The tongue design is one of the most important features in a boot or shoe. The tongue area of your shoe does three things—prevents water from leaking through to your foot, allows easy entry when putting boots on, and helps you adjust the fit.

There are three kinds of tongue designs—the *gusseted tongue,* including the bellows feature; the *overlapping tongue;* and the *split tongue.* Gusseted and overlapping tongues are used in mountaineering, backpacking and hiking boots. Most leisure and athletic shoes have a split tongue.

A gusseted tongue has a piece of leather across the tongue area. It can be made from a separate piece sewn in, or it can be a true bellows, in which the tongue is continuous, one with the upper. Bootmakers make the bellows tongue by thinning the leather so it will bend and fold like a bellows. In bellows and gusseted tongues, a padded tongue is also sewn underneath.

Gusseted and bellows are the most effective designs for keeping out water. They also affect the way your boot fits, especially if it has a bellows

tongue. As the bellows tongue is pulled tight, it presses down on the instep—the arched part of the foot in front of the ankle. This in turn presses the heel firmly into the heel pocket of the boot. It's a desirable feature for most people because it helps keep the heel firmly in place. Loose heel fit is one of the biggest causes of blisters.

Conversely, some people have a very high, sensitive instep. They may find the pressure from a bellows tongue unpleasant. If this happens to you, buy boots with a different tongue design.

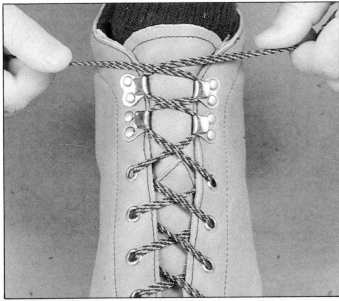

This lightweight hiking boot has a lacing system using eyelets on the bottom and hooks on the top.

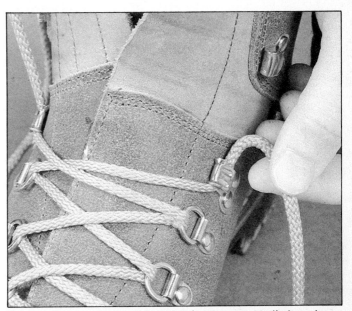

Backpacking and mountaineering boots are usually laced with D-rings on the bottom and clinch hooks on top.

You may have to buy boots with an overlapping tongue. This has a split front, but when laced, the two sides substantially overlap, providing good protection from water. Like the bellows tongue, the overlapping tongue can also affect fitting.

Narrow-footed hikers may not be able to lace their boots tight enough. When the overlapping flap hits the lacing hooks on the opposite side, the boot cannot be tightened further.

A simple split tongue design is used on boots not needing a complete water barrier. Halves of the upper are drawn together across the tongue, but they don't overlap. This design may also include a gusset.

Lacing—Boots and shoes are closed with laces drawn through eyelets, D-rings or hooks. Athletic and leisure shoes usually have eyelets. Boots have a combination of eyelets, D-rings or hooks. Backpacking and mountaineering boots usually have D-rings on the bottom half and hooks on the top. Heavier boots may have double-riveted hooks.

Some boots have a special hook, called a *clinch hook,* halfway up the laces. With this hook, you can lock lace tension, making it easier to lace the top half without having the bottom loosen. It also allows you to lace the bottom and top of the boots to two different tensions.

When hiking up a steep grade, it is common to loosen the top half slightly to reduce pressure on the front of the ankle. When going downhill, tighten it back up to keep your foot from sliding forward to the toe.

Nylon laces are the best choice. Cotton laces will eventually rot. Leather laces stretch, rot and break.

Leather

Leather is by far the most common material for all kinds of outdoor shoes and boots. Even shoes with fabric uppers use a lot of leather in construction. Because leather is so important, we discuss in detail how leather is prepared and what kinds of leathers are used in footwear.

HOW LEATHER IS MADE

Leather-making from animal hides is prehistoric. Ancient Egyptian carvings depict tanners at work. By 500 B.C. the Greeks had developed leather-making into a well-established trade. Over succeeding centuries, leather-making has evolved from a craft into a scientific industry.

Today, hides go through nearly 20 operations. Some of the most important are cleaning, unhairing, tanning, fatliquoring, splitting and drying. Many of these operations have a direct bearing on the kind of leather you'll have in your boots.

Tanning—This happens after the hides have been thoroughly cleaned. The hides are put into a large rotating drum with a chromium sulfate solution. This is called *chrome tanning.* It's a process *all* leather goes through.

The most obvious reason for chrome tanning is to make the leather insusceptible to rot. But it has other beneficial results. The leather becomes more resistant to abrasion and deterioration from chemicals and heat. It has a greater ability to flex without breaking and to endure repeated cycles of wetting and drying.

Some leather undergoes a second tanning process, usually called *vegeta-*

ble tanning. Hides are again placed in revolving drums, this time with an extract derived from trees and shrubs such as sumac, hemlock, oak and spruce. This second operation gives leather solidity and body.

Fatliquoring—More than any other process, fatliquoring determines how firm or soft a leather will be. In this step, leather fibers are lubricated so that, after drying, they are capable of sliding over one another. In addition to regulating the flexibility of leather, fatliquoring increases its tensile strength—the ability to withstand stretching.

Leather is fatliquored with either oils or waxes. Oils make it soft. Waxes make it firm. Outdoor-equipment catalogs sometimes refer to boot leather as *oil-tanned* or *wax-tanned,* both misleading terms. Leather is treated with waxes or oils during fatliquoring, not tanning. A more accurate description is to say that leather has been either *oil-treated* or *wax-treated.*

Splitting—As cows vary, so do hide thicknesses. To produce a piece of leather of uniform thickness, the hide is split by a machine. Splitting produces two halves of leather. The outer, or hide side, is called *full-grain leather.* The inner half is *split leather.*

Full-grain leather has greater density than split, with all the resulting positive characteristics. It is stiffer, more waterproof, and more abrasion-resistant.

Split leather can show a great variation in quality. If it is cut from very near the hide surface, it will have enough density to be used in light, flexible boots. Lower-quality split leather is used for linings and other leather goods. Split leather is not naturally waterproof, so manufacturers must treat it with wax or oil to make it more so.

All mountaineering, backpacking and most hiking boots are constructed with full-grain leather. Manufacturers can use it either *smooth-out*—in which the grain, or hide, side faces out—or *rough-out,* in which the flesh side is outward.

Boots for rugged use, including mountaineering and backpacking boots, usually have rough-out leather. This keeps the smooth grain side, the leather's ultimate waterproof barrier, inside the boot and away from abrasion. Smooth-out leather isn't suitable for rugged uses because the "skin" is

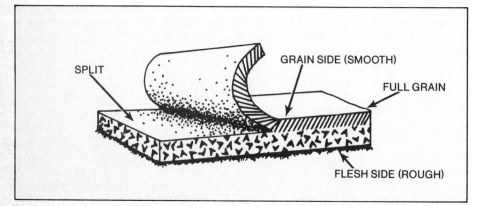

During manufacture, leather is split. The full-grain (hide) side is sturdy, abrasion-resistant and waterproof. The split (inner) side is pliable but lacks natural waterproofing. Full-grain leather can be used with either the smooth or the rough side facing out.

on the outside and abrasion may cause permanent damage, allowing water to leak through. Smooth-out leather is fine for hiking and leisure shoes, though, because there is usually little chance of abrasion.

Fitting

Boots and shoes *must* fit well! The goal in fitting footwear is to give your feet the most comfortable environment possible. When you shop for boots, make up your mind to accept nothing less than excellent fit.

Size is the first consideration in fitting boots. Second is design. Not every boot design will fit everyone's feet well. Each boot is molded over a *last,* a wooden or plastic form, that gives the upper its shape. Two boots of exactly the same size may fit your feet differently because the uppers are designed differently and made from different lasts. If you are unable to find a good-fitting boot or shoe in a certain style, try a different one.

A common mistake is to buy a boot that's heavier than you need. For example, if you are planning light trail hiking with a small pack, it's pointless to buy a mountaineering boot. It will be stiff and heavy, making the break-in period longer and compounding fitting problems.

HOW TO GET A GOOD FIT

Be sure that you fit a pair of boots carefully and correctly. The wrong fit can make hiking uncomfortable, and even painful. Here's how to do it right:

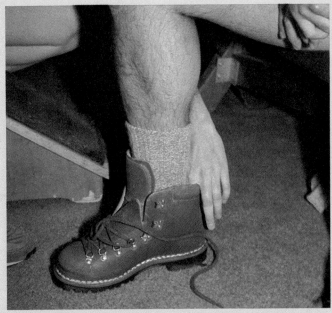

1) Test length by pushing your toes to the front. You should be able to insert your index finger behind your heel. Do this with the boots unlaced.

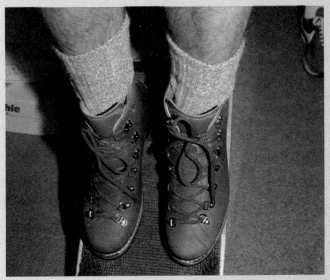

2) Lace up your boots and stand facing down a slanted platform. Your feet shouldn't slide forward.

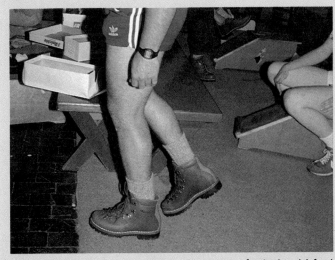

3) When you walk around the store, your feet should feel snug but not tight. If you lean or rock forward, the heel shouldn't rise more than 1/8 inch.

4) Test width after getting a good heel fit. The ball of your foot should be in a neutral position, neither bunched nor loose.

FITTING IN PERSON

If you shop at a store that carries outdoor footwear and has knowledgeable salespeople, they will probably have a method to test if a boot fits well. A good system for fitting yourself is on page 27.

Have the type of socks you'll typically use with the footwear. This can be one heavy-duty pair of wool socks, or a pair of olefin socks and medium-weight wool socks used together.

Many people have problems with heel fit, and it pays to be aware of this. A common misconception is that Europeans make their boots with wider heels than do American manufacturers. Actually, there are no differences between the heel fit of American and European boots.

FITTING BY MAIL

You may be more insecure about ordering boots and shoes through the mail. However, most retailers who sell shoes through the mail have become expert in sizing-by-mail techniques. Carefully follow all the directions given in the mail-order catalog. You should be able to get a boot that fits well.

The method used by REI is to have you outline your larger foot with a pencil held vertically. Be sure to do this while wearing the sock combination you would normally wear with these boots. REI has insole patterns in stock for each style and size of boot and shoe they carry. Experts match your outline to these insole patterns and choose the best-fitting size.

REI and other reputable mail-order dealers carefully check your traced foot pattern to make sure you get a boot that fits.

A FINAL CHECK

Always double-check newly purchased boots or shoes by wearing them indoors for a few hours before you go outside. If you feel pressure points or excessive rubbing, return the boots. Those problems won't go away; they'll get worse. Most reputable retailers will give full credit for footwear returned in new condition, but only partial credit for those worn outdoors.

BREAKING IN BOOTS

There is no miracle method for breaking in boots. If you read other books, you'll find that some authors and outdoor experts have their own preferred method, such as filling your new boots with water, or treating the uppers with oils or waxes. These methods may help get your boots *ready* to break in, but the only way to actually do the job is by wearing them and walking around.

Take a few short hikes to begin with, gradually increasing the distance as your boots begin to break in. The most important change comes when the sole flexes more easily. The other major change is that the upper gradually conforms to the shape of your foot.

Care & Maintenance

Four main factors deteriorate boots and shoes most—abrasion, heat, water and the wrong kind of waterproofing.

ABRASION

In the normal course of boot and shoe wear you can't avoid abrasions completely. Boots get nicked and scuffed while hiking. Even walking around the city exposes your shoes to countless bumps and nicks. It's important to buy a boot or shoe built to withstand the abrasion you'll encounter.

Rough-out leather is the most durable material of those mentioned, which is why it's used in mountaineering and backpacking boots. Smooth-out leather stands up to the occasional bumps that come with trail hiking. And for city walking or car camping, either fabric or leather shoes should do the job if they're made well.

HEAT

Excessive heat reduces leather life. Never expose your shoes to temperatures hotter than your skin can tolerate. And don't dry boots over a campfire, stove or heater. If your boots get wet, stuff them with newspaper to draw out the moisture and store them in a cool, dry place until dry.

It's obviously not as easy to dry your boots if they get wet in the field. Take them off when you can, wipe them out and place them under cover to dry. If you have to wear them wet, wipe them as dry as you can and then put on a pair of dry socks. The warmth from your foot will speed drying, and your socks will absorb some of the moisture from the boot. As your socks become soaked, change to a dry pair.

WATERPROOFING LEATHER

You waterproof boots to help the leather maintain its original properties. Applying the wrong kind of waterproofing will damage and destroy a leather's useful characteristics.

Waterproofing Leather Uppers—Earlier in this chapter, we described how leather is either wax- or oil-treated during fatliquoring. It's important to know which treatment your boots received. Most mountaineering and backpacking boots have been wax-treated. Hiking boots and leisure shoes have probably undergone oil treatment. If you are unsure, ask the salespeople at the store that sold you the boots. Or, carefully read the mail-order catalog.

Boots made with wax-treated leather must be waterproofed with a *wax* waterproofing. The best is made from beeswax because it stays flexible at low temperatures. Paraffin waterproofing is less satisfactory because it eventually dries and cracks, resulting in leakage.

You can seriously damage wax-treated leather by applying an oil-based waterproofing such as mink oil, Neatsfoot oil or shoe grease. Oils may soften and stretch wax-treated leather, making it more susceptible to leakage and lessening needed ankle support.

It's OK to apply oil-based waterproofing to an oil-treated leather. But, oil-based products are not long-term waterproofers. They are *conditioners*. Oil floats on water, and if the boot gets very wet, the conditioners will wash out. Wax waterproofing can be applied to all kinds of leather without any detrimental effects, so we recommend it.

The best way to apply either wax or oil waterproofing is with moderate heat—no warmer then direct sunlight or a hair dryer at a low setting. Using a soft rag, work the waterproofing into the leather so that it can't rub off during use. Then apply heat so the waterproofing soaks in fully. Waterproofing will be easier to apply to rough-out leather than smooth-out leather.

A recent innovation is silicone-base waterproofing. REI sells it under the name *Ultra-Seal*. Other retailers use different names.

Silicone is an oil, but it is so water-repellent that it won't soften wax-treated leather. The silicone is combined with substances that make it penetrate and adhere to leather—it can't be washed out by water.

Don't use silicone-base spray waterproofings. They contain propellants and solvents that break down cement used in sole lamination.

Waterproofing The Seams And Welt—You need to pay extra attention to these areas. Buy a liquid *seam sealer* specifically designed for this purpose, so it won't harm the synthetic thread used in stitching. It should have good adhesive qualities because seams are subject to abrasion that can wear off the waterproofing. For this reason, you'll need to reapply seam sealer after a rough trip.

Treating The Inside— Perspiration salts from your feet make leather brit-

tle, which can lead to cracking. If the cracking becomes bad enough, foot blisters may result.

Avoid the problem by using a product that softens the interior leather without stretching it. We recommend a brand called *Inner Guard*. It also prevents mildew and interior rot, the two biggest causes of boots falling apart from the inside.

TREATING GORE-TEX UPPERS

Don't apply *any* waterproofing to a Gore-Tex laminated upper because it contaminates the Gore-Tex, reducing its breathability. You can keep the leather parts of the upper looking good by applying shoe polish. This also applies to athletic shoes made with Gore-Tex uppers. Athletic shoes with plain nylon or canvas uppers cannot be waterproofed.

RESOLING AND REPAIR

Most well-built and well-maintained boots can be resoled several times. If your boots have worn soles, but the uppers are in good shape, it's both economical and practical to resole them.

Your local shoe repair shop can handle repairs on leisure shoes and some hiking boots. Repairing and resoling mountaineering and back-packing boots require special expertise and equipment. You may be able to find a local shop with the experience to resole your boots. If not, check with a local sporting-goods store for a shoe-maker that does work by mail.

You can apply Ultra-Seal silicone waterproofing with just the heat of your fingers.

Wax waterproofing can be applied to all kinds of leather. Moderate heat helps the waterproofing soak in.

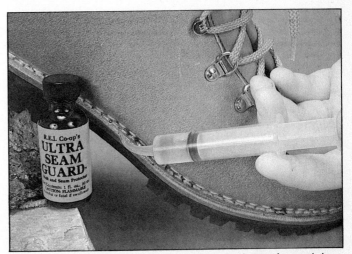

Boot seams are especially vulnerable to leakage. A special seam sealer applied with a syringe provides good protection.

Sleeping Bags

3

A sleeping bag is a heat container. It's designed to trap a layer of still air around your body, so you can warm it. This warmed air is the insulating layer. The thicker and calmer the layer of air, the better job of insulating the bag does.

When sleeping bag designers speak of a bag's *loft,* they're talking about the maximum height the insulation fluffs to. There's a direct relationship between loft and maximum warmth of a sleeping bag. The more loft, the warmer a bag will be.

Sleeping bags differ not only in the amount of loft they have, but also in weight. If you need a light sleeping bag for backpacking or for another sport in which light weight is important, you'll need to choose one of the lighter insulating materials we discuss. You can also use other methods to increase a bag's warmth with only a small weight gain. Radiant-heat-barrier liners and vapor-barrier liners are two examples. They're discussed later in this chapter.

Selection

When choosing a sleeping bag, it's important to carefully analyze your intended use and choose the best bag for your needs. Sleeping bags are made in many different grades of warmth and weight. You may not need the warmest bag in the store—in fact, few people do. If you're a backpacker, warmth and weight are equally important. If you want a bag for car camping or sleeping indoors, weight doesn't matter. In these cases, you need a bag that provides appropriate comfort and warmth at the price you can afford.

Six main factors should affect your purchasing decision—the warmth of a bag, its weight, compressibility, quality of materials, workmanship and cost. Without ignoring any of the categories completely, decide which are more important and determine your need in each. You may be able to make compromises in some areas. In others, your requirements may be rigid.

Sleeping bags are divided into three categories—recreational, backpacking and expedition. We base these on warmth, weight and design features.

RECREATIONAL BAGS

Recreational bags are one-season bags designed for summer camping, car camping or sleeping indoors. They will keep you warm at temperatures near, but not below, freezing. They are filled with down, PolarGuard, Hollofil or a polyester filling.

Because they have less insulation than expedition and backpacking bags, recreational bags are the least expensive of the three categories described here. But this doesn't necessarily mean that quality is sacrificed. Many manufacturers make recreational bags with the same high standards of quality and workmanship as their warmer models. The only difference is that the design, shape and loft of the insulation make them most

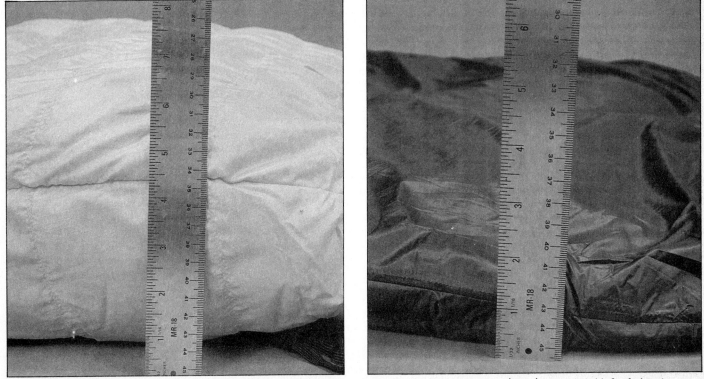

This down-filled expedition bag (left) has a total loft of about 8 inches. The backpacking bag (right) has a total loft of about 5-1/2 inches. Choose a sleeping bag with appropriate loft for your needs.

appropriate for use in moderate temperatures.

Most recreational bags are made with sewn-through construction. Because this is a relatively simple design, these bags can usually be made by machine. Also, they are usually shaped rectangularly. This is comfortable, though not as thermally efficient because there is too much room for body heat to escape.

BACKPACKING BAGS

Backpacking bags are the favorite of most outdoor enthusiasts because of versatility. They're warm enough for all but the coldest conditions and are designed to be light and compressible. Models vary, but most keep you warm in temperatures as cold as 5F.

Most backpacking bags are suitable for three-season use, meaning they will keep you warm in spring, summer and fall. Summer temperatures are mildest and, in most parts of the country, only occasionally drop below freezing. In spring and fall, you can expect the temperature on many nights to drop near or below freezing. Winter bags must be designed to keep you warm in temperatures reaching far below freezing. Of course, much depends on where you live and at what altitude you'll be using the bag.

Manufacturers try to build backpacking bags that are both warm and light. For this reason, backpacking bags meet the needs of most climbers, hikers and cyclists—people who have to carry their sleeping bags. Backpacking bags are filled with down, PolarGuard, Quallofil or Hollofil.

EXPEDITION AND WINTER BAGS

Expedition bags are made to the highest standards of warmth and quality. Because warmth is paramount, designers may sacrifice weight to achieve extra insulation. The comfort zone of these bags extends below 5F, and they may have a total loft of seven inches or more.

Special design features contribute to their warmth. There are no sewn-through seams, which could cause cold spots. A hood and collar reduce heat loss from the head and shoulder area. Zippers are backed with a generous insulating tube.

Expedition bags are filled with either down or polyester insulation of PolarGuard or Quallofil. If you are a high-altitude mountaineer or winter camper heading into a cold, hostile climate, an expedition bag is necessary. But for more hospitable temperatures, it may be too warm. A sleeping bag that cooks you at night can be just as uncomfortable as one that is too cold.

Materials

We recommend that you consider not only the kind of insulation a bag has, but also the materials used in the outer shell and inner lining. All three have an effect on a bag's cost, warmth, durability and comfort.

SHELL MATERIALS

A sleeping bag's outer shell must do three things—resist abrasion, allow moisture to pass through so perspiration can escape, and keep the insulation from escaping.

Nylon is used most often in outer shells. In past years, ripstop nylon was used most, but it has been largely replaced by nylon taffeta. The switch is simply one of changing tastes. Both fabrics are good shell materials, being light, breathable and abrasion-resistant. If you are unfamiliar with outdoor fabrics, see Chapter 1.

Poly/cotton, a polyester/cotton blend, is used in lower-priced recreational bags. Being much heavier than nylon, it is used mostly for recreational bags because weight isn't a prime consideration. Poly/cotton mildews if it gets wet and is not properly dried.

Preventing Leakage—Obviously, you don't want the bag's insulation to leak out. To this end, nylon is *calendered*. The fabric is pressed with heated metal rollers to close small pores.

Another method of preventing leakage is to use fabrics with a tight weave. The higher a fabric's *thread count,* the more tightly woven it is. Nylon fabrics used in shells usually have a thread count of 112x100 or 160x90. Both are effective. For a discussion of thread count, see Chapter 1, page 5.

You can check to see how insulation-proof a shell is before you buy the bag. Rapidly rub your hand across the fabric. If tiny fibers of insulation work their way through the material, you can be suspicious of the bag's quality. A sleeping bag that loses insulation will eventually lose loft and warmth.

A drawstring hood is found on most backpacking and expedition bags. You can draw it tight to reduce heat loss from your head.

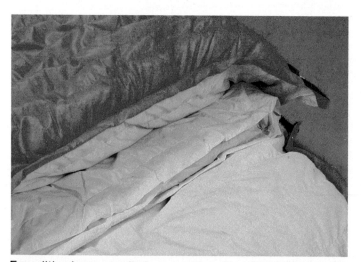

Expedition bags usually have a collar of insulated tubes sewn to the inside lining. This helps reduce heat loss around your shoulders.

In an inexpensive sleeping bag, the fabric may allow insulation to work its way through the shell. Top-quality bags don't do this because the fabric is calendered, has a high thread count, or both.

INNER-LINING MATERIALS

An inner lining must be breathable, insulation-proof and comfortable. Linings are made from either nylon, nyl-silk, cotton or a nylon/cotton/polyester blend, such as trinyl or Tri-blend.

The major difference between nylon and a nylon/cotton/polyester blend is comfort. They are equally breathable and insulation-proof, but blends have a softer feel. Cotton is used on lower-priced bags when weight is not important.

INSULATION

Sleeping bags are insulated with either a natural or man-made material. Down has been proven to be the most effective natural insulation. Man-made insulation is usually made of polyester fibers crimped to make a resilient insulating layer.

Down Insulation—As described in Chapter 1, down is the undercoating beneath the feathers of waterfowl. The thousands of tiny fibers and filaments on each plumule of down form clusters of tiny air pockets that trap air, forming a blanket of dead air.

Down used in sleeping bag insulation comes from either geese, ducks or a combination of the two. Popular knowledge claims that goose down is superior to duck. Actually, the differences are small—goose down lofts only about 10% higher than duck. Duck down can be an excellent sleeping bag insulation.

Some manufacturers advertise that their bags are filled with goose down only. Others extol the virtues of using duck down, or a combination of duck and goose. Don't worry about which type the bag is filled with. You can be certain that reputable manufacturers use a good insulation.

Down offers the best warmth-to-weight ratio of any insulation. Properly cared for, the down inside a sleeping bag will probably outlast the shell and lining. Furthermore, its extreme compressibility accounts for its popularity with backpackers. They need to save space wherever they can.

You're likely to find all sorts of descriptive words used in catalogs and on bag labels. Some of the most common are *Prime Northern, AAA Prime* and *New Prime Quality*. These are strictly sales and advertising words and are not recognized by the Federal Trade Commission as specific descriptions of grade or quality.

One accurate way to check on the lofting ability of down is to find out its *filling power.* Many manufacturers and retailers state this figure in their catalog descriptions. They compute it by placing an ounce of down inside a cylinder. A slightly weighted piston is allowed to sink until it comes to rest on the lofted down. This simulates the weight an outside shell puts on the insulation. The volume filled by the down is then measured. Nearly all sleeping bag manufacturers use down with a filling power of about 550 cubic inches.

Plenty has been written about the poor insulation provided by down when wet. To be sure, this is a major consideration when buying clothing, but it is much less important in sleeping bags. Your sleeping bag will seldom get soaking wet. Modern stuff sacks, packs and tents provide good protection from the elements.

MEASURING THE COMFORT RANGE OF YOUR SLEEPING BAG

Even though there is no industry standard, many manufacturers state the intended comfort range of their sleeping bags by providing the lowest temperatures the bag is designed for. If this information is not available, you can estimate how warm a sleeping bag will be by measuring its loft.

Here's how: Zip up the bag, lay it out and give it some time to fluff up. Measure the height from the floor to the top of the bag by holding a ruler alongside.

Remember, though, that when you are inside the bag, only the insulation on the top half will keep you warm. You flatten the insulation under you. Some designers put 60% of the insulation on the top half; others use only half.

The accompanying table is based on top insulation only, so take 50% to 60% of the total loft you measured and compare it with the figures in the table. It will give you a general idea of the lower temperature of the bag's comfort range. Most manufacturers use *more* insulation than shown in this table.

MINIMUM TEMPERATURE AND INSULATION THICKNESS

Temperature	Insulation Needed (inches)
40F	1-3/4
30F	2-1/4
20F	2-3/4
10F	3-1/4
0F	3-3/4
−10F	4-1/4
−20F	4-3/4
−30F	5-1/4

Source: U.S. Army Quartermaster Corps

Man-Made Insulation—So-called synthetic insulation is widely used in sleeping bags. Because it is heavier than down, it has a lower warmth-to-weight ratio. A sleeping bag filled with synthetic insulation must be about 20% heavier to provide the same insulation value as down. Synthetics don't compress as well either.

Even so, they have many beneficial features relative to down. They are less expensive. They are odorless, non-allergenic and mildew resistant. And when wet, they retain most of their lofting ability.

Currently, four quality man-made insulations are used in bags—Hollofil II, Hollofil 808, PolarGuard and Quallofil. Some less-expensive bags are labeled just *polyester fill.* Such un-branded filling comes from polyester remnants left from other uses—cut and shredded polyester cord from tire-making, for example. They lack the lofting capacity and durability of brand-name fillings.

PolarGuard is a long, continuous fiber that is made into stable batts. Its stability allows it to be used in bags without internal baffles, a feature that saves weight and allows the insulation to fluff to maximum loft. PolarGuard is a bit more expensive than Hollofil and won't compress as well.

Hollofil II and Hollofil 808 are identical except for one thing. Hollofil II is silicone-treated to allow the fibers to move past each other easily, produc-ing a softer, more down-like feel.

As the names suggest, both types of Hollofil fibers are hollow. See page 14. The fibers are much shorter than those in PolarGuard, giving a loose insulation that must be contained in a nylon mesh to keep it from shifting around the bag. This means little in light, sewn-through bags, but for warmer, heavier models with more than two layers of insulation, the re-sulting weight gain is significant. That's why manufacturers usually use PolarGuard instead of Hollofil for their warmest models.

Hollofil II and 808 have the same good warmth-to-weight ratio as PolarGuard.

Quallofil, a relatively new synthetic insulation from the makers of Hollofil, promises to become very popular. Fibers are not just hollow. They have cross bars that divide the hole into four parts. This makes a stiffer, more resilient fiber that lofts more effective-ly than other synthetics. Early tests show it gets 10% to 15% more loft for a given weight than either Hollofil or PolarGuard.

Design Features

The right type of insulation is only one of several factors to consider when choosing a sleeping bag. The way the bag is designed and put together is just as important. Con-struction methods vary, depending on whether down or man-made insula-tion is used. The amount of insulation used also partially determines the most appropriate design.

CONSTRUCTION METHODS FOR DOWN BAGS

Down is a loose type of fill, so down bags must be made to keep the insula-tion distributed evenly around your body. You don't want it to *migrate* be-cause this results in too much down collecting in one place and not enough in others, giving the bag *cold spots.* There are four main types of down bag construction—sewn-through, box, slant-tube and V-tube.

Sewn-Through Construction—This method uses stitching lines to hold the down in place. Down is spread evenly throughout the bag. The inner and outer shells are stitched together. It's satisfactory for recreational and summer bags, but because sewn-through seams contain no down, cold spots result.

Box Construction—This is the sim-plest method that uses *baffles.* A baffle is a wall of fabric that divides the bag into compartments, prevent-ing down migration. Properly de-signed, each compartment should allow the down to loft to its full height, completely filling the space.

Baffles are made of many different materials—nylon tricot, ripstop nylon, stretch fabrics or gauze-like netting. When you examine the bag from the outside, it's difficult to know what material was used in the baffles. The best way to assure quality con-struction is to buy only from reputable manufacturers. You can be sure they use the highest-quality materials and construction methods. Generally, if all observable characteristics are top-quality, so are the rest.

In box construction, the compart-ments are formed by baffles sewn at a 90° angle to the shell. The problem with this method, and the reason many manufacturers have abandoned it, is that the down may not fluff up enough to fill each compartment. If this happens, down can migrate to one corner of the box, producing a cold spot at the other side.

Slant-Tube Construction—Slant-tube design solves the problem of cold spots because the sides of the baf-fles are at a 45° angle. This creates an overlapping effect, so every seam is backed by some insulation. The tubes are typically narrower than those used

PolarGuard is unique among man-made insulations. Because the stable batts are like building insulation, the bag doesn't require internal baffles.

CONSTRUCTION METHODS FOR DOWN BAGS

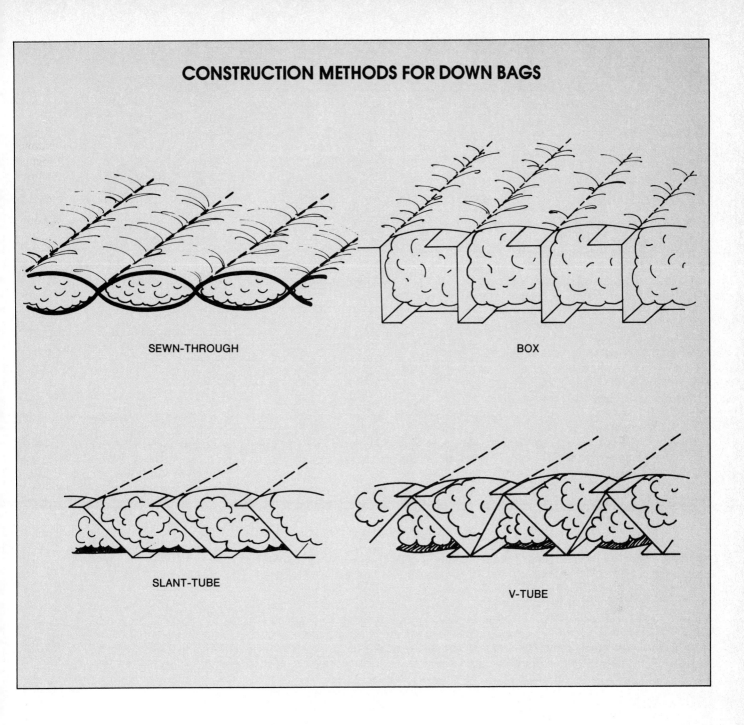

SEWN-THROUGH

BOX

SLANT-TUBE

V-TUBE

in box construction. This better holds the down in place, allowing even lofting and preventing any migration into corners. And because baffles are at a 45° angle, they lie down easier when compressed.

V-Tube Construction—This is the most effective, but heaviest, down bag construction method. Baffles are sewn in a zig-zag pattern so that each compartment has a triangle shape. Every seam is backed with a down-filled compartment.

The extra weight and expense needed to construct a V-tube bag make it most appropriate for expedition bags, in which weight is sacrificed to achieve extreme warmth.

Distribution Of Down—Most down bags have more down on the top of the bag than the bottom. This is because bottom insulation is often rendered ineffective when you lie on it, crushing it flat. Still, it's necessary to put some insulation on the underside because most people roll around

during sleep. If there were no bottom insulation, you'd get cold every time you rolled on your side.

The top and bottom sections of most down bags are separated by a side-wall, or side-block, baffle, running the length of the bag, opposite the zipper. Bags without the side-wall baffle give you a handy option. You can shift the down to put even more on top than bottom, or vice-versa. It's a good way to regulate the comfort of the bag.

CONSTRUCTION METHODS FOR SYNTHETIC BAGS

Sleeping bags using man-made insulation require different construction methods. Because synthetic insulation comes in batts, baffled compartments are unnecessary. The batts need only to be anchored in place. The four major kinds of construction are sewn-through, double-quilt, sandwich and shingle.

Sewn-Through Construction—The sewn-through method used on synthetic bags is much the same as that used in down bags. A batt of insulation is quilted to the outside shell and inside liner by stitching all the way through the batt. This produces cold spots along the seams, of course, which makes it an appropriate method for summer bags only.

Double-Quilt Construction—A double-quilt bag combines two sewn-through layers. One batt is quilted to the outside shell and the other to the inside liner. When the bag is assembled, seams are staggered. Each seam is backed with an insulation layer. There should be no cold spots.

Sandwich Construction—You'll find this method in many of the warmest sleeping bags. It uses at least three layers of PolarGuard. Two layers next to the inside and outside shells are quilted in place with sewn-through stitching. Then, a middle layer, or two, is fixed in by stitching along the edges—called *edge stabilization*. The inner layer(s) of PolarGuard are free-floating, sewn through only at the edges.

This lets them attain their highest levels of loft without being held down by stitching. Also, the small amount of air between insulation layers adds some insulating value.

Layers in sandwich construction are *cut differentially*. This means that the inner layers, with a smaller diameter to cover, are cut shorter. In this way, the layers are kept from pressing against each other, which would hinder lofting ability.

Shingle Construction—In the shingle method, batts of insulation are sewn in at angles, much like the baffles in a slant-tube bag. Because batts overlap each other, there are at least two layers of insulation at any point, and no sewn-through seams.

Distribution Of Insulation—Like down bags, synthetic bags will often have more insulation on top than bot-

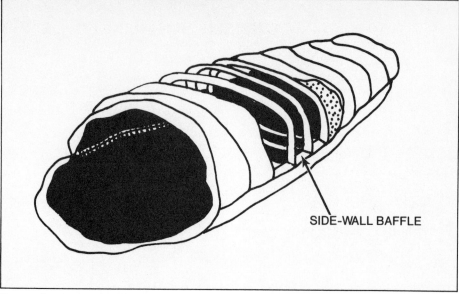

Generally, the top and bottom sections of a down bag are separated by a *side-wall* baffle. It keeps top insulation from shifting to the bottom. Manufacturers usually put more insulation on top, where it does more good.

tom—and for the same reason. For example, a PolarGuard expedition bag may have four layers on the top and only three on the bottom.

SHAPE

Three basic sleeping bag shapes are used—mummy, modified mummy and rectangular. Of course, you'll find many variations on these basic shapes.

Mummy—The true mummy shape is the warmest and lightest of all shapes because it conforms most closely to your body. The close fit keeps inside air circulation to a minimum, reducing heat loss. Mummy bags have a hood to provide a tight closure around the head and neck. This lets you expose only part of your face.

Because of the close fit, people who toss and turn in their sleep may dislike a mummy bag. When you roll over, the bag rolls with you. Mummy bags have been used mainly in the military, where comfort has never been a great consideration.

Modified Mummy—This design is a compromise between the mummy and the rectangular type. Because it is cut wider overall than the mummy, a small amount of insulating efficiency is lost. But most people find the added comfort more than compensatory. Most modified mummy bags have hoods.

Rectangular Bags—Rectangular bags are best-suited to summer use. Because of the generous fit, there's

plenty of air circulation inside the bag, something that's OK in mild temperatures but unsatisfactory if the temperature gets near or below freezing. The large amount of extra room makes these bags very comfortable.

FOOT BOX

Well-designed mummy and modified mummy bags have a high spot built in the bottom of the bag to allow more room for your feet. This *foot box* is more than just a comfort feature. Without the extra room, your feet would press against the inner lining, compressing the insulation and producing a cold spot.

Many sleeping bags have a separate foot piece across the foot of the bag. This piece should be insulated and baffled, so the insulation doesn't fall to the bottom of the section.

DIFFERENTIAL CUT

Earlier in this chapter, we discussed how layers of batting are cut differentially—those on the outside are cut larger to arch over inner layers. Well-designed bags also have inside lining and outside shells cut differentially. Because the inside lining covers a smaller diameter than the outside shell, it can be cut smaller. This allows the insulation to fully loft and eliminates cold spots that can occur if the inner shell presses against the outside.

Differential cut is most important

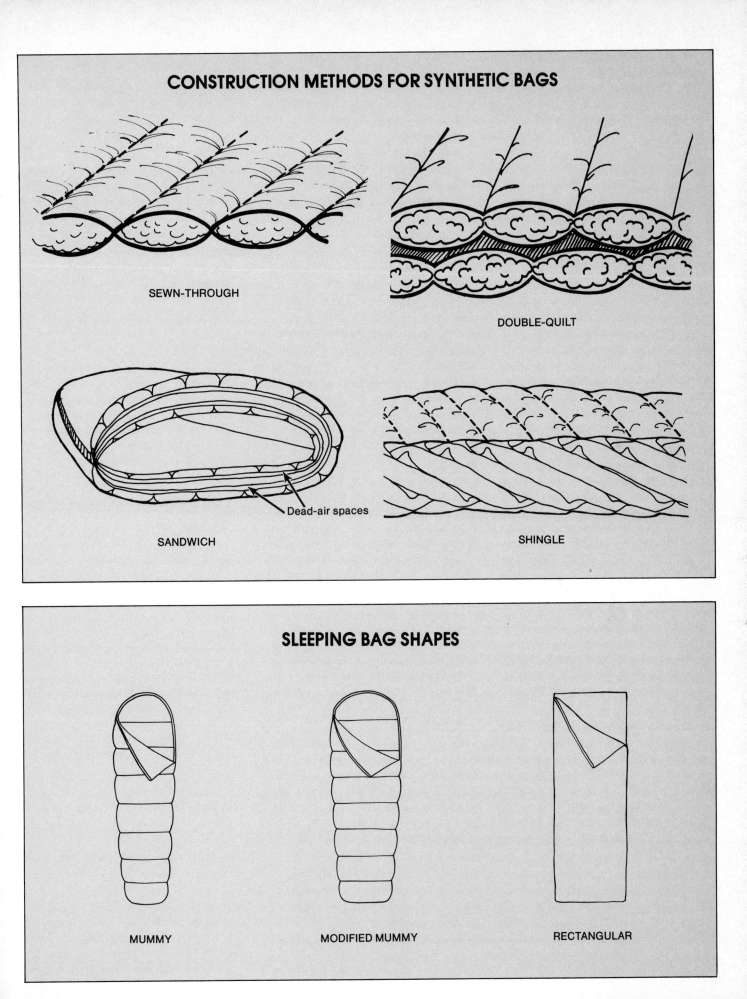

CONSTRUCTION METHODS FOR SYNTHETIC BAGS

SEWN-THROUGH

DOUBLE-QUILT

SANDWICH

Dead-air spaces

SHINGLE

SLEEPING BAG SHAPES

MUMMY

MODIFIED MUMMY

RECTANGULAR

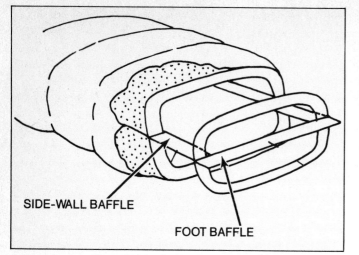

SIDE-WALL BAFFLE

FOOT BAFFLE

A foot box supplies plenty of room for your feet so they don't compress the bag's insulation and cause a cold spot.

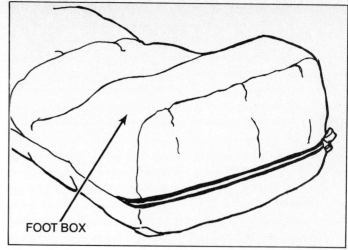

FOOT BOX

Many sleeping bags have a separate foot piece across the bottom of the bag. It should be baffled so insulation doesn't fall to the bottom.

in mummy and modified mummy bags. Rectangular bags use shells that lie parallel to one another. They don't benefit from a differential cut.

ZIPPERS

Sleeping bag zippers are made of either nylon or metal. Nylon types are used on most top-quality bags. Metal zippers—found only on less-expensive bags—are heavier, conduct cold and run with more difficulty. Nylon tracks easily, is very light and, because it won't corrode, has a long life.

Nylon zippers come in two designs—*toothed* and *coil*. Differences are not major. Toothed zippers are easier to start, which is a consideration in cold weather. Coil zippers are self-repairing. You can retrack them by pulling the zipper back across the break. Whether you have a toothed or coil zipper, it should be large enough that it runs easily. Numbers 5, 7 and 10 are most common.

Most modern bags have full-length zippers running either all the way down the side, or down the side and across the foot. In a true mummy bag, the zipper is three-quarters length and is located on top.

A two-way zipper increases the bag's comfort range. Most people are mainly concerned with choosing a bag that will keep them warm. However, some bags can be *too* warm in mild weather. A zipper that you can open from the bottom for ventilation helps cool you down if you get too hot.

Many bags are designed to allow attachment with a second bag. If you are looking for this feature, make sure the bags are designed to match. The two zippers must be the same size and style. One bag must have a right-handed zipper, the other, a left.

Heat can be lost through the zipper, but the problem can be solved by an insulating tube called a *draft tube*. It stops heat loss and drafts along the zipper line and also keeps you from rolling against a cold zipper while you sleep.

Some draft tubes are stitched all the way through the outer shell. This produces a sewn-through seam, and the inevitable cold spot. A better method is to sew the draft tube to the inside lining only. The draft tube should be stitched to the top side of the bag to fall down across the zipper line.

A *zipper stiffener* is a strip of nylon tape stitched to the draft tube alongside the zipper. It prevents the zipper from catching and ripping the shell fabric. It also helps to tie a string, cord or piece of nylon tape to the zipper handle, making it easier to find the zipper in the dark or grab it with cold hands.

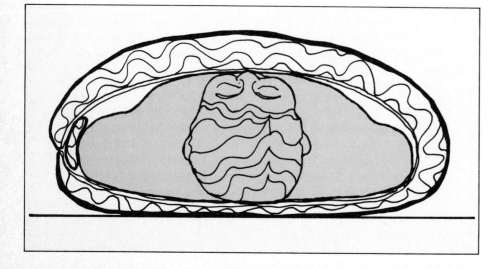

In a bag with a differential cut, the outside shell is cut wider than the inside lining, allowing insulation to loft fully.

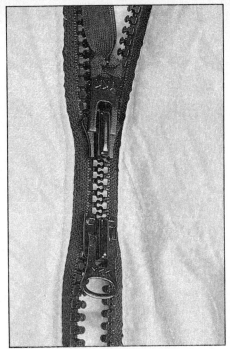

The two-way zipper increases the versatility of your bag by allowing you to open the bottom for ventilation.

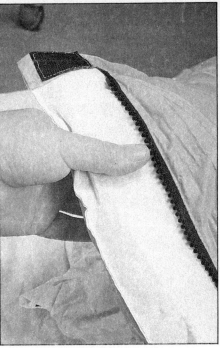

A generously insulated draft tube prevents heat loss through the zipper.

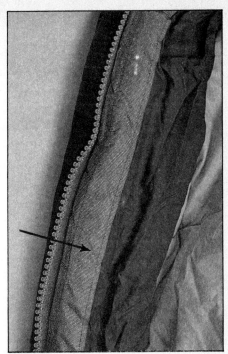

The nylon zipper stiffener (arrow) stitched to the draft tube prevents the zipper from catching on the shell fabric and tearing it.

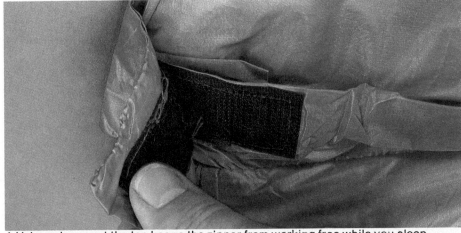

A Velcro closure at the top keeps the zipper from working free while you sleep.

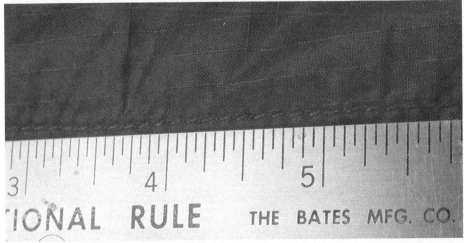

Inspect a sleeping bag's stitching before you buy it. Seams should be sewn evenly with 8 to 10 stitches per inch.

STITCHING

The way a sleeping bag is put together largely determines its life span. It pays to closely examine the workmanship that went into any bag you're considering.

The ends of the zipper should be bar-tacked for increased strength. Seams that must endure extra stress, such as those along the zipper and hood drawstring, should be double-stitched. Count the number of stitches per inch in several seams—8 to 10 per inch is best. A smaller stitch count indicates potentially weak stitching. Too many stitches may weaken the fabric because needle holes have the effect of cutting it.

DRAWSTRINGS AND CORDS

Most sleeping bags have a drawstring closure around the head to close the bag tightly, retaining body heat. A *toggle* fix-lock device or leather washer will keep the drawstring tightened without knots.

Some bags, especially recreational designs, have string or tie tabs sewn into the foot to aid in rolling them up. This is valuable if you roll your bag, instead of stuffing it. This feature can also be used to hang up your bag.

Accessories

After you've found a bag that suits your main needs, you may want to consider buying some accessories to increase your bag's efficiency and comfort range. Some of the accessories are liners or oversacks, sleeping pads or air mattresses, pillows, stuff sacks and ground cloths.

LINERS

Cotton-flannel liners have long been used to keep sleeping bags clean. If your body touches the liner instead of the sleeping bag, it's the liner that gets dirty, not the bag. If you want to use a liner for this purpose, your bag should be equipped with interior snaps or ties to hold the liner in place. Without these, the liner is likely to get twisted and tangled. No liner is worth having if it keeps you awake at night. Cotton liners are most often used in recreational bags.

A radiant heat barrier liner of Tex-o-lite reflects body heat. With it, you can lower the comfort rating of your bag 20F and thereby winterize a summer bag.

Some forward-thinking people have started using liners for another purpose—keeping warm. Adding a liner to a standard three-season bag can increase its temperature range at least 20F, effectively turning it into a winter bag.

Several modern liners accomplish this with minimal weight and bulk. One type is called a *radiant-heat barrier.* It consists of a fabric, usually trinyl—a soft, comfortable polyester blend backed with *Tex-o-lite.* The Tex-o-lite reflects body heat, but still breathes enough to allow perspiration to pass. Radiant-heat barriers are so effective that you'll probably want to use one for winter or cold-weather camping only.

A second type of liner, a *vapor bar-*

Vapor barriers of coated nylon, useful in sub-freezing temperatures, can lower the comfort rating of your bag at least 20F by preventing evaporative heat loss.

The oversack (top) is insulated with PolarGuard and Tex-o-lite to add extra warmth to your bag for cold weather. The uninsulated oversack (bottom) is made of Gore-Tex laminated fabric to protect you from rain, fog and dew.

rier, also has a specialized application. It's a waterproof liner worn inside the bag to prevent evaporative heat loss by enclosing you in coated nylon. In moderate temperatures it's desirable for your perspiration to ventilate through the bag, but the resulting heat loss is what the vapor barrier is designed to stop.

The prospect of sleeping inside a waterproof cocoon doesn't sound pleasant to most people, but studies show that it's not as wet as you might expect. After a certain level of humidity is reached, your body ceases most perspiration.

Vapor barriers are useful in subfreezing temperatures only. In these conditions, perspiration may not pass through a radiant-heat barrier before it freezes. After it turns to ice inside the bag, it can later thaw, soaking the insulation. A vapor barrier prevents this.

OVERSACKS

An oversack is used on the outside of the bag to provide extra warmth or shelter. An insulated oversack acts much like a liner, making the bag more comfortable in cold temperatures. It can turn a summer bag into a usable three-season bag and a three-season bag into an effective winter one.

Uninsulated oversacks of Gore-Tex or coated nylon, often called *bivouac sacks* or *bags,* are designed as small, lightweight shelters from wind, rain, snow and dew. Climbers carry them for planned as well as emergency nights out in the open. They are popular with cyclists because of their light weight. Hikers trekking in a dry climate often carry them as an emergency shelter in case of unexpected rain. Though they provide some additional warmth, they're designed mainly to protect you from rain.

AIR MATTRESSES AND SLEEPING PADS

Sleeping bags don't work especially well without some sort of insulation under them. The bottom insulation gets compacted under your body, losing most cushioning and insulating value. Air mattresses and sleeping pads help solve the problems.

Air Mattresses—They're mainly built for comfort, not warmth. They do a good job of cushioning you from lumpy terrain, such as rocks, roots

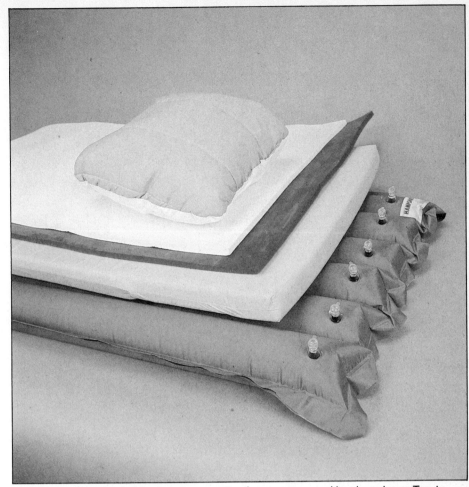

Here's a selection of sleeping accessories for campers and backpackers. Top to bottom—a pillow filled with Hollofil, Ensolite, Blue Foam, Therm-A-Rest pad and air mattress.

and holes in the ground. But they do little to insulate you from the cold ground. The air inside is far from still. In fact, there is so much movement that air mattresses create their own little weather systems.

Even so, air mattresses have their uses. You can use one in tandem with an insulating pad for sleeping on the ground, and of course, you can use one alone for sleeping indoors.

Make sure that your air mattress is durable enough for the uses you'll put it to. Plastic mattresses are made for pool floating, not outdoor sleeping. Instead, get one made of coated nylon or vinyl. Some have separate tubes that you fill individually. If one deflates, the rest stay inflated.

Insulating Pads—If you'll be sleeping on the ground, get a foam sleeping pad. The millions of tiny cells in a foam pad trap a layer of dead air, acting as effective insulation.

Pads are made of either *closed-* or *open-cell foam.* Closed-cell foam does not absorb moisture. Two common types are Ensolite, a polyvinylchloride foam, and Blue Foam, a polyethylene material. Each is durable, extremely light and offers some padding in addition to good insulation.

Open-cell pads are thick and soft. They absorb moisture and must be encased in a waterproof cover. Because inch-for-inch they don't insulate as effectively as closed-cell pads, they are cut thicker to give equal insulation. Two inches of open-cell foam provide about the same insulating value as a half inch of closed-cell foam.

A third type of pad combines the best features of an air mattress with an insulating pad. The Therm-A-Rest pad consists of an open-cell foam pad, a waterproof cover, and a valve. When the valve is opened and the pad unrolls, the foam "inflates" automatically. You can make it firmer by blowing in more air. To pack away the pad, open the valve and roll up the pad to force out air.

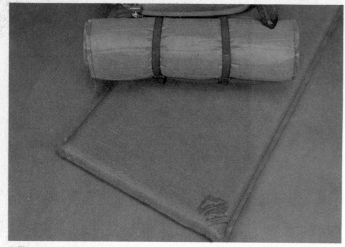

A Therm-A-Rest pad takes up more space when rolled than either Ensolite or Blue Foam, but it offers more sleeping comfort.

Choose the stuff sack that best meets your needs. The smallest sizes are for backpacking. The largest are storage bags to keep your bag stuffed loosely between trips.

Therm-A-Rest pads weigh a bit more than either Ensolite or Blue Foam and are bigger packed. They are quite a bit more expensive than other pads, too. But if sleeping comfort is what you're after, the investment is well worthwhile.

PILLOWS

The question of whether to use a pillow or not is strictly personal preference. Many people can't get a good night's sleep without one. If it's true for you, bring one along when hiking or camping.

For car camping, bring a pillow from home. For backpacking, two types are common. The simplest is the *air pillow*. Also available is a specially made backpacker's pillow of nylon filled with Hollofil. Air pillows suffer the same problem as air mattresses—they offer little or no insulation. Insulate yours by laying your head on a spare shirt or sweater.

The least expensive and most historically proven backpacking pillow is a stuff sack filled with extra clothing.

STUFF SACKS

A stuff sack keeps your sleeping bag dry when you carry it on a pack. It also protects it from abrasion. This is of utmost importance to backpackers and climbers who expose their sleeping bags to branches, rocks and repeated settings on the ground.

Stuff sacks are usually made of coated, waterproof nylon. They should have a storm flap with a drawstring and toggle closure. Some manufacturers sew a handle on the

bottom, a handy feature for removing your sleeping bag from the sack. When choosing a sack, make sure the one you buy is large enough for your sleeping bag. Try it out by stuffing the bag into it.

GROUND CLOTH

Never place your sleeping bag directly on the ground. A ground cloth keeps the bag clean and protects it from abrasion. Even if you're using an air mattress or sleeping pad, use a ground cloth underneath. Most people roll off their pad occasionally.

Of course, if you're sleeping inside a floored tent, a ground cloth is unnecessary.

The least-expensive ground cloth is a sheet of plastic. Coated nylon cloths cost a little more but make up for it in durability and compactness.

SLEEPING ATTIRE

What you wear at night affects the warmth of your bag. There are no hard-and-fast rules about the best combination of clothing to wear when sleeping.

Of course, the more clothing you

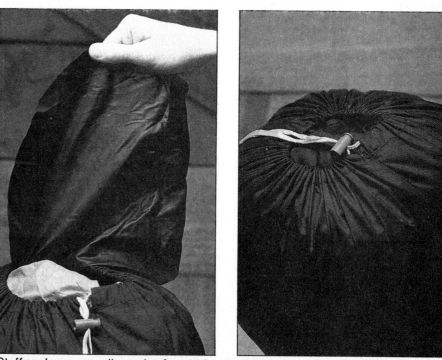

Stuff sacks are usually made of coated, waterproof nylon. They should have a generous storm flap (left) that closes tightly with a drawstring and toggle (right).

HOW TO WASH A DOWN BAG

It's a good idea to wash your down bag annually to remove dirt and restore the down's lofting ability. Here's how:

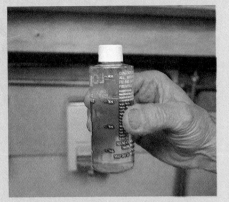

1) Use only soap made specially for down. Any detergents, even mild ones, strip away down's natural oils.

2) Pour in about an ounce of soap for one bag.

3) Stir the soap into lukewarm water.

4) Slowly push your bag under the water.

5) Work in the soap completely by pushing and gently kneading your bag until it's clean.

6) To rinse, drain the tub and run in repeated fillings of clear water, while pushing and kneading all of the soap out.

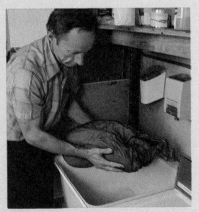

7) Lift your bag out of the tub by cradling it from the underside.

8) Place it in a dryer. Tumble at low heat with a clean tennis shoe thrown in to help fluff the down.

9) When completely dry, the down will be light, fluffy and free of clumps.

wear, the warmer you'll be. If you have the clothing with you, why not put it to 24-hour use? On the other hand, too many clothes can be uncomfortable. You'll have to experiment to find the most comfortable combination.

The single most effective piece of clothing for sleeping is a hat. In a sleeping bag, your head is the only place exposed to heat loss. Reduce some of that heat loss by wearing a watch cap.

In very cold weather, many campers keep their clothing in their sleeping bag for the night so it's warm and toasty in the morning. Climbers often clean their boots and then keep them warm at the foot of their bag. Carry along a small stuff sack for this purpose.

Sleeping Bag Care & Maintenance

A sleeping bag should have a long life. There are several easy steps to keep yours in top condition.

Keep your bag as dry as possible. If it does get wet, dry it as soon as you can. This is especially important for down bags. If left wet for a long time, down's microscopic fibers and filaments may rot, reducing the insulating power.

Handle a wet bag carefully! It's very heavy, and if lifted from the top, baffles may tear. When turning a wet bag, support it from the bottom. Never grasp the outside shell.

You can dry a down bag in a dryer. Tumble it at low heat until completely dry.

A second way to extend your bag's life is to keep it clean. Body oils attract dirt, which reduces the lofting power of any insulation, especially down. We recommend that you wash your bag annually.

Finally, never store your sleeping bag in its stuff sack. It's best to put it in a large storage sack or box that doesn't compress the down or polyester fibers.

WASHING

Sleeping bags get dirty, inside and out. Dirty insulation has reduced lofting power, and a dirty shell can be uncomfortable. Washing a bag makes it more pleasant to sleep in and can actually restore some of the lofting ability of the insulation. Because correct washing procedures are different, we've divided the directions into two categories—down and synthetics.

Washing Down—Natural oils in down give it resiliency and contribute to its lofting power. The major risk in cleaning it is stripping oils away, permanently reducing loft.

You can either dry-clean or handwash your down bag. If you use a dry cleaner, find a professional shop with experience cleaning down products. It pays to be very selective. Never use a coin-operated dry cleaner. The wrong treatment will strip each plumule of its fibers.

Let your dry-cleaned bag air out for at least a week. Unevaporated solvents can be toxic and may last long after

cleaning is complete.

A better and safer idea is to handwash your bag. *Never machine-wash it.* The baffles will tear if handled roughly.

Put the bag in a tub half full of lukewarm water. Use only soap specially made for down. Detergents, even mild ones such as Woolite, strip oils. Work in the soap completely by pushing down and gently kneading the bag. To rinse, drain the tub and run in repeated fillings of clean water, while pushing and kneading all the soap out.

To dry, start by *pressing* out as much water as possible. A heavily soaked bag is an invitation to damage when you lift it. Don't wring it out, just press firmly. Pick up the bag from the underside. Never grab it from the top—you may tear the baffles.

Not only is it faster to dry the bag in the dryer—the constant tumbling also keeps the down from clumping together. Tumble your bag at low heat with a clean tennis shoe thrown in to help fluff the down. When completely dry, your down insulation will be light, fluffy and clump free.

Washing Synthetic Bags—PolarGuard, Hollofil and Quallofil sleeping bags can be handwashed with a mild soap or machine-washed in a commercial *front-loading* machine. Do not use a top-loading agitator! Use warm or cold water.

Air-dry the bag until most of the water has evaporated. Then transfer the bag to a large, laundromat-sized dryer, set at low temperature, for the final drying.

Packs

4

Packs are used in nearly all outdoor sports. Backpackers, canoeists, camera buffs, travelers, skiers and day hikers use packs of varying sizes and designs to carry equipment and clothing. When selecting the pack you need, the first thing to consider is its intended use. Before you go shopping, answer these questions:

1) In what kind of activity will you be using your pack? Hiking, canoeing, traveling or skiing?

2) What will be the duration of most of your trips? One day, overnight or several days?

3) What kinds of equipment and how much will you need to carry? You may need a pack that can carry an extra-large load or have attachments for specialized equipment, such as a camera tripod or mountain-climbing equipment.

What is the ideal pack like? First, it meets your needs well. For example, if you're going on weekend hiking trips only, you won't need the biggest pack in the store. If you plan on using your pack for strenuous activities like cross-county skiing or mountain climbing, you'll need a model that doesn't interfere with body movement.

Second, the ideal pack is comfortable. Packs come in different sizes, and each model fits differently. You may have to shop around for a good-fitting pack just as you would for a good-fitting pair of boots.

Finally, the ideal pack should be durable. Materials and workmanship should guarantee that, if it's used properly, your pack will provide years of good service.

A pack that fits well makes your outings comfortable. A large variety of packs is available.

We've divided the selection of packs into the following groups— external-frame packs, internal-frame packs and rucksacks. At the end of the chapter, we discuss some specialized packs, too. These include children's packs, belt pouches, fanny packs, baby carriers and soft luggage.

You'll be able to find an appropriate pack for any outdoor endeavor. Rucksacks (top) are best for day outings. Frame packs (bottom left) are the most popular choice for overnight trail hiking. Internal-frame packs (bottom right) are best for strenuous activities like off-trail hiking or mountaineering.

External-Frame Packs

An external-frame pack consists of a frame—usually made of aluminum—an attached pack bag, shoulder straps and a hip belt. This type is the most popular choice for trail hiking because it provides excellent weight distribution, allowing you to carry heavy loads comfortably. The frame carries the weight high, putting the center of gravity over your hips. This allows you to walk erect in the optimum hiking posture.

Another feature making the external-frame design excellent for trail hiking is that the frame holds the bag away from your back, increasing ventilation and comfort on long hikes.

But external-frame packs aren't the best choice for all kinds of hiking. In rough terrain with heavy underbrush,

the high-riding external frame can catch on branches. The high profile also causes problems in active sports such as cross-country skiing or mountaineering. With the weight held so high, a shift in the pack may throw you off balance.

FRAME DESIGN

Most pack frames are made of high-strength aluminum alloy tubing. The best frames are made of *aircraft-quality* aluminum, in which molten aluminum alloy is extruded through a die. Inexpensive pack frames may be made of *furniture-grade* tubing, a seamed tube that may not endure rough use.

Tubes are joined together in several ways. Top-quality frames are either welded or joined together with metal couplings. Two of the best welding methods are the tungsten-inert-gas weld (TIG) and the heliarc weld. In less-expensive frames, tubes may be soldered or held together with plastic connectors.

Because any welding process destroys some of a tubing's strength at the joint, quality pack manufacturers use extra-strength tubing. Even after welding, the tubes remain sufficiently strong.

Stiff vs. Flexible Frames—Manufacturers have different theories on how to best carry loads. Most believe stiff frames work best. Others produce a flexible frame, believing that a pack that flexes as you walk is the most comfortable. Currently, there is no consensus of opinion on which works best.

Generally, welded frames in a ladder-like design are stiff. Frames put together with metal couplings are more flexible. Overall, though, the quality of workmanship and materials is more important than the particular construction method. If your pack is made by a quality manufacturer, you can choose the pack frame you find most comfortable and be confident that it's both well-made and durable.

Frame Shape—External-frame packs fall into one of three basic shapes—straight, S-shaped and hip-wrap.

The *straight frame* is seldom used anymore, except in inexpensive packs. The major disadvantage of a straight frame is that it doesn't fit the curve of your spine. At the bottom it digs into your hips, and at the top it is too far away from your shoulders. When heavily loaded, a straight-frame pack has a tendency to pull you backward.

Most modern frames are *S-shaped,* a design that is only slightly more expensive to make than the straight frame. Vertical tubes are bent to approximate the natural bend of your spine. The tubes bend away from your spine.

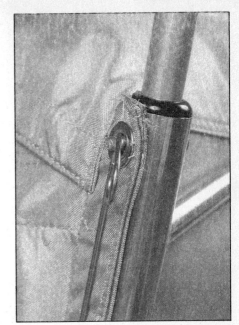

The pack bag is attached to the frame by a clevis-pin arrangement—a strong, secure and durable system.

hips and in toward your shoulders, producing a close fit between the pack and your torso.

Hip-wrap frames are S-shaped with an added "twist." At the bottom, the vertical tubes sweep forward to enclose the hips. In a different hip-wrap design, horizontal tubes are attached to the vertical tubes, and these enclose the hips.

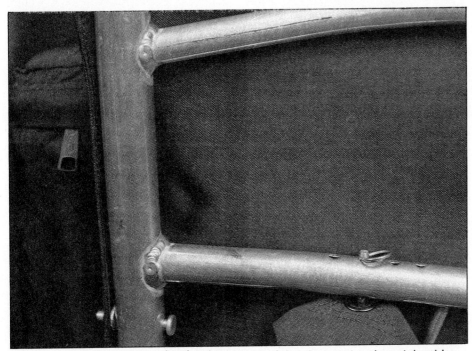

Here's a tungsten-inert-gas (TIG) weld. It's one of the strongest and most durable methods for welding aluminum frames.

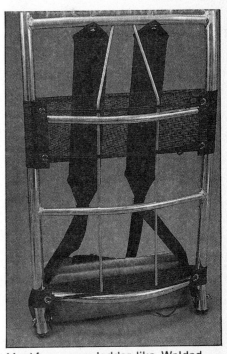

Most frames are ladder-like. Welded frames like this one are stiffest. Frames put together with metal couplings are more flexible.

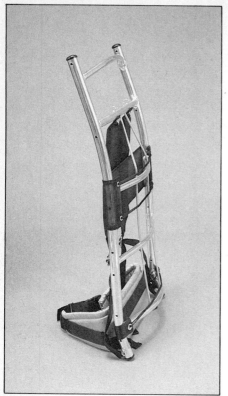

The most common frame design is S-shaped. It's more comfortable than a straight frame because the bent tubes conform better to your back.

Proponents claim that the hip-wrap design provides a more comfortable ride by bringing the center of gravity more directly over the hips. To do this, a hip-wrap frame *must* fit well. If it is either too narrow or too wide, the frame won't work effectively. Again, the best strategy is to try several different frames and decide for yourself which is the most comfortable for your body. Fitting a pack is described later.

Frame Extensions—Many frames have a curved frame-extension bar at the top. It is useful for lashing extra equipment to the top of your pack. With some packs, you can buy a separate frame extension and attach it to your pack when you need the extra capacity it offers.

Internal-Frame Packs

An internal-frame pack consists of a pack bag, at least two internal *stays* to give rigidity, shoulder straps and a hip belt.

Internal-frame packs grew from the need of mountaineers, bushwhackers and cross-country skiers for a large pack that would hug the body and have a relatively low center of gravity. Because internal-frame packs ride relatively low, they don't throw you off balance like a high-riding external-frame pack can. But because the internal-frame pack hugs your back, you can get uncomfortably warm. For this reason, the external-frame pack is still more popular for trail hiking. But, for active sports in rough terrain, the internal-frame pack is usually best.

Internal-frame packs have become very popular as travel packs, too. They're less bulky than external-frame packs and don't have any external framing that can be broken by catching on obstructions or by rough handling.

You'll sometimes hear internal-frame packs called *soft packs*. Technically speaking, if the pack has a set of stays sewn into the pack bag, you should consider it an internal-frame pack. Soft packs have no frame. Some large-capacity soft packs are available, but most manufacturers put internal stays in their soft packs to make them true internal-frame packs.

FRAME DESIGN

The stays of an internal-frame pack offer some rigidity, but the pack is

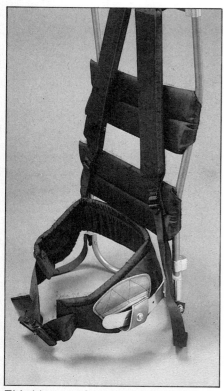

This hip-wrap frame has horizontal bands that enclose your hips. In other hip-wrap frames, the vertical frame tubes sweep forward on both sides of your hips.

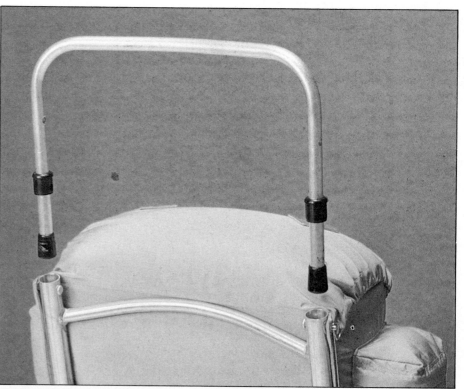

Some packs have an integral frame extension. On others, such as the one shown here, you can get an optional extension. The extension has no structural function but is useful for lashing extra equipment to the top.

still much more flexible than an external-frame pack. The internal frame consists of lightweight, flexible aluminum or plastic stays in either a parallel or X configuration. The stays are sewn into sleeves in the back of the pack bag.

Stays are designed to flex as your body moves. Some manufacturers bend the stays slightly to conform to your spine. It's sometimes possible for you to bend the stays to fit your body better, but do this only with the advice and assistance of a knowledgeable salesperson.

The differences between the parallel and X configurations are still being debated. The parallel design probably flexes more freely, but the X design offers better load control because the stays reach to the corners of the pack bag. To decide for yourself, try on both kinds with a full load and select the design that's more comfortable.

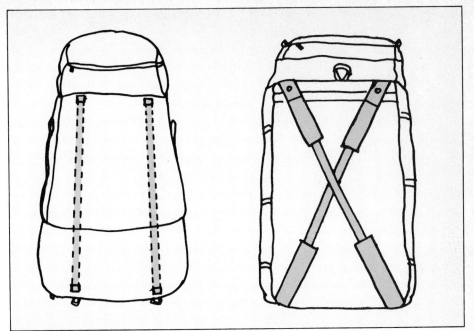

The parallel design flexes more freely than the X type, but it doesn't offer as much load control.

Internal-frame packs ride lower and hug the back more closely than external-frame packs. Because there's little air space in back for ventilation, trail hiking with one can be hot. Even so, the lower center of gravity makes internal-frame packs best for active sports like mountaineering or skiing.

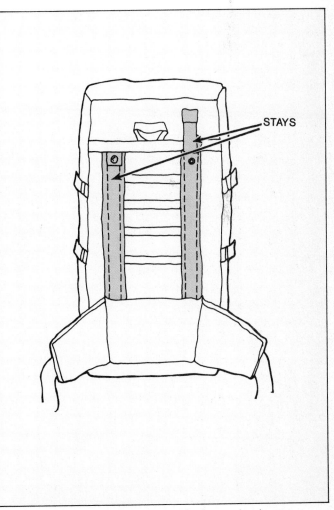

An internal-frame pack's structure features aluminum or plastic stays sewn into sleeves.

Rucksacks

Rucksacks are available in a wide range of sizes. Most have smaller capacities than frame packs and are designed to carry less than 20 pounds. A few rucksacks are large enough that a clever packer can fit in enough gear to take overnight or on multi-day hikes. But rucksacks have outgrown the world of hikers. They're now used by students, bicyclists, tourists and others to carry everyday supplies.

DESIGN

The design of most rucksacks is much less complex than that of frame packs. Lacking a frame of any sort, they depend on the bulk of their contents to give them rigidity. Rucksacks ride most comfortably when they are fully loaded. So, if you need to carry only a few items in your rucksack, it will feel most comfortable if you pack in a sweater to fill up the empty space. Or, consider having rucksacks of different sizes.

Suspension Systems

This is the method used to attach the pack to your body. Nearly all packs use three basic parts in a suspension system—hip belt, shoulder straps and back bands.

Modern pack manufacturers design their packs so most of the weight is carried by your hips, which are more heavily muscled than your upper torso and shoulders. With the weight of the pack centered over your hips—rather than pulling back from your shoulder—it's easy to walk erect.

Because the suspension system is primarily responsible for a pack's comfort, some experts consider it the most important part of a pack. For this reason, we closely examine each part of the suspension system, pointing out the differences you're likely to find.

HIP BELT

The idea that a pack's weight should be carried on the hips is not new. In fact, the inventor Merriam proposed the idea back in 1886, but it wasn't until the early 1960s that the hip belt began showing up on mass-produced packs.

Origins—The well-known pack designer Dick Kelty is credited with producing the first commercially available packs with hip belts. As the story goes, the idea came to him while hiking with some friends. Somebody called for Kelty's attention: "Hey Dick, look—no hands!" he exclaimed. The friend had stuck the ends of the pack frame in his back pants pockets. The pants were supporting the weight of the pack and taking the burden off his shoulders.

The first hip belts were unpadded, two-piece belts. They were attached to the bottom ends of the frame tubing and buckled in front of the hips. The belts did their task though they often bruised the user's hips. Two-piece belts are still made, but they are now well-padded.

More common is the one-piece

Rucksacks are true multi-use packs. They're used by day hikers, students, cyclists, travelers and photographers to carry everything from groceries to schoolbooks.

A correctly fitted pack puts most of the weight on your hips, which are stronger than your shoulders.

padded design—the belt fully encircles the hips, attaching to the pack at its rear, and buckling in front. By circling your waist, it distributes the load of the pack better than a two-piece belt. Properly constructed and fitted, the belt should rest *on top* of your hip bone, carrying as much as 75% of the pack's weight, and not interfering with your walking motion.

Hip belts should be padded with closed-cell foam, so they won't soak up water and perspiration. It's also a good idea to find one equipped with a quick-release buckle enabling you to remove the pack quickly in case of an emergency.

On external-frame packs, the hip belt attaches to the two bottom ends of the frame. Internal-frame packs may have either a one- or two-piece belt system. In either case, the belt is stitched directly to the pack bag.

Because rucksacks are not designed to carry much weight, they usually don't have a hip-belt suspension system. Instead, they have an unpadded waist strap that stabilizes the load rather than supporting any weight.

SHOULDER STRAPS

Pack weight not supported on your hips is carried by your shoulders. This is why your pack should have *padded* shoulder straps. Again, the best padding is closed-cell foam sewn into sleeves that are inside the strap. Some manufacturers make sleeves with a differential cut so the material inside the strap doesn't bunch up on your shoulder.

You can adjust shoulder straps by loosening a buckle and shortening or lengthening the straps. Essentially, this moves the pack toward or away from your shoulders if the pack is centered over your hips and the waist belt is secure. Make sure that the nylon used in the straps isn't so slippery that it slides through the buckle under stress.

Most often, the straps on an external-frame pack fasten to a shoulder-level crossbar on the frame.

Shoulder straps should be padded with closed-cell foam, sewn into sleeves. Notice the clevis-pin attachment common to frame packs.

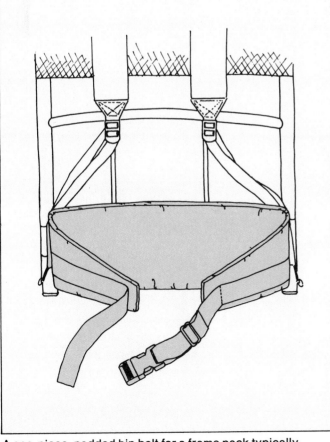

A one-piece, padded hip belt for a frame pack typically attaches to the two bottom ends of the frame.

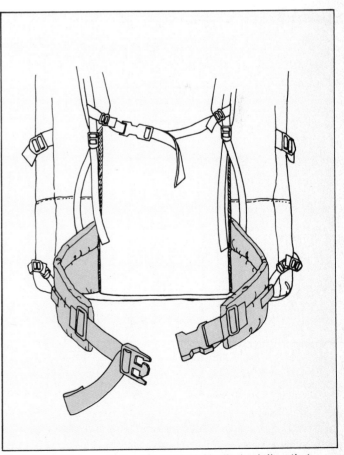

On internal-frame packs, the hip belt is stitched directly to the pack bag.

Occasionally, designers use a *yoke system*, in which the straps curve over your shoulders, cross in back, and attach to the bottom of the frame. An additional strap connects the tops of each shoulder strap to the frame crossbar. This connecting strap is adjustable, which allows you to determine how close the pack rides to your shoulders.

Internal-frame packs use the same two shoulder-strap systems. But instead of the straps being attached to a frame, they are sewn into the pack bag. Make sure that the straps are well-reinforced with multiple lines of stitching and patches of leather, seatbelt webbing or extra fabric.

Which is better, the conventional shoulder strap system or the yoke design? Again, there's disagreement. But by having two options you're able to find the type best-suited for you. Try on different shoulder-strap systems and choose the one you find most comfortable.

Many internal-frame packs have more elaborate suspension systems than those found on external-frame packs. This is because some manufacturers produce only one size of a given model, depending on an elaborate adjustable-strap system to adapt the pack to different body sizes.

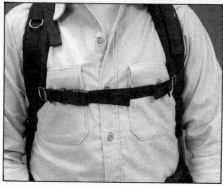
Many internal-frame packs use a sternum strap to keep the shoulder straps secure.

Sternum Strap—Many internal-frame packs have a sternum strap, which connects the two shoulder straps across your chest, midway between the base of your throat and your stomach. It keeps the shoulder straps from sliding too far down on your shoulders. By loosening or releasing the strap, you can vary the way your shoulder straps ride.

Sometimes, even after manipulating straps, you may find that a given sternum strap won't fit you right. This sometimes happens if you are very tall or short. In this case, try a different pack.

BACK BANDS

This is what your back rests against while you wear the pack. In external-frame packs, back bands are usually made of nylon fabric, wrapped around the frame and tied with cord. This keeps the pack bag slightly away from your back.

The Pack Bag

Pack bags share common characteristics, whether they are attached to an external frame, part of an internal frame or a rucksack. Here, we discuss the materials used in pack bags, their loading systems and construction methods. We also point out some useful features available on pack bags.

CAPACITY

A pack bag should have sufficient capacity to hold all of your equipment. Generally, the larger the pack bag, the more expensive it is. The largest bags have a capacity greater than 4000 cubic inches, and a few huge ones let you stuff in 6000 cubic inches. Such bags are used for very long hikes or mountaineering expeditions.

Pack bags with a capacity between 3000 and 4000 cubic inches are popu-

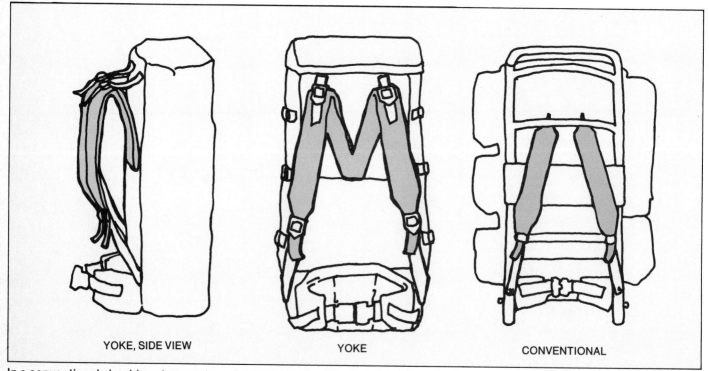

| YOKE, SIDE VIEW | YOKE | CONVENTIONAL |

In a conventional shoulder-strap system, the straps are fastened at shoulder level. In contrast, yoke straps pass over the shoulders, down the back, and fasten lower down on the pack.

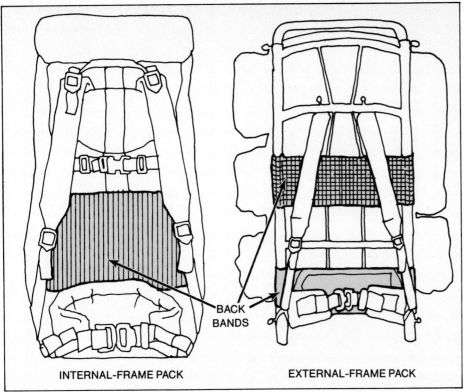

INTERNAL-FRAME PACK   EXTERNAL-FRAME PACK

BACK BANDS

The back band of an internal-frame pack is a pad stitched to the bag. Back bands on an external-frame pack are usually nylon fabric or mesh wrapped tightly around the frame and secured with cord. Because external-frame packs have an airspace between back band and bag, they are cooler than internal-frame packs.

lar for two- or three-day use. Smaller models are best for day hikes.

Both internal- and external-frame packs are available in a full range of sizes.

MATERIALS

Most pack bags are made from either nylon pack cloth or Cordura nylon. Cordura is more abrasion-resistant and is often used in conjunction with pack cloth as reinforcement on the bottom of the pack. Internal-frame packs are often made entirely of Cordura because mountaineers and skiers need the strongest possible pack.

Many packs are made of coated nylon fabric. But even if your pack is made of coated fabric, it probably isn't waterproof. Needle holes along seams and zipper lines will readily admit water. You can seal the seams yourself, but this is a laborious and not completely effective process. It's better to use a poncho or waterproof pack cover if you need to protect your equipment from heavy rain or river spray.

A waterproof pack cover is the most effective way to keep your equipment dry in rainy weather.

Choose a pack with a bag large enough to hold the equipment you need. But don't automatically buy the largest pack. Larger packs are generally more expensive, and it's a waste of money to buy space you don't need.

LOADING SYSTEMS

Most packs are loaded either through the top, when the pack is standing upright, or through front panels, opened while the pack is lying on the back side.

Top-loading frame packs usually have a hold-open device that makes it convenient to load gear. Internal-frame top loaders have a drawstring and toggle that close the pack's top opening. You'll also find a storm flap that straps down over the top. It should be large enough to keep out dirt, sticks, water and snow.

A few top loaders, especially some internal-frame packs, have an extension sleeve that you can pull up if you need to carry an extra large load. Some extension sleeves are so long that when they are pulled out to full length, the pack can be converted into a *bivouac sack*—a one-person shelter. This feature shows up most often on internal-frame packs designed for mountaineering.

Front-loading, also called *panel-opening,* packs are becoming more and more popular. The major advantage is that the design allows several compartments. You can open one compartment to get something without disturbing the contents of the entire pack. It's easier to find things, too, because you don't have to reach down inside the bag from the top.

Front-loading bags are usually closed by either a horizontal or semicircular zipper, or a combination of the two. Some front loaders have compression straps that allow the pack to be cinched up, reducing pressure on the zippers.

The major drawback to front loaders is that the pack must be set on its back if you want something. It's inconvenient in muddy, wet or snowy terrain. In these cases a top loader is definitely better. But for hiking in primarily dry country, or for traveling, front loaders are more convenient.

Some packs combine top- and front-loading features. The bag is divided into two compartments, a bottom one that opens with a horizontal or semicircular zipper, and a top-loading upper compartment that has a drawstring and flap.

The debate about which bag design is best has lingered for years. Both are still available, so obviously each has advantages. Most hikers seem to prefer divided bags for the ease in

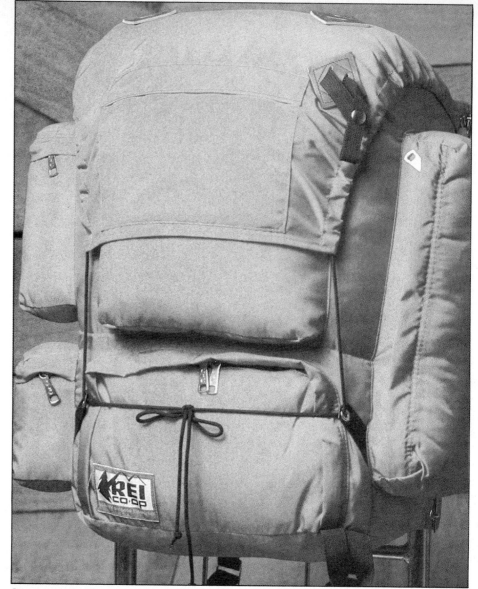

Some packs have both front- and top-loading features. The upper half of this one loads from the top, the bottom half through a front zipper.

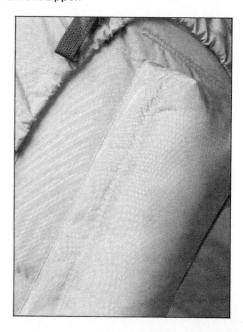

Well-made pack bags have two lines of stitching on all seams subject to stress. Also look for a nylon coil zipper with a storm flap to keep out rain. Outside pockets like these are the best place to store small items you need often.

which equipment can be organized. The single-compartment bag is clearly best for carrying large, bulky equipment.

CONSTRUCTION METHODS

A well-made pack bag will last for years. To get a good one, it pays to closely examine the seams all around the bag to make sure that they have been properly sewn. See that the stitching isn't too close to the edge seams. Under stress, such seams could pull apart. Look for even stitching, about 8 to 10 stitches per inch. A seam with fewer stitches is likely to be weak. One with more than 10 per inch may be weakened due to too many needle holes.

Some bags have two or more stitching lines at stress points. This is especially important where shoulder straps are sewn onto internal-frame packs and rucksacks, and where any accessories such as buckles, straps and ice-axe holders are attached.

Reinforcing fabric or leather patches should be sewn on where there might be a lot of abrasion—such as the pack bottom—where straps are sewn to the bag, and where you might lash gear.

Nylon or cotton-wrapped polyester thread is used most often in pack stitching. Nylon is stronger, but cotton/polyester thread is easier to work with. In addition, it swells when wet, helping to keep water from leaking through needle holes.

Coil zippers are best for packs because they run smoothly around curves and corners. Zipper ends should be bar-tacked.

ACCESSORIES

Most packs have accessories attached to the pack bag. They can be permanent or removable. Some come as standard equipment. Others are optional. Obviously, it's unwise to pay for features you'll never use. Find out exactly what you need and buy only that.

Pockets—These are definitely handy. They're the best place to store small items that must be readily available or would be lost in the bulk of the main compartment. Nearly every large pack comes with external pockets sewn onto the bag.

Internal-frame packs often have a large pocket built into the storm flap on top of the bag. Because these packs

A leather crampon patch is useful for attaching crampons and other accessories to the outside of your pack.

An ice-axe loop is the most convenient way to strap your axe to the outside of your pack.

are designed primarily for rugged use, they usually don't have side pockets that could catch on rocks and branches. But external-frame packs will have several side pockets and perhaps a front pocket, too.

Make sure that the pockets have coil zippers protected by a storm flap to keep out rain.

Detachable accessory pockets are available for some packs. With them you can customize your pack to occasionally carry extra loads.

Ice-Axe Loop—Ice-axe loops are most frequently found on internal-frame packs and rucksacks designed for mountaineers who need to strap an ice axe to the outside of the pack. The loop consists of a simple strap of nylon webbing sewn to the rear of the bag. You insert the axe point downward, then turn it around so the point is up. Secure ice axe shaft to the pack with a strap and buckle.

Crampon Patches And Lash Points—Typically, these are the pieces of leather stitched to the pack bag, through which cord or straps can be strung for tying accessories. They are often used to tie crampons onto the outside of the pack, eliminating the risk that the sharp points will puncture equipment inside your pack. Sleeping pads, camera tripods and tent poles are other items you can tie to lash points.

Compression Straps—If you don't have a full load in the pack, you'll want to cinch up the pack with com-

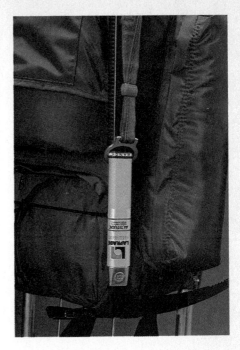

pression straps. This is useful because internal-frame packs and rucksacks don't ride well unless they're full. With the compression straps tightened, the load is kept closer to your back.

Fitting A Pack

Fitting a pack correctly is as important as fitting a pair of boots to your feet. With a well-fitting pack, you'll be able to carry a lot of weight comfortably. It pays to be selective, so try on several different packs with the features you want. If possible, try a pack in the field, by borrowing or renting a model you're interested in. If you've tried on and used a pack, and it still doesn't feel comfortable, don't buy it.

When trying on packs in a store, make sure that you put some weight in the pack bag. Otherwise, the pack "floats" on your back, and you can't tell how it will feel fully loaded. Most stores have sandbags or other weight available for such a purpose.

Most models of external-frame packs come in several different sizes. Manufacturers often publish fitting guidelines that list the recommended frame size for your height. You can generally rely on these guidelines. However, if you have a small torso for your height, you may need a smaller pack than called for. Always try on a pack and, if possible, different sizes, too.

FITTING A FRAME PACK

Here are the four main steps to fitting a pack with conventional suspension:

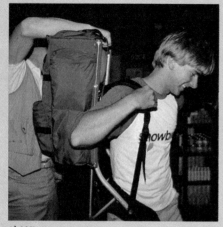

1) When trying on a pack, make sure there's some weight in the bag.

2) Adjust the shoulder straps to the correct length.

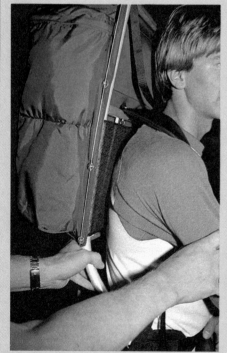

3) After the straps are adjusted, they should run level from the top of your shoulder to the frame.

4) Hunch your shoulders and tighten the hip belt. If the frame is the right size, the belt should rest comfortably on top of your hip bones.

Of course, if you are ordering your pack by mail, you won't be able to try it on. In this case, rely on the fitting charts provided by the retailer. Most reputable outdoor-equipment suppliers that sell by mail have developed reliable sizing guidelines. And if the pack you order doesn't fit just right, they'll exchange it for the right size.

Fitting A Pack With Conventional Suspension—Put the pack on and adjust the straps so the point at which they attach to the frame is level with the top of your shoulders. Next, with your shoulders hunched, fasten the hip belt around the *upper* part of your hip bone. When you relax your shoulders, the pack should settle and the weight rest primarily on your hips.

Now, examine yourself in a full-length mirror. The shoulder straps should still be approximately straight over your shoulders. If they angle sharply downward, the frame is too short. If they angle up, the frame is too large.

Fitting A Pack With Yoke Suspension—You'll need to use a slightly different method. Since the shoulder straps connect to the frame at the bottom, you'll need to check to see that they hug your shoulders closely. Next, look at your back. If there's space between the straps and your back, the pack may be the wrong size, or the straps may need adjustment.

Fitting A Hip-Wrap Frame—These are more difficult to fit than S-shaped frames. Not only must the frame be the right height, but the side bars must fit your hips just right.

If the bars are too far apart, the hip belt slides down. If they are too narrow, the bars will rub, bruising your hips and interfering with your stride. It's sometimes possible to bend the side bars of a hip-wrap frame. But you should never do this without the advice of a knowledgeable salesperson. Not all hip-wrap frames are made to be adjustable.

Fitting An Internal Frame Pack—Internal-frame packs may have either a conventional or yoke suspension system that is adjustable. Use the same fitting methods described for external-frame packs. The major difference is that internal-frame packs usually offer more adjustments and are therefore easy to fit, as long as you have some expert advice.

Loading A Pack

All packs, whether internal-frame, external-frame or rucksacks, are loaded basically the same way. Slight variations exist for particular packs and activities.

First, load the heaviest items close to the top of the pack and place them so they are next to your back. This puts the pack's weight closer to and over your hips—your center of gravity. This allows you to stand erect without the pack pulling you backward.

Second, pack the items you are likely to need first in a handy place. This includes rain gear, maps, snack food, camera and an extra sweater or coat. Sometimes you can store these items in outside pockets.

Third, take care to balance your load. If you pack a heavy item on one side of the pack, balance it with another heavy item on the other.

Internal-frame packs cling close to your body and are inherently more stable than external-frame packs. Even so, be careful about where you pack the heaviest items. For hiking in easy terrain, pack them near the top. For rugged use, lower the weight a little to increase the pack's stability. Every pack rides differently, so it's a good idea to experiment with different loading techniques until you find one that works best for you.

Packing a rucksack can be either simple or even more complicated than loading frame packs. Rucksacks are used for myriad city tasks, including carrying groceries, books, camera equipment and an extra sweater.

In such situations, most users simply pack in the few items they're carrying and head off. But for longer excursions, day hikes and bicycle rides, carelessly packed rucksacks are uncomfortable. Sharp objects dig into your back, and a partially packed rucksack doesn't ride as well as a full one.

To make your rucksack ride better, pack the heaviest items near your back so they don't pull back on your shoulders. Wrap sharp items in a sweater, extra shirt or coat to protect your back. And if you have extra space, you'll get a more comfortable ride by stuffing in a light piece of clothing to fill empty space and give the pack more rigidity.

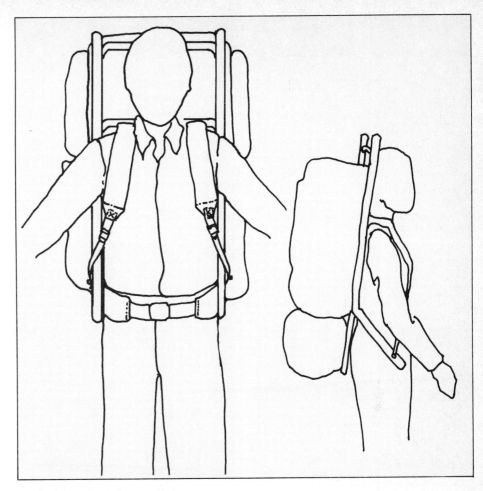

Hip-wrap frames must be the right height, and the side bars must be the correct width for your hips. If the bars are too wide, the belt slips down. If too narrow, the bars rub against your hips.

Here's the correct way to load your pack for a comfortable hike. When the heaviest items are next to your back and near the top of the bag, most of the weight is over your body's center of gravity.

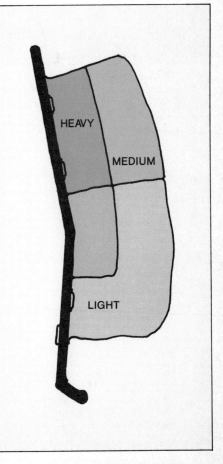

Children's Packs

Children who are old enough and enthusiastic about hiking usually want to carry their own packs. Parents of hiking children have discovered that it's important to limit the weight they have to carry. Usually, children are content to carry a lunch and some clothing.

It's important to find a pack that fits. The best choice for many children is to outfit them in a *junior-sized* rucksack.

When the child is about four feet tall, he can start using a children's frame pack. Several manufacturers produce adjustable models that have either telescoping frames or a system with straps that can be set at different widths.

Fitting packs for children is the same as for adults. Don't buy a pack that's too big in the hope that the child will grow into it.

Baby Carriers

Two kinds of baby carriers are available. Soft carriers are suitable for newborns to three-year-olds. Frame carriers are best for older children.

Soft carriers cradle the child in front of you. They're the only pack that should be used before the baby can hold its head erect. And, they're most comfortable when the child weighs less than 20 pounds.

Frame packs carry the baby on your back, usually facing forward. The baby must be able to hold its head up. There is usually space underneath for storage.

Belt Pouches & Fanny Packs

You use a belt pouch on your pack to carry small items such as an extra camera lens or filters, sunglasses, or a map and compass.

Fanny packs have larger capacity. They strap around your waist, with the pack usually carried in back. Some photographers, though, turn them around so the pack is in front. It's a handy way to carry extra lenses, filters and film, instead of carrying them in a large pack that would have to be removed to get equipment.

Cyclists and skiers also use fanny packs to carry food, a few tools or extra clothing.

Soft Luggage

Waterproof nylon or canvas soft luggage is gaining ground on leather luggage. Cost is one reason, convenience another. Soft luggage is ideal for short-distance travel in which light weight and maneuverability are important. Travelers to foreign countries find that soft luggage is easy to handle on and off trains, buses and taxis. When properly packed, it stands up well to airline handling, too.

Soft luggage comes in many different designs—duffle bags that can be either hand- or shoulder-carried, garment bags, suitcases, shoulder bags and briefcases.

When you consider soft luggage, look for the same high-quality construction you look for in packs. Stitching should be even, stress points should be reinforced and double-stitched, and zippers should be bar-tacked.

The frame carrier (left) is best for an older infant who can hold his head up. A soft carrier (right) is the only kind to use before the infant can do this by himself.

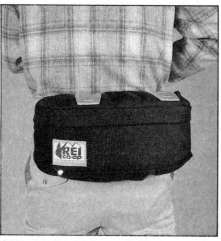

Although there are exceptions, fanny packs usually fit best with the pack in back.

Soft luggage is great for lightweight traveling.

These internal-frame packs can be converted into a suitcase or shoulder bag. A removable zippered flap covers the pack straps when not in use.

Tents & Shelters

5

In most parts of North America, overnight camping requires a tent. Like clothing and sleeping bags, tents protect you from wind, rain, cold, snow, sun and insects.

In the past few years, tents have undergone radical changes. Modern, lightweight fabrics provide outstanding protection from wind and rain. Flexible aluminum and fiberglass poles are used for external support, making possible new designs that offer more headroom than traditional designs.

Successful tent manufacturers must be architects, engineers and sewing experts. Building a tent is a complicated business. The tent must be durable and extremely stress-resistant. It must use space efficiently. And it should be as light and compact as possible.

Because tents are designed for specific uses, it's important to decide which of your outdoor activities require a tent. It is unlikely that one tent provides everything you need, so be prepared to make a few compromises.

For example, a small, low tent stands up to strong winds, but it offers less headroom. A tent with plenty of insect netting is comfortable for summer use, but it may not provide enough warmth for spring and fall camping. Modern dome and arch tents provide good headroom, but they require more poles. These use space and add weight in a pack.

Here are five questions to ask your-

self before you go shopping for a tent. We apply these five questions to the discussion of different kinds of tents, materials and construction methods.

1) What is your most frequent use—backpacking, car camping or mountaineering?

2) What type of weather will your tent have to face?

3) How many people have to sleep in the tent?

4) Are there any special features you need, such as insect netting or extra room for equipment?

5) How much money are you willing to spend?

Categories

There are three tent categories—camp, backpacking and mountaineering. The key to finding the right kind of tent is to decide what you need it for most. If you need it for just one activity such as car camping or one-season backpacking, selection is simplified. But, many people use a tent for different activities, and if this includes you, choosing is more difficult.

Tents share common design and construction methods, as well as many of the same materials and fabrics. First we discuss different kinds of tents, then go into the various materials, designs and construction methods used.

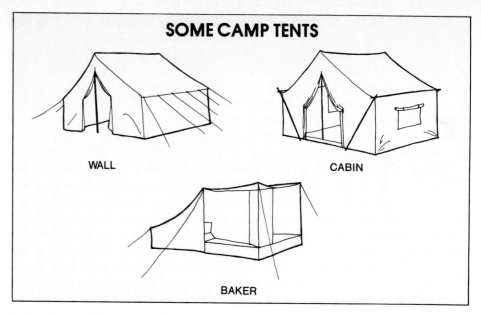

SOME CAMP TENTS

WALL

CABIN

BAKER

CAMP TENTS

These are designed for car campers, canoeists and others for whom weight is not the most important factor. The lightest camp tents, for four or more people, weigh about 15 pounds. Heavyweight models may tip the scales at over 50 pounds! Weight depends on materials, size and design.

There's a trend toward lighter, more compact camp tents, partially because many car campers drive small cars and don't have room for a huge tent. Some of the smaller camp tents can be used by large groups of backpackers who can share out the load of a heavy tent.

Camp tents are often used for extended trips. They have features that make long stays pleasant—plenty of headroom, insect netting in windows, awnings that extend out the front door, and sometimes, netting-enclosed screen rooms for sleeping out on balmy nights. Some camp tents have a separate *rainfly*—a waterproof cover.

Camp tents are made of either canvas, cotton/polyester, nylon or a modern fabric called *Evolution 3*—a three-layer laminate of spun-bonded polypropylene. It's considered a replacement for canvas.

You'll find four basic shapes of

Camp tents have plenty of head room and floor space, making them perfect for family outings.

Umbrella tents usually have external poles and an awning over the front door.

camp tents—umbrella, cabin, wall and baker.

Umbrella Tents—They're recognized by the pyramidal shape and square floors. Modern umbrella tents have an external, free-standing frame that provides ample interior space. Many come with an awning you stake outside the front door, providing extra protection in the rain and sun.

Cabin Tents—Also called *cottage* tents, cabin tents are the roomiest of all camp tents. Three external poles support walls and a sloping roof. Although the center pole is in the middle of the front door, most cabin tent doors are so large that it's easy to step around the pole. Awnings and screen porches are easy to add to a cabin tent.

Wall Tents—Basically, a wall tent is an A-frame design with vertical walls, not slanted, to increase headroom. The tent is supported by either two vertical end poles, or two end poles plus a horizontal ridgeline pole. Sides are staked out with guy lines. Again, a separate awning may be added to the front.

Baker Tent—The baker tent is a modified lean-to. It has a large front wall that can be staked up with poles to make an awning, or collapsed to enclose the front of the tent. Some models of the baker tent have the awning outfitted with insect netting to make a screened-in room in front of the main tent.

Baker tents were originally designed to take advantage of the warmth of a fire built in front of the tent. You may still see people doing it, but it's unsafe. Sparks can easily set fire to equipment stored inside.

This free-standing, modified dome tent is an example of some of the exciting new designs available to backpackers and mountaineers. It sleeps 6 and weighs only 12 pounds.

BACKPACKING TENTS

This category is the largest and most varied. A good backpacking tent should be light and compact enough to carry in a pack, rugged enough to survive storms, durable enough to last for years, and well-ventilated for comfortable sleeping.

The selection of backpacking tents covers emergency tube tents and tarps, small bivouac sacks, and elaborate domes, tunnels and A-frames that sleep one to six, or more, people.

Shopping for a modern backpacking tent is fun. In addition to the long-proven A-frame design, you'll find domes, tunnels, and sweeping, soaring shelters that defy description. Of course, esthetics is not the most important consideration in selecting your tent—function is—but it's exciting to know you can buy a tent that's both functional and beautiful.

Most people prefer tents that set up quickly and easily, requiring few guy lines and stakes. A current trend is to produce a tent that stands by itself—called *free-standing*—supported by an exterior "skeleton" of aluminum or fiberglass poles. You can set it up in one place, then pick it up and move it to a new site. Stakes and guy lines are not needed to hold the tent up, but they may be necessary to anchor it in strong winds.

Whether you choose a free-standing tent or one requiring guy lines and stakes, your tent should have a pole system sturdy enough to endure strong winds and moderate snow loads. Backpacking tents are not designed to withstand the Arctic blasts a mountaineering tent can survive, but they should be able to withstand some hostile weather. A-frames, domes and tunnels can perform well in strong winds.

Coated, waterproof fabrics are not practical materials for tent canopies. Regardless of how well they are

In contrast to bulky camp tents, backpacking tents are light and compact enough to carry on a pack.

A free-standing tent is self-supporting. You can lift it to move it to a new location or upend it to shake out dirt, leaves and pine needles.

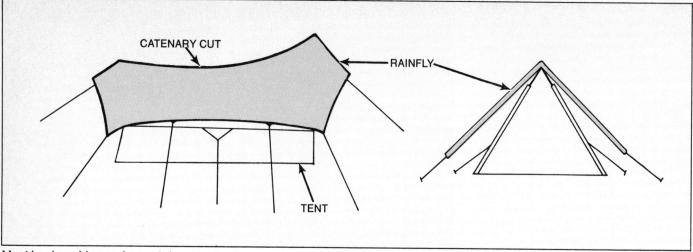

Most backpacking and mountaineering tents use a double-wall design. The breathable tent canopy is protected by a waterproof rainfly, with an air space in between.

vented, some water vapor will condense on the coated fabric and may drip back on you. We don't recommend inexpensive tents made exclusively of waterproof fabrics.

Well-made backpacking tents have *double-wall* construction. (Tents made of Gore-Tex are an important exception and are discussed later in this chapter.) They include a breathable tent canopy protected by a waterproof rainfly that fits over it, producing an air space in between.

Precipitation that hits the rainfly flows harmlessly to the ground. Moisture from inside the tent passes through the inside wall and evaporates in the air space or condenses on the bottom of the rainfly and drips to the ground.

Most backpacking tents have a waterproof floor, zippered doors, insect netting and other features that make them practical for varied conditions. With some of these features in mind, we've divided backpacking tents into six types.

Tube Tents—This tent is a simple plastic tube. You erect it by running a line through the tube and tying each end to a tree. Most tube tents hold only one person. If you want, you can add grommets to it so the tent can be staked taut.

The main attractions of tube tents are simplicity, light weight and low price. They can be used effectively as an emergency shelter, or for hiking in regions where rain showers are short and infrequent. They won't stand up to strong winds or heavy rains.

Because the waterproof material won't allow moisture to escape, the ends must be left open for ventilation. If you encounter both rain and wind, you have the unpleasant choice of either leaving the ends open and having rain blow in, or tying them shut and enduring sauna-like conditions.

Tarps—These do some things very effectively, but unfortunately, many people try to make them do things they were never designed for. You can set up a tarp with a combination of poles, guy lines and nearby trees. They provide good protection from sun, dew and light rain. They are also useful as a ground cover under a sleeping bag or tent. If you own a small tent, you can use a tarp to protect packs that must be left outside at night. Car campers find them useful for sheltering the camp picnic table, or as an additional tent awning. Hikers in dry climates carry them for emergency shade and shelter from occasional rain showers.

Tarps do not offer adequate protection in harsh weather, so don't use one if you backpack above timberline or hike in regions where you might encounter prolonged wet weather. Tarps

A tube tent is an effective emergency shelter.

Use a tarp for good protection from the sun or a light rain.

This bivouac sack is made of Gore-Tex laminated fabric and weighs only 2-1/2 pounds!

The A-frame tent is simple, stable and weatherproof. These two models are free-standing. The tent at the left is set up with a rainfly over the canopy.

The external framework of a dome tent provides stability in strong winds. The shape sheds rain and snow.

Tunnel tents have a low profile that gives them superior performance in strong winds.

are one-season shelters. They may not stand up to the wind, rain and occasional snow of spring and fall.

The least expensive tarps are made of plastic. They're waterproof and durable enough for covering equipment, or as an emergency shelter. For durability, get one that is at least 0.004 inch (4 mils) thick.

If you plan to use your tarp frequently, invest in one made of coated nylon. Those equipped with grommets and tie loops are easiest to set up. No matter what kind of tarp you buy, practice putting it up at home a few different ways before you take it into the field. You will probably have to buy poles, stakes and guy lines separately.

Bivouac Sacks—These shelters occupy a midpoint between sleeping bag covers and tents. Bivouac sacks are used primarily by those who need a one-person tent and are willing to trade lack of interior space for extreme light weight and compactness.

Mountaineers and touring cyclists are two of the bivouac sack's most loyal users. Alpine mountaineers sometimes have to sleep in small places because lack of space makes it impossible to set up a conventional tent. Cyclists use them because a larger tent adds too much weight.

They're made of either waterproof nylon or Gore-Tex laminated nylon. They have waterproof, coated-nylon floors and two hoop-like poles that keep the sack erect.

A-Frame Tents—The A-frame is the most basic of all tent designs. Edward Whymper, the first to scale the Matterhorn, reportedly made the first

backpacking tent in 1862. His design was an A-frame.

Designers have made numerous modifications and changes since then, but the basic shape remains. A-frame tents are triangular-shaped, supported at each end with poles and staked out with guy lines. With the current trend toward free-standing tents, the A-frame design is used less now than it was previously. But it is still functional because it stands up well to strong winds and effectively sheds rain and snow.

Some tent manufacturers produce a free-standing A-frame, eliminating the need for staking out the tent with guy lines. The design uses two A-frame poles at each end, with a central pole running the length of the center ridge of the canopy.

Most quality A-frames are double-wall tents. A detachable, specially fitted rainfly is usually included with the tent. Some inexpensive A-frames are made of coated, waterproof fabrics. We don't recommend them. It's better to spend a little more and find an A-frame with double-wall construction.

The sturdiest A-frames use two poles at each end, in a design that leaves the door open and adds extra stability in the wind. A single, or *I-pole,* arrangement is simpler and faster to set up, but it is unstable in any sort of wind. I-poles should be guyed in two different directions to give them stability. One drawback is that the I-pole obstructs the tent entrance.

The best A-frames features a *catenary cut*—a built-in sag along the top

ridge of the tent and fly. It allows you to pitch the tent tightly. This eliminates loose fabric and flapping in the wind. The catenary cut is usually supplemented by *pullouts*—tie loops along the side of the tent that allow you to stake out the sides, further tightening the fabric.

Dome Tents—This design marked the first departure from the standard A-frame tent. In the early 1970s, dome tents were revolutionary. Now they are commonplace. Manufacturers have modified and improved the standard dome shape, producing dozens of specialized versions.

Dome tents provide more head and shoulder room than an A-frame with the same floor space. And, their rounded profile effectively stands up to strong winds, rain and heavy snow.

All domes have a free-standing exterior framework of fiberglass or aluminum poles, which means that you can pick one up and move it to a new location without taking it down. Even though the tent will stand without guy lines, we recommend that you stake it down to prevent it from blowing away when you aren't in it. In strong winds, use guy lines to help the tent keep its shape.

Most domes are made of breathable nylon, with a fitted rainfly for protection in wet weather.

Since the appearance of the first dome, many variations have been produced. The *wedge* is smaller than a full dome, using only two arching poles. It has a rectangular floor instead of the hexagonal or octagonal shape of the standard dome. Newer still are shapes with one side cut high for easy entry, and the opposite side tapered down. Various manufacturers make this design, each calling it by their own name, such as the Sierra Designs Sphinx and the Moss Trillium Tent.

Tunnel Tents—Tunnel designs offer superior performance in strong winds. They share many of the characteristics of domes—extra inside space due to the hemispheric shape; taut, curved profile; and exterior pole structure. Some are free-standing.

Tunnels are usually long and narrow, with a low profile. Tall people, who sometimes find too little leg room in a dome, find that the tunnels have ample room at the foot and head. You can store extra equipment at each end, too.

They are made with either Gore-Tex laminated nylon, or breathable nylon with a rainfly.

MOUNTAINEERING TENTS

Mountaineering tents are for four-season use. They're designed to withstand strong winds, rain and snow. You'll find two types—small, low-profile tents for use at exposed, high-altitude campsites by two or three people; and large, base-camp models designed to house many people in spacious comfort.

Mountaineers face the possibility of storms confining them to their tents for days at a time. Therefore, mountaineering tents have many house-keeping features—such as a lot of storage space—that make them comfortable for long stays.

In addition, a snow-tunnel entrance not only helps keep snow out of the tent, but is also a good place to put packs. Cookholes, a handy feature for winter and cold-weather camping, are crescent-shaped, zippered openings in the floor. With a cookhole, you can cook inside without the worry of spilling food or fuel on the tent floor.

Most mountaineering tents are of A-frame, dome or tunnel design.

Materials

Tents are made from two components—fabric and poles. Material choice basically depends on your intended use.

If you do your shopping from a quality mail-order or retail store that specializes in outdoor equipment, you can be reasonably sure the tent you buy will be made of top-quality materials.

FABRICS AND WORKMANSHIP

Nylon, canvas, cotton/polyester and plastic are the tent fabrics used most. Each has its place, based on function and cost requirements.

The ideal tent fabric is light, durable, waterproof and breathable. Although the ideal fabric hasn't been invented yet, there are some very good ones. When used in the proper tent design and for the appropriate activities, they provide excellent protection.

Many states have enacted laws requiring tent fabrics to be flame-retardant. Typically, the tent material is treated with a flame-retardant substance. Nearly all manufacturers can treat nylon and canvas fabrics so that they meet these requirements. However, Gore-Tex fabrics and plastic can't be made flame-retardant.

Be aware that flame-retardant doesn't mean fireproof. A flame-retardant tent will burn if exposed to flame long enough. And, even if your tent doesn't catch fire, there are other pieces of equipment inside that may ignite. Common sense dictates that you avoid cooking and open flames inside your tent whenever possible.

Just as important as the choice of fabric is the quality of workmanship used in sewing the fabrics. Double-stitched, flat-felled seams are the strongest way to connect pieces of fabric.

Stitching should be even and without puckers, crooked seams or large needle holes. High-quality tents have from 6 to 12 stitches per inch. More than 12 weakens the fabric, less than 6 won't be strong enough.

Cotton/polyester thread works better than nylon. Nylon is so strong that it can cut the fabric when the material is under great tension. In cotton/polyester thread, polyester provides strength. The cotton swells when wet to fill the needle holes and add some waterproofing.

Tents must be reinforced at stress points, and different tent styles have different stress points. A-frames put the greatest stress on peaks, poles, guy-line pullouts and stake loops. External-frame tents have stress primarily on the pole joints and the sleeves the poles run through.

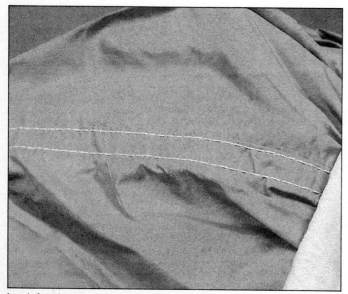
Look for double-stitched, flat-felled seams. They're the strongest and most durable for tents.

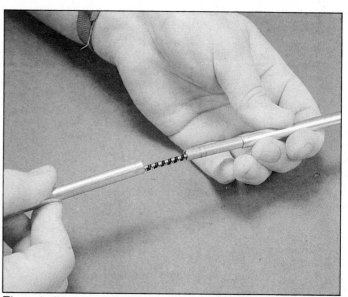
These hollow-aluminum tent poles are connected by shock cord. Pieces can't be lost, and the poles are easy to set up.

The most common method of reinforcing a tent seam is to sew in a double layer of fabric. Look for it when you inspect a tent. For a complete summary of seams, stitching and sewing techniques, refer to Chapter 1.

Plastic—Plastic is used in storm shelters, tarps and tube tents. It's heavy, non-breathable and waterproof. Though it may not be an appropriate choice for rugged backpackers or mountaineers, plastic works well for certain car-camping and backpacking needs. You can stretch it over poles and stake it out to make a tarp tent or shelter. Plastic doesn't stretch well, so it can't be pulled tight. This restricts its uses to areas where wind isn't a problem.

Plastic's major deficiency is its lack of durability. Even heavy, 4 mil (0.004 inch) plastic tears and punctures easily. The only trade-off is that it's inexpensive.

Canvas—It's durable, water repellent and breathable. When wet, fibers swell, sealing out most of the rain. However, in a hard downpour, some water may still leak through in the form of a fine mist. Touching the fabric may cause a leak due to capillary action.

Because canvas is very heavy, it is most often used for camp tents. When wet, it becomes even heavier. In addition, wet canvas is subject to mildew and rot unless dried completely before storage.

Nylon—Backpacking and mountaineering tents are almost exclusively made of nylon. It's light, durable, moderately breathable and mildew-resistant.

You'll find two types of nylon commonly used for tents. Taffeta is the heaviest and most abrasion-resistant. It's used in floors and some walls and roofs. The second kind, ripstop, is easily recognizable by the reinforcing threads criss-crossing the fabric at about quarter-inch intervals. Ripstop is lighter than taffeta but not as resistant to abrasion. For this reason, ripstop is used primarily for tent canopies.

To be waterproof, nylon must be coated, usually with a polyurethane coating. Coated nylon is used for tent floors and rainflies. Coated fabrics are heavier than non-coated ones.

Gore-Tex Laminated Fabrics—As mentioned, Gore-Tex is a Teflon film laminated to fabric. It has millions of tiny pores large enough to allow vapor to escape yet too small to permit water drops to enter.

The best Gore-Tex tent materials are three-layer laminates. The outer layer is usually nylon, the middle layer Gore-Tex, and the inner layer polyester *nexus,* an absorbent polyester fabric. The nexus is absorbent enough to hold condensation. It passes through the Gore-Tex pores and doesn't drip back on the tent's occupants.

The three-layer laminate adds to the weight of each yard of fabric, but because Gore-Tex tents are waterproof, you don't need a separate rainfly. The overall weight and packed size are comparable to other backpacking tents of the same size. The tent on page 59 uses Gore-Tex.

Gore-Tex is effective in small two- and three-person tents only. If the air pressure inside the tent isn't greater than the pressure outside, vapor will condense on the inside fabric rather than being pushed through the pores.

The only way to build up the interior pressure is to raise the temperature inside significantly higher than the exterior temperature, a situation that occurs most often in small, unvented tents. If vents are opened, the pressure drops, and the vapor condenses on the colder, inside surface of the tent fabric.

Other Tent Fabrics—Cotton/polyester fabric is used in many camp tents. It mildews less than canvas, is lighter, and less susceptible to deterioration from ultraviolet radiation from the sun.

Evolution 3 may eventually displace canvas as the best material for camp tents. It is made of three layers of polypropylene, so it breathes and repels water better than canvas. Water drops cannot get through the three layers of closely woven fibers, but water vapor escapes easily. Evolution 3 weighs only a third as much as canvas, too.

POLES

Most modern tents use either aluminum or fiberglass poles. Aluminum poles come in two forms, rigid, heavy poles used in camp tents, and flexible, hollow poles for backpacking and mountaineering tents. In mountaineering and backpacking tents, the pole pieces may be internally connected by shock cord. This way you'll never lose a piece of the pole, and it's also easy to set up.

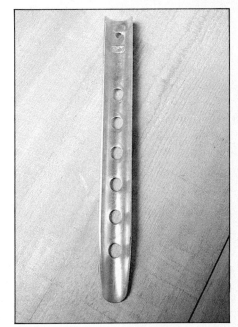

A plastic stake (top) works best in soft ground. A wire stake (center) is effective in medium-to-hard soil. Snow stakes (bottom) have holes so the snow freezes through to add holding power.

The flexible poles necessary for domes and tunnel tents are made from a special aluminum or fiberglass. A few years ago, fiberglass poles were solid, heavy, and had the problem of sticking together. Now, most are hollow. The result is a strong, light pole as good as an aluminum one.

STAKES

For stability, all tents should be staked down. Even free-standing models should be staked so they won't blow away in strong winds. Stakes may or may not be included with your tent.

Two factors determine the usefulness of a stake—the material it's made from and its shape. The best stakes are made from either aluminum or plastic.

Flat, broad stakes are necessary for loose ground. Narrow, thin stakes work best in hard ground. *Snow stakes* are broad stakes with holes for snow to freeze through. This adds extra holding power, making them the best choice for soft snow.

DESIGN FEATURES

The most appropriate use for a tent is only partly determined by its shape, size and materials. You should also consider what special features are included. Some of these are necessary for effective use of the tent. Others are just handy extras.

Rainfly—If your tent is made of an uncoated fabric, especially nylon, you'll need a rainfly. Most quality tents come with a detachable, fitted rainfly included in the purchase price. Rainflies are always made of a coated, waterproof fabric.

To work correctly, the rainfly must be separate from the tent. Moisture passes through the tent fabric and dissipates in the air space between the two layers. If the rainfly were laid

Rainflies are made for all types of nylon tents.

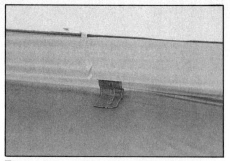

The waterproof portion of a tent floor should extend about six inches up the sides of the tent. It offers protection from water that gets past the rainfly.

directly on the tent fabric, it would work no better than a tent made of waterproof fabric.

Gore-Tex tents don't need rainflies because the tent fabric is waterproof and breathable. Canvas and Evolution 3 tents generally don't need them either. However, these fabrics protect you only in moderate rain showers. If you're planning to use a camp tent in places where you can expect prolonged heavy rainfall, it's a good idea to invest in a plastic or coated-nylon tarp to cover the tent.

Floors—Most modern tents have waterproof floors. These are made of nylon taffeta, oxford nylon (a heavy nylon cloth similar to pack cloth) or canvas. All can withstand a lot of abrasion.

The waterproof tent floor should extend far enough up the sides of the tent to be covered by the rainfly. This *bathtub floor* offers protection from splashes, drips and mud. Any seams on your tent floor should be sealed before the first use and resealed at least once a year.

Vents—Double-walled tents should have several vents. These should be near the top of the tent to allow warm air, steam and carbon monoxide—if you are cooking inside—to escape.

Cooking inside your tent is not recommended, but occasionally you may need to bring your stove inside the tent to escape hostile weather.

In addition to the fire hazard, burning camp stoves consume oxygen. In a tightly sealed tent, this not only devours your oxygen, but also generates byproducts of poisonous carbon dioxide and carbon monoxide. In this case it's important to always leave plenty of vents open. This is especially important if you have a Gore-Tex tent, which you're likely to keep tightly sealed to maintain inside pressure.

Guy Lines—Many tents, including A-

frames, tunnels and most camp tents, require guy lines in order to stand erect or withstand strong winds. Free-standing tents often have a flexible, exterior pole structure that allows them to bend with the wind. Even though they may not blow down, they might flex enough to interrupt your sleep. Guy lines will help free-standing tents hold their shape.

Nylon cord is the best guy-line material. Be sure to carry extra stakes for the guy lines.

Zippers—Nylon coil zippers work better than metal, which are usually found on inexpensive tents. Nylon zippers slide easier, are temperature-proof, lighter and noncorrosive. Two-way nylon zippers, with tabs on the inside and outside, are most convenient.

The two most common zippered-door configurations are the triangular and curved-arch. Tent shape determines which design works better. Both triangular and curved-arch zippers offer easy venting. All you have to do is lower the top zippers a few inches. You can open an arch zipper with just a sweep of your hand. And if your tent has insect netting in the door, it's convenient if the netting zippers follow the same pattern as those on the tent.

All tent zippers should be double-stitched and bar-tacked at the ends.

Netting—Depending on the season and locale, insect netting may be the most important feature your tent can

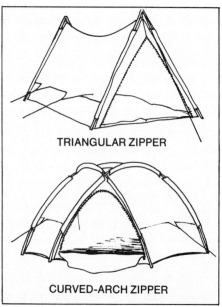

TRIANGULAR ZIPPER

CURVED-ARCH ZIPPER

A-frame tents usually have a triangular zipper. Dome and tunnel tents use a curved-arch design. Both provide easy venting.

have. The best is tightly knitted "no-see-um" netting. It obscures vision a little more than mosquito netting, but the added protection from tiny biting insects is worth it. Dark-colored netting is a little easier to see through than lighter material. Color makes no difference in protection from insects.

If you need a tent that is absolutely bug-proof, be sure you can completely close the netting with zippers so spiders, scorpions and crawling insects can't enter. Check to make sure there is no hole where zipper ends meet.

Some manufacturers produce tents with large sections of netting on the roof and sides, an ideal design if you are backpacking or camping in a warm, dry region. There's plenty of ventilation, and in good weather, the view of stars and moon through your tent roof gives you the satisfying feeling of sleeping out in the open. In case of rain, you can quickly set up the rainfly.

Snow Tunnels—A tunnel is a sleeve usually made of waterproof material that is sewn into the end of the tent and closed with a drawstring. In cold, stormy weather, it enables you to get in and out of the tent without tracking in snow or letting it blow in. Tunnels are also used to store extra equipment.

Vestibules—This is a canopy or extension of the rainfly that reaches beyond the door. Most vestibules must be purchased separately and are attached to the tent's poles and staked out.

Vestibules are used for storing extra equipment and cooking. You'll see them most often on mountaineering tents. If you are planning an extended backpacking trip into a region where there may be long stretches of wet weather, a vestibule may be a useful feature. But most backpackers find the modest increase in convenience not worth the expense and added weight—usually a pound or two.

Housekeeping Features—Some tents have interior pockets, clotheslines and cookholes. These features are designed primarily for those who spend long periods of time in their tents, such as mountaineers or backpackers waiting out a storm.

Pockets provide a place to put small objects, such as sunglasses, socks and gloves, that are easy to misplace inside a crowded tent. Use a clothesline to hang a flashlight, candle lantern or small wet items.

When you're inside a tent, dark-colored insect netting (right) is easier to see through than light-colored netting (above).

A vestibule extends out from the tent door, offering extra space for cooking or storing equipment.

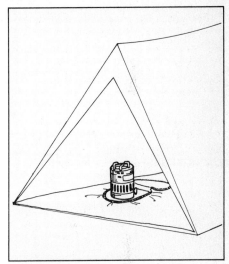

A zippered cookhole in the tent floor of mountaineering tents allows you to cook inside without worrying about spilling fuel on the floor.

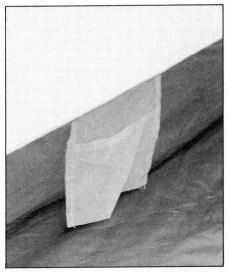

Interior tent pockets help keep a tent tidy.

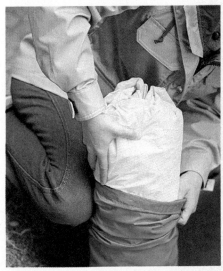

A waterproof stuff sack is essential for your tent.

Stuff Sack—Most quality tents come with a fitted stuff sack. You may prefer to carry your tent, poles and stakes in separate sacks to give you more flexibility when loading the tent into a crowded pack. A waterproof stuff sack is useful to protect the other things in your pack from a wet tent.

Care & Maintenance

A well-made tent is a lifetime, and life-saving, investment. With proper care, it should stand up to rugged use for years. Tents are like cars in that some regular maintenance can forestall major problems and greatly increase lifespan.

WATERPROOFING

Unless you know otherwise, you should assume that your tent's seams require sealing. Special sealers are available for Gore-Tex and coated nylon fabrics. Periodic resealing is necessary. For most users, once a year is adequate. If you are putting your tent through heavy use, it may be necessary to reseal seams two or three times a year.

Canvas and Evolution 3 camp tents require seam sealing, too. The best way to seal seams is to set up the tent on a dry, sunny afternoon. Follow the directions on the seam sealer you use. Then allow plenty of time for the sealer to dry.

STORAGE

Dirt, rocks and twigs can abrade tent fabric. Therefore, before you store a tent, brush out and sponge up any dirt.

Always dry a tent completely before storing it. This is especially important for canvas tents, which mildew easily. Nylon tents have cotton/polyester thread that is susceptible to mildew. The best way to dry a tent is to set it up in your yard. If that's impossible because of rain, hang it on an inside line.

CLEANING

Tents rarely need washing. If they become soiled, clean them with a sponge and mild detergent. Vigorous washing wears away seams and may weaken the bond between the waterproof coating and the fabric.

MAKING REPAIRS

Sometimes things go wrong. A tent pole may break or be lost. Guy lines can snap. Fabric can tear or be burned.

For these reasons, it's a good idea to carry a repair kit so you can make minor repairs in the field. Include an extra pole section, some nylon cord to replace guy lines, an extra stake or two, and a roll of duct or rip-stop repair tape to repair tears and holes or to splint a broken pole. If you're heading out for an extended backpacking trip, carry an extra piece of tent fabric and a needle and thread.

You can repair minor problems, such as small tears and burns, at home. If you don't feel competent to do it yourself, contact a qualified sewing expert or send the tent back to the manufacturer for repair.

Major failures might be covered under the warranty. Even if they aren't, be sure to contact both the manufacturer and the retail store where you purchased the tent. Responsible manufacturers want to know how their tents function. And if there's a design problem, the sooner they know about it, the sooner they can correct it in future models.

One of the greatest drawbacks to purchasing an inexpensive tent from a manufacturer who really isn't serious about the tent business is the lack of warranty, repair service and spare parts. Nearly everyone loses or breaks a tent pole sometimes. If you can't find a replacement that fits, the tent may become useless.

Be sure to sweep out your tent before folding and stuffing it. Dirt, rocks and twigs can wear out fabric.

Stoves, Cooking Equipment & Food

6

Whether you backpack, car camp, cross-country ski or canoe, you need to stay warm, dry and well-fed. Staying warm and dry in the outdoors is discussed in previous chapters. In this chapter, we tackle the subject of food and cooking equipment.

It's a happy topic. Eating well in the outdoors is remarkably rewarding. Few things are more enjoyable than a good meal at the end of a long day in the outdoors.

As with other subjects of this book, your choice of food and cooking equipment is largely determined by your intended activity and individual needs. You should ask these questions:

1) How many people will be served?

2) How long is your trip?

3) What's the nature of your activity? Will you have to carry all your gear on your back? Or can it be stored in a canoe, kayak or in the trunk of your car?

4) How strenuous will the trip be? Extra effort means you'll need more food than usual.

5) Do the members of your group have special food preferences?

6) Are you traveling into an area where campfires aren't allowed?

Obviously, your needs will be slightly different for every trip you take. But with the wide range of stoves, cookware and foods available, you'll have no trouble finding what you need. Taking extra care to eat well in the outdoors is worth the effort.

Stoves

Cooking over a stove is oftentimes better than cooking over a fire. Stoves are easier to start in wet weather. The amount of heat is controllable. Foods generally cook faster. And, stoves create no environmental damage.

Stoves are now considered practically a necessity for backpackers. Many popular backcountry destinations no longer have adequate supplies of firewood. In some fragile wilderness areas, campfires have been prohibited. Backpackers must carry their own stoves. Fires are still acceptable in

A camping stove (left) offers large fuel capacity, multiple burners and easy starting. A backpacking stove (right) is smaller, lighter and more portable.

campgrounds accessible by car, but campers should plan on either bringing their own firewood or buying it at the site. For this reason, most car campers now cook over stoves and save their firewood for a social fire in the evening.

Stoves come in a wide variety of sizes and designs. We've divided them into two categories:

1) Camping stoves are too large to carry in your pack, but are suitable for car camping, picnics, and some canoeing and rafting activities.

2) Backpacking stoves are designed to be light and compact enough to carry in your pack.

No matter which type you want, there are several things to consider when looking for a stove.

FUEL

Fuels have different burning characteristics, prices and availability. Most stoves can burn only one kind of fuel. Your choice of fuel will largely be determined by how much it costs to run your stove and how easy it is to buy more fuel.

White Gas—Also called *naphtha,* white gas is a special, additive-free version of gasoline. It is highly volatile, which is both good and bad. White-gas stoves light quickly, and spilled white gas evaporates, leaving little odor. On the other hand, white gas is extremely flammable, so it re-

quires careful handling, especially when you refuel and start the stove.

Though white gas used to be available at many gas stations, fire regulations now discourage gas station owners from storing it in bulk. Typically, you now have to buy it in commercially packaged one-gallon cans, available in most sporting-goods stores, backpacking shops and some hardware stores. Coleman and Blazo are two brand names of white gas. These products are filtered clean, an

Most white-gas stove and lantern owners buy their fuel in one-gallon cans from sporting-goods stores, backpacking shops or hardware stores.

important consideration because dirt and other impurities can clog the stove.

White-gas stoves operate inexpensively—for only pennies per hour. Though white gas is widely used in the United States, it's difficult to find in foreign countries. If you're planning to use your stove for foreign travels, we recommend a kerosene or butane stove instead.

Kerosene—It's the most widely available fuel in foreign countries. Because it's not as volatile as white gas, in cold weather you have to preheat it before burning it. This makes kerosene stoves more difficult to start, but once burning, kerosene actually burns hotter than white gas.

Spilled kerosene doesn't ignite easily, is slow to evaporate and leaves a disagreeable odor. Kerosene costs less than white gas, but since both are so cheap the difference is insignificant.

Alcohol—Unlike most other stove fuels, alcohol is not a petroleum product. It can be made from many substances, including corn and other grains.

Alcohol is much less volatile than either white gas or kerosene, so it doesn't burn as hot. However, this makes it OK for use in boats, where there would be a high risk of explosion if a more flammable fuel were spilled below deck.

Butane—This gas comes pressurized in steel canisters called *cartridges.* The main advantage of butane stoves is convenience. In addition, butane is easy to light. It's under pressure in the cartridge, so all you have to do is hold a match to the burner and turn the valve on. When a cartridge runs out, you just detach the spent one and load a full replacement. You don't have to handle a liquid fuel.

Butane is affected by both temperature and elevation. At sea level, it won't vaporize when the temperature drops below freezing. However, if you move to higher elevations, where atmospheric pressure is lower, the fuel vaporizes more easily. It's then possible to light a butane stove even when the temperature is well below freezing.

The major drawback to using butane cartridges is that as fuel is used, the heat output gradually declines. It may take twice as long to boil water with a nearly empty cartridge as it does with a full one. Another drawback is its expense due to packaging.

These four models represent the most commonly used backpacking stoves: White-gas stoves (top left) are compact, and the fuel burns very hot. Kerosene stoves (top right) should be your choice if you're backpacking or camping in foreign countries. Butane stoves (bottom left) use pressurized canisters so they're simple to start. Alcohol stoves (bottom right) are often used by boaters because alcohol is a safe fuel.

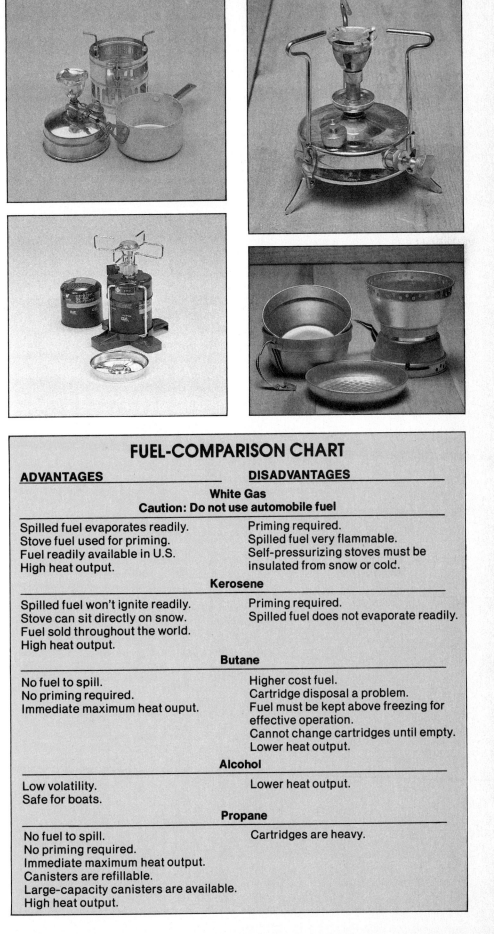

Propane (LP Gas)—Like butane, propane comes in canisters. Propane must be stored under extreme pressure. This makes the canisters larger and heavier than butane cartridges. Propane canisters, however, can be refilled at any gas station offering propane service for recreational vehicles.

Propane burns hotter than butane and will vaporize at temperatures down to −40F at sea level.

Because the canisters are so heavy, propane is impractical for backpacking stoves. It's widely used in stoves designed for picnicking and car camping.

Solid Fuel—A few stoves use solid fuels, such as wood chips, wax pellets and Sterno fuel. They aren't popular for outdoor use, due to low heat output. But solid fuel can give adequate heat to cook foods in an emergency.

WEIGHT AND PACKING EASE

Backpackers need a light stove that's compact enough to fit into a pack. The lightest backpacking stoves weigh about a pound—without fuel—and can fit in the palm of your hand when parts are nested. Because car camping stoves don't need to be

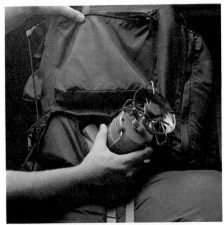

Backpacking stoves are compact enough to fit easily into your pack.

FUEL-COMPARISON CHART

ADVANTAGES	DISADVANTAGES
White Gas	
Caution: Do not use automobile fuel	
Spilled fuel evaporates readily.	Priming required.
Stove fuel used for priming.	Spilled fuel very flammable.
Fuel readily available in U.S.	Self-pressurizing stoves must be
High heat output.	insulated from snow or cold.
Kerosene	
Spilled fuel won't ignite readily.	Priming required.
Stove can sit directly on snow.	Spilled fuel does not evaporate readily.
Fuel sold throughout the world.	
High heat output.	
Butane	
No fuel to spill.	Higher cost fuel.
No priming required.	Cartridge disposal a problem.
Immediate maximum heat ouput.	Fuel must be kept above freezing for
	effective operation.
	Cannot change cartridges until empty.
	Lower heat output.
Alcohol	
Low volatility.	Lower heat output.
Safe for boats.	
Propane	
No fuel to spill.	Cartridges are heavy.
No priming required.	
Immediate maximum heat output.	
Canisters are refillable.	
Large-capacity canisters are available.	
High heat output.	

packed long distances, they are bigger and much heavier.

No matter what your activity, though, it's wise to buy a stove that folds into a compact unit and doesn't have protruding parts. Even large backpacks and car trunks can get crowded, so you'll be glad your stove can pack compactly.

STARTING

Outdoor stoves vary widely in starting ease. Some can be fired with a twist of the valve. Others require pumping. And some have to be manually primed to help the fuel vaporize. When shopping for a stove, make sure you find out how it starts.

Butane And Propane Stoves—These are the easiest to start. Simply strike a match, hold it next to the burner and turn the valve on. Because the fuel is pressurized in the canister and comes out as a gas, it should light easily.

White Gas And Kerosene Stoves—These liquid fuels need to be vaporized before they will light. There are several ways to do this.

Camp stoves are usually lit directly at the burner. Before lighting, you pump the tank manually to vaporize some fuel, which travels to the burner. When first lit, the flame burns with a cold yellow color. As the vaporizing tube—the tube connecting

Camp stoves usually have a built-in pump that pressurizes the tank and allows starting without manual priming.

the fuel tank and burners—heats up, the fuel begins vaporizing automatically. The flame soon turns blue, suitable for cooking.

Some liquid-fuel backpacking stoves are equipped with pumps, but even these must be *primed*. You do this by pumping the plunger a few times until a small amount of liquid squirts out. It collects in a pool in the priming cup directly below the vaporizing tube. When this is lit, it heats the tube, vaporizing some of the liquid fuel inside the tube.

Backpacking stoves without a pump are primed manually. Most manufacturers recommend cupping the

tank in your hands, which warms the gas inside until it expands and runs out into the priming cup. This method works most of the time, but many backpackers have developed alternate—some say superior—methods.

An eyedropper is often used to draw the priming fuel directly from the tank or from an auxiliary fuel bottle. The fuel is squirted into the priming cup and then lit. Another method is to squirt a little jelly fire starter in the priming cup.

If you've never done it, manually priming a stove may seem complicated. Actually, after a little practice, you'll be able to fire up your stove quickly.

EFFICIENCY

Most backpacking stoves can boil water at least as fast as an electric range. But not all boil water at the same rate. Some are significantly faster than others. If you need to boil water quickly or melt snow for water, boiling speed is important. For most outdoor users, however, the differences aren't critical.

What is important is the stove's ability to continue working well when exposed to strong winds and cold temperatures. Wind pushes the flame off to the side, diverting heat away from the cooking utensil. It also cools its

Butane stoves are among the easiest to light. Simply strike a match, hold it next to the burner and open the valve.

Many backpacking stoves have to be primed manually. Typically, you burn some fuel in the priming cup to heat the vaporizing tube. Many backpackers squirt a small amount of gas into the cup from a squeeze bottle or eyedropper.

Large camp stoves often have a built-in windscreen that significantly increases stove efficiency in breezy weather.

Backpacking stoves are built to be light and compact, so few have the elaborate windscreens of camp stoves. This model, however, has a small screen that does a good job.

surface. In addition, cold temperature hampers the performance of nearly all stoves.

Windscreens—Large camp stoves typically have a built-in windscreen that unfolds when you open the stove for use. With the windscreen in place, all you have to do is turn the stove to make the windscreen effective.

Backpacking stoves, however, are built for light weight. They don't have windscreens as elaborate as camp stoves. Some have a small built-in windscreen, or a separate screen that you can put up in windy weather. Other stoves sit inside a cookset that offers some protection. One even comes with a very effective collapsible foil screen you can set up to completely enclose the stove and pot.

Cold-Weather Performance—Among the stoves mentioned here, butane stoves are most severely affected by cold weather. In fact, at sea level butane fuel doesn't vaporize at temperatures below freezing.

It's possible to warm the cartridge up with your hands, but it's a nuisance, requiring you to remove your gloves and hold the cartridge—an unpleasant task in cold weather. Even at temperatures just above freezing, the butane fuel may come out of the cartridge at a reduced rate.

White-gas and kerosene stoves operate well in cold weather, as long as you don't place the tank directly on snow or very cold ground. For this reason, many backpackers carry a small insulating pad on which to put their stove.

Propane vaporizes and performs well at extremely cold temperatures.

STABILITY

Two- and three-burner camp stoves are usually very stable. However, one-burner backpacking stoves are another matter. They often stand on spindly legs, holding the pot high off the ground. It's easy, in a moment of inattention, to knock over your stove, spilling food and creating a fire hazard.

When you consider that backpackers often put their stoves on uneven ground, it's all the more reason to shop around for a stove that offers good stability.

SAFETY

Always use your stove cautiously and according to the manufacturer's instructions. Most accidents involving stoves occur because the user was careless or used the stove improperly.

Safety must always be a major concern. The greatest dangers occur when you handle liquid fuel and when you start the stove. You should also be careful when refilling a stove that burns liquid fuel—white gas, kerosene or alcohol.

The most common mistake in starting a stove is to put in too much fuel for priming, which can cause a flare-up when you light the match. To be safe, start the stove outside, away from tents, open fuel bottles or other flammable objects. Never allow small children to handle camp stoves.

Washers and screw-in fittings occasionally loosen, becoming potential safety hazards. Frequently check connections to make sure all are tight.

In addition to the precautions already mentioned, here are some more you must remember:

1) Don't enclose a stove in rocks or a windscreen so tightly that heat is reflected back to the tank. It may become too hot, possibly resulting in an explosion.

2) Don't remove a butane cartridge from an operating stove before the cartridge is completely empty.

3) Don't operate a stove inside a tightly sealed tent. Without proper ventilation, the carbon monoxide produced by a stove can build up to potentially dangerous levels.

4) Don't handle fuel containers carelessly. For example, hikers have started fires by knocking over their uncapped fuel bottles near an operating stove.

ACCESSORIES

Some stoves are designed to be used with special accessories. Car-camping stoves come with the greatest array, including ovens that sit over

The Coleman backpacking stove is available with an optional cookset of two pots, a lid and a windscreen. This cutaway view shows how parts nest.

the burners, stands to hold the stove at waist height and auxiliary, extra-capacity fuel tanks.

If you buy a backpacking stove without a tank pump, you can buy a separate *mini-pump* that screws onto the tank of some stoves. The mini-pump aids starting by allowing you to pump out the priming gas.

Some backpacking stoves are compatible with a cookware set. The stove fits into a pot/base that helps give it stability and acts as a windscreen. The entire unit then nests inside several pots and the lid for efficient packing.

THE ENTIRE SYSTEM

It's unlikely you'll find a stove that does everything well. Stoves have strong and weak points. Because you'll probably have to make some trade-offs, it's vital to decide which features are most important to you and buy a stove that satisfies them best. Is light weight your biggest priority? Ease of starting? Stability? Ability to operate in cold temperatures? Fuel availability? Consider these before purchasing a stove.

Gas, Butane & Propane Lanterns

Lanterns are most often used by car campers, canoeists, river rafters, those with rustic cabins and as an emergency source of light. In addition, some backpackers are now using small, lightweight lanterns. Having a little light in the evening is worth the extra weight, particularly if you are headed out on a weekend hike.

FUEL

Lanterns run on either white gas, butane, propane or kerosene. It makes sense to buy a lantern that runs

on the same fuel as your stove. It's possible to control the light of butane and propane lanterns, but white-gas lanterns run at one speed—full blast.

Backpacking lanterns are powered by white gas or butane. Larger car-camping models run on white gas, butane, kerosene or propane. If you have a propane camp stove, it's possible to connect your lantern into the same fuel tank, by means of a special fitting.

OPERATION

Fuel-powered lanterns produce light by means of a silk *mantle,* a lace-like globe positioned over the gas flame. Because mantles are fragile and easily crushed in the everyday tasks of carrying, packing and repacking your lantern, it's wise to carry extras. They're inexpensive and available where you bought your lantern.

SELECTION

When shopping for a lantern, ask many of the same questions you did when looking for a stove. Do you need a lightweight, compact lantern for backpacking? Or, is it more important to buy a larger, brighter car-camping model? Be sure to buy one that's easy to start, stable and runs on a convenient and relatively inexpensive fuel.

Fuel Bottles

Liquid fuel for gas stoves and lanterns must be carried in a metal container. Glass isn't suitable because it can break, and plastic may allow small amounts of gas to evaporate. Because many campers carry water in plastic bottles, it's a bad idea to put fuel in a container resembling a drinking-water bottle.

The most popular fuel bottle for backpackers is made of aluminum and has a secure cap and rubber gasket. Car campers can use larger fuel containers, perhaps even the one-gallon can the fuel came in. It's safest to carry not much more than the fuel you'll need, so you may want to buy a small one-liter or half-liter bottle for short trips.

Aluminum bottles have either a plain or anodized finish. The colored, anodized finish is corrosion-resistant. **Fuel-Bottle Accessories**—Because it's nearly impossible to pour fuel directly into your stove's tank without spilling, you'll need to buy an acces-

A camping lantern (left) provides a good source of light for car campers. A backpacking lantern (right) weighs less and is small enough to fit into your pack.

A vented pour spout fits on the cap of an aluminum fuel-bottle cap. It makes tank refilling easier.

sory to help you refill the stove. Popular among backpackers is the vented pouring spout that fits on top of your fuel bottle. It allows you to direct a small stream of liquid fuel into the tank. The pouring spout can also be used to pour a small amount of fuel into the priming cup to prime the stove.

Also popular is a small plastic or metal funnel. For a little more money, you can buy one with a filter—extra insurance against allowing any impurities into your stove.

Cookware

No matter what your outdoor activity, you'll be able to find cooking equipment, utensils and food-storage containers to make outdoor eating pleasant. Backpackers and others who need to save space and weight need cookware that's simple, light and fulfills several functions. Car campers, rafters and some canoeists can afford to carry more weight.

Consequently, they can choose from a wider range of products—or bring some from home! It all depends on the kind of food you'll be cooking and how important it is to save weight and space.

Shopping for outdoor cookware and eating utensils doesn't need to be complicated. Basically, pots and pans should be large enough for your needs, light, compact, resistant to spilling and tipping, durable, easy to clean, and if possible, have many uses. Utensils and storage containers should be easy to use, durable and lightweight.

We've divided the cookware section into two parts:

1) Cooking equipment and utensils, made up of pots and pans, plates, cups and silverware.

2) Food containers, including water bottles, plastic bags, squeeze tubes and food-storage containers.

COOKING EQUIPMENT AND UTENSILS

This category includes all the equipment you'll need to actually do your cooking and eating—from coffee pot to spoon.

Materials—Most outdoor cookware is made of aluminum, stainless steel, regular steel or cast iron.

Aluminum is very light and a good heat conductor. Some aluminum cookware is coated with a non-stick coating that helps tremendously when it's your turn to wash dishes. Aluminum pots and pans are easily dented, but they can be pressed back into shape. Because of its light weight, aluminum is best for backpackers and mountaineers.

Stainless steel is a poor heat conductor, so we don't recommend it for outdoor cookware. The part of the pot that sits right over the flame may be red hot, but the corners can be almost cold. Stainless steel is widely used in domestic pots and pans, but these have a jacket of copper on the bottom to help distribute heat.

Steel cookware is heavier and more durable. It distributes heat more effectively than stainless steel, so food is less likely to burn.

Cast iron offers outstanding heat distribution, but it's very heavy. This limits its use to car camping and other activities in which weight isn't a consideration.

Pots—Your choice of a pot, skillet or frying pan depends on what kind of foods you'll be cooking.

Many backpackers do no more than boil water for dried food and instant soups and beverages. For them, a pot is all that's needed. There's a wide range of sizes, from less than one quart to 10 quarts or larger.

Be sure to buy a pot that's big enough for your largest meals, one that will allow you to stir the contents without spilling over the sides. Most backpackers find that a two-quart pot is big enough.

Most outdoor pots are lifted by *bails*—the arched handles reaching over the top of the pot—rather than by handles. Some bails are made to lock in an upright position, but even these are likely to get too hot to lift. It's a good idea to bring along a pot holder. Or, get a clamp-like pot lifter that grips the edge of the pot for lifting or steadying when pouring.

It's also a good idea to buy a pot that comes with a lid. When the lid is on, food cooks faster, and you're less likely to spill the contents when you lift the pot.

Aluminum cookware comes in a variety of designs and sizes. Because of its light weight and ability to conduct heat, it's popular with backpackers.

Pots come with (left) or without (right) bails. The pot on the right uses a detachable gripper.

A pressure cooker is especially useful for cooking at high altitudes. This model has an interior divider so you can cook several foods at once.

Water for instant coffee, tea or cocoa can be boiled in either a pot or a coffee pot. Hikers often save weight by boiling water in the same pot they make dinner in.

Frying Pans—Bring one if you want to fry potatoes, pancakes, fish or eggs. Aluminum frying pans or griddles are available for backpackers. Some backpacking models have folding or detachable handles that help you pack them into small places.

Pressure Cookers, Reflector Ovens And Dutch Ovens—A pressure cooker is especially handy at high altitudes, where the low atmospheric pressure can extend cooking time. At 5000 feet, for example, water boils at only 203F. Since it's heat that cooks food, it may take 50% longer to cook your food completely if you can't get your water up to a high temperature.

A pressure cooker is a sealed system that increases air pressure within the pot, effectively lessening cooking time. If you're cooking for a lot of people on a backpacking trip, consider a lightweight aluminum model. Larger, heavier models are available for those who don't need to save weight. Some have internal dividers that allow you to cook several foods at the same time.

The reflector oven appeals mostly to car campers, rafters and canoeists. With a bit of practice, you can use it to bake biscuits, muffins, and, for those with the gourmet touch, pies and cakes. The oven uses reflected heat from an adjacent fire to bake the food, which is placed on a center shelf.

Car campers also like the Dutch oven. It's a cast-iron or aluminum kettle that's shaped to stand over a bed of coals. It effectively cooks like an electric crockpot—great for slow-simmering foods such as soups and stews.

Cookware Sets—Cookware comes individually or in sets. Sets typically include cups and plates. Small sets for one or two people may include two pots, plates and cups, plus a lid that can double as a frying pan. Larger sets may have enough equipment for eight or more. These usually include several pots, including a large 10-quart size, several frying pans, plates and cups. Most cookware sets are designed so individual pieces nest to save space.

Accessories—If you'll be cooking over a fire, you may need a grate. There are lightweight aluminum models designed for backpackers and larger, heavier models for car campers.

Be sure to plan what utensils you'll need. Usually this includes spatulas, cooking knives, forks and stirring spoons. Most car campers can bring along everything they need from home. Backpackers have to cut corners to save weight, possibly using their pocket knife as a cooking knife and a regular spoon for stirring food.

Make sure you have a can opener if your menu calls for any canned food.

Eating Utensils—Outdoor plates, bowls and cups are usually made from aluminum, stainless steel or plastic. Eating utensils are made of stainless steel, plastic or even ultra-light materials such as polycarbonite.

Whether you bring a full-place setting of a plate, cup and bowl depends on what kind of food you'll be eating, how much space you have, and how much weight you want to save. Backpackers often carry just a spoon, bowl and cup. Some do all of their eating out of a cup.

Everyone seems to have his own idea about which kind of cup works best. Many prefer the stainless steel

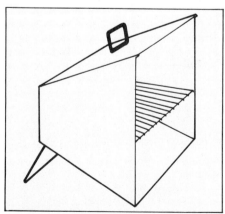

A reflector oven uses reflected heat from a fire for baking.

A Dutch oven is practical for cooking slow-simmering foods like stew and soup. The oven sits on fire coals, and more coals can be placed on the lid.

Sierra Cup, which works well for hot drinks because it doesn't conduct heat to your lips. Others like a simple plastic mug. Brass-plated cups may be popular gift items, but they'll burn your lips the first time you sip a hot drink.

Whether or not you bring along a full place setting depends on what you prefer. Most backpackers don't bring this much.

FOOD CONTAINERS

There are dozens of different kinds of containers, bags, bottles, squeeze tubes and jugs for carrying food and water. Most are made of plastic, polyethylene (poly) or aluminum.

Liquid Storage—Only a few traditionalists still carry aluminum canteens. Most hikers now use narrow- or wide-mouth polyethylene bottles with a screw cap. They come in various sizes from one ounce to two quarts or larger.

They're handy for more than carrying water. Wide-mouth bottles are ideal for carrying honey, cooking oil, juices and even liquid detergent.

Some anodized aluminum "bottles" that are lacquered on the inside are suitable for carrying juices and other drinks without imparting a metallic taste to the drink. However, it's not a good idea to carry drinks in any container that resembles a fuel bottle.

Large plastic jugs, with a capacity of up to five gallons, are ideal for carrying water to your campsite from a distant water source. Hikers prefer the collapsible models that fit in a pack. Car campers have more space, so rigid plastic jugs are better because they're easier to carry and pour.

Food Storage—If you're concerned with saving weight and space, it pays to measure out the food you'll need. Repack it in smaller food containers. There's no need to carry along pounds of extra pancake mix, oatmeal and coffee.

You can store food in a variety of containers. Plastic works best because it won't break, is lightweight and is made into dozens of different sizes and designs. Most outdoor enthusiasts avoid glass, due to weight and potential breakage.

Closable plastic bags are ideal for carrying nuts, candy, spices and powdered mixes. Lightweight sandwich bags puncture easily, so we recommend heavy-duty storage bags.

Round or square polyethylene boxes with snap-on or screw lids can carry crushable foods that would be too messy to carry in plastic bags—foods such as fruits and vegetables, peanut butter, jam and eggs. Poly squeeze tubes are excellent for peanut butter, jam, honey and margarine.

Small poly vials and surplus 35mm film canisters are the best way to carry salt, pepper and other spices.

Outdoor Menus

There's no doubt about it—food is important in the outdoors. The hard work, fresh air, scenery and camaraderie of the outdoors undeniably make good food taste great. When choosing food for outdoor activities, consider the following:

1) What is your intended activity? Will you carry all your own food, or will some be carried by horses, in canoes or by car? Obviously, if you're going to carry all your food on your back, you need lightweight foods. Since weight is no problem for car camping, you can probably bring along a cooler full of many of the same foods you'd eat at home—whether they're frozen, canned or fresh.

2) How strenuous is your activity? If you're going to be burning a lot of calories by hiking, climbing or paddling, you'll need to make sure your menu supplies enough calories to keep you going.

3) How long is the trip? The longer it is, the more certain you must be that the food provides necessary daily nutrients. There's probably little danger of undernourishment on a weekend hiking trip. But on longer trips—a week or two or more—you'll need to make sure you're eating a balanced diet.

4) What kind of foods do you and your friends enjoy eating? Everyone

Plastic bottles, jugs and squeeze tubes are useful for carrying water and storing drinks, honey, cooking oil, jam and jelly.

has different tastes, so consider them when planning outdoor menus.

In this section, we first take a brief look at how calories and nutritional needs affect your purchasing decisions. Then we discuss various choices in outdoor foods, including both specially prepared backpacking foods and foods that you can buy in a supermarket.

CALORIES

If you're healthy now, you're probably already eating a well-balanced diet. It's unlikely that you would develop any serious nutritional deficiencies on a two- or three-day trip. The most important factor in planning your menu in this case is to make sure that your foods provide enough calories.

A calorie is a unit used to measure the potential energy provided by a food. Nutrition books available at book stores and libraries can tell you how many calories are provided by different kinds of food. Often, the food's

A refillable, washable squeeze tube is the neatest way to carry small amounts of sticky foods.

package will provide caloric information, too.

There's tremendous variation among different foods. Fruits, vegetables, and fish are relatively low in calories. Nuts, candy and some grain and dairy products give more calories per weight.

If you eat too many calories, the surplus is stored in your body as fat tissue. Too few calories mean that you're burning fat to provide energy. Cutting down on calories may be desirable if you're dieting, but in the outdoors, it just leaves you feeling hungry, weak and grouchy.

How many calories do you need? The answer depends on many factors, including your age, sex, weight and the outdoor activity. Young people need more calories than older people. Men burn more calories than women. The heavier you are, the more calories you'll need. And, of course, strenuous activities burn more calories than sedentary ones.

For example, a 170-pound man carrying a 30-pound pack and hiking at 3 miles per hour may burn 270 calories an hour. The same man may burn only 100 calories per hour while doing camp chores such as gathering wood or setting up a tent. Even while sleeping, he continues to use calories,

about 20 an hour. This is just an example, of course. Your caloric needs will undoubtedly be different.

Therefore, it's difficult to say exactly how many calories your outdoor meals should provide. Some experts estimate that 3000 to 4500 calories per day is a good starting point if you're an adult participating in vigorous exercise, such as backpacking. From this standard, you can then adjust for the variables mentioned earlier. For example, the 3000 calorie estimate applies mostly to women; the 4500 calorie estimate to men.

Our best advice is to learn from experience. If you didn't bring quite enough food on one trip, simply increase portions the next time out. Similarly, if you overestimated caloric needs one time, it's easy to cut down.

NUTRIENTS

When you've decided how much food to bring, make sure you bring the right kinds. Your food should provide six nutrients—carbohydrates, protein, fat, vitamins, minerals and water.

Carbohydrates—These are your basic source of energy. Foods providing *simple* carbohydrates and quick energy are sweet—candy, honey and fruit. *Complex* carbohydrates, provided by

grains, cereals, noodles, rice and potatoes, take longer for your body to break down, but they are a longer-lasting source of energy.

Protein—You need it to build and repair cells. Your body can't store protein, so you should eat a small amount with every meal.

Although many people know this, protein is still one of the most misunderstood nutrients. It doesn't provide any energy—carbohydrates do that. You don't need more protein in your diet when you are physically active. Most Americans eat far more protein than they need anyway, so protein deficiency is generally not a great problem.

You get protein from two sources—animal products such as meat, cheese, milk and eggs, and plant sources such as some beans, nuts and grains. Protein from animals is readily usable by the body. Plant proteins are good sources of *complete* protein only when certain combined. For example, legumes (peanuts, beans, dried peas) make complete protein only when combined with either seeds (sunflower or sesame seeds), nuts (walnuts, pecans, almonds) or grains (wheat, corn, oats).

Textured vegetable protein (TVP), a soybean product, is used as a meat

These foods are rich in carbohydrates—your basic source of energy in the outdoors.

Many of these foods are good sources of protein, vitamins and minerals. Some of the fresh foods shown here are ideal for car camping and weekend backpacking trips.

substitute in many backpacking foods. It can be processed and flavored to resemble meats.

If you're interested in planning a meatless outdoor menu, we recommend further reading on nutrition and protein combinations from one of the books recommended on page 158.

Fat—Contrary to what you may read in some diet books, fat is a necessary and important nutrient. It carries fat-soluble vitamins into the blood stream, provides a cushion around internal organs, supplies a source of stored energy in case energy from carbohydrates runs out, and helps keep you warm.

Peanuts, oils, margarine, butter, cheese, red meat and whole milk are good sources of fat.

Vitamins And Minerals—These regulate many bodily functions and guard against disease. Fruits, vegetables, meat and dairy products are good sources of minerals and vitamins. If you've been eating a balanced diet before you head into the outdoors, it's unlikely that you'll have any problems with vitamin or mineral deficiencies.

Water—Technically, water isn't a nutrient, but it's essential that you drink plenty of it to maintain normal bodily processes. It provides a base for body fluids and provides vital cooling during hot, strenuous activity.

The Four Food Groups—It's admittedly difficult to calculate how much of each nutrient is provided by each food you bring on your trip. A better and simpler way is to plan your menu according to the four food groups.

Nutritionists have divided foods into four groups—milk (including cheese, yogurt and other dairy products), meat (including eggs, fish, poultry and some protein-rich vegetables eaten in combinations providing complete protein), fruit/vegetable and bread/cereal.

By eating foods from all groups each day, you'll be getting a balanced diet. Here's the plan most widely recommended by nutritionists:

Two servings each day from the milk group.

Two servings each day from the meat group.

Four or more daily servings from the fruit/vegetable group.

Four or more daily servings from the bread/cereal group.

OUTDOOR FOODS

Planning your outdoor menu is just the first step. The second is deciding what form of food to buy. If you're headed for an extended backpacking, canoeing or climbing trip, you may need a full menu of dried, lightweight foods. On a shorter trip, you may be able to combine some fresh food with your dried foods. For car camping and other activities in which weight isn't a concern, it's possible to shop much as you would at home, buying primarily fresh foods.

Dried Foods—Modern-day hiking has become popular partly due to advances in dried food. It's possible to hike for days, carrying just a few pounds of non-perishable food, something that was unheard of when food was heavy, bulky and spoiled quickly.

Four processes are used to dry food—conventional drying, vacuum drying, freeze drying and spray drying.

Conventional Drying works well for such staples as noodles, rice, onions and other vegetables. About 80% to 90% of the moisture is removed by placing the uncooked food on a conveyor belt and running it through an oven. If you have a food dryer, you can do this yourself.

Vacuum Drying can remove up to 96% of a product's moisture. Fresh food is placed in a vacuum chamber and heat is applied, causing the moisture to evaporate. This process is primarily used for fruits such as apples, apricots and peaches.

Freeze Drying is the most complicated method. It is generally agreed that freeze-dried food retains the texture and taste of fresh food better than other drying methods.

First, the food is frozen rapidly. Second, it's put in a vacuum-heat chamber. In the process, the frozen water turns into a gas without ever becoming liquid again. Freeze drying is used most often with vegetables and meat to produce tasty foods that reconstitute quickly when you add boiling water.

Spray Drying is used for liquid products such as milk and eggs. The liquid is sprayed as a fine mist into a heated chamber, where it dries into a powder and is collected. You reconstitute it by adding water.

Purchasing Dried Foods—You'll find dried foods in supermarkets and hiking, sporting-goods and outdoor-equipment stores.

DRINK LOTS OF WATER—BUT BE CERTAIN THAT IT'S CLEAN

Unfortunately, not all mountain water is pure and clean. Horses, sheep, cattle and men have fouled many streams. It pays to be very careful about the water you drink in the backcountry.

Generally, you can trust water that flows directly out of a snowfield or glacier. But beware of slow-moving streams, especially if they flow through or near popular campsites, heavily used trails, or areas where horses and sheep have been held.

When in doubt, boil your water, or purify it with iodine-based tablets. See Chapter 11 for information about water-purification accessories.

This selection of specially packaged freeze-dried food is just a part of the wide variety of lightweight foods you can find in most outdoor and sporting-goods stores.

Dried foods are available in individual packages or as part of a complete-meal package. Complete meals are great if you're cooking for large groups.

Outdoor-equipment stores are likely to sell food that is specially packaged for backpackers. Usually, you just need to add water, bring the food to a boil and simmer for a while. Some freeze-dried foods require no cooking at all. Just pour hot water into the package to reconstitute the food. It takes only a few minutes.

The current variety of backpacking foods resembles a gourmet's collection of favorite recipes. Main dish entrees such as Almond Chicken in Wine Sauce, Beef Bourguignon with Noodles, and Mushroom Pilaf; separately, packed fruits and vegetables; beef jerky, bacon bars, omelettes and instant cheesecakes, ice cream (!) and other desserts are just a few of the choices. Some manufacturers pack these different foods together into complete-meal packages, including a main course, beverage, side dish and dessert.

However, most hikers prefer to choose their foods individually. This way they don't end up with too much, too little or foods they don't like. Even so, complete meals are a popular option for large groups.

Some dried foods are available in bulk, packed in 10-pound tins. Repackaging into smaller, meal-sized pouches is usually necessary, but bulk buying is a good budget option for those who backpack a lot or plan menus for large groups.

If you're looking for an inexpensive way to buy dried food, don't overlook your neighborhood supermarket. Many everyday convenience foods are actually dried foods. They're great as lightweight outdoor food.

Among the food you'll find on supermarket shelves is quick-cooking oatmeal, pancake mix, dried fruit, powdered drink mix, instant coffee, cocoa, dried milk, instant potatoes, rice, pudding, gelatin desserts, biscuit mix, crackers, cheese, peanut butter and dried sausage.

Because supermarket foods are often packaged in sizes large enough to last a family for days, you may need to repack the foods and mixes into smaller plastic bags or containers. Be careful to always read the labels, or at

Supermarkets also carry a variety of lightweight, dried foods. Typically, they're less expensive than specially packaged backpacking food.

least bring them along. Some foods require milk. You can always bring dried milk. And others may need to be baked.

Even a gourmet or ethnic food shop can provide you with delightful and unusual choices in outdoor foods. Exotic dried meats, fruits, vegetables and noodles are some of the delicacies you'll find. Eating in the outdoors doesn't have to be a Spartan exercise in self-denial.

Retort Packaging—This packaging has also been called, accurately, a flexible tin can. The food, usually entrees like stew, chili and stroganoff, are put (usually in their raw state) into a flexible three-layer polyester, foil and polypropylene pouch. The air is drawn out of the pouch, and it is sealed. Then the entire package is cooked.

Retort packaged foods are usually quite tasty, but because the moisture hasn't been removed, they are heavier than dried foods. However, retort foods are certainly lighter than canned foods. They can be warmed in hot water or eaten cold.

Fresh Foods—There's still a place for fresh foods when backpacking. Nothing will replace the luscious sweetness of fresh fruit, the taste of real milk and the savory sizzle of fresh meat.

Long-distance backpackers and cyclists often say that standard dried foods don't provide enough fiber and roughage. Adding a small amount of fresh food can combat that problem.

The two major problems with taking fresh food on your trip are

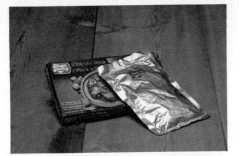

Retort packaged food is heavier than dried food, but considerably lighter than canned. Retort packaging retains the food's liquid content, sealed inside a light, vacuum-sealed pouch.

perishability and weight. You have to look at your planned trip and decide—first, will the food stay fresh enough? And second, are you willing to carry the extra weight? Sometimes, it's worthwhile to carry a few extra pounds to put together an outdoor feast.

Finally, read cooking directions carefully. "No cooking required" shouldn't be taken literally. You still have to boil water. Some dried foods, especially those you buy off the supermarket shelves, may require a combination of milk and water to reconstitute them. You can still use them, of course, by bringing along some instant milk to add to the mix, but you should know this before you leave home. With some products, it may be best to test before you take them along.

BE AN INTELLIGENT CONSUMER—READ THE LABEL

You can discover a lot by reading the label on packaged food. Government regulations require the food processor to tell you what you're getting.

First, look at the name of the food. Is it *Stroganoff with Beef* or *Beef Stroganoff?* How about *Dumplings with Chicken* or *Chicken Dumplings?*

United States Department of Agriculture (U.S.D.A) regulations specify that to be labeled *Beef Stroganoff,* the product must have at least 45% beef content, while a product labeled *Stroganoff with Beef* can have as little as 21% beef.

Second, look at the list of ingredients. The U.S.D.A. requires that they be listed in descending order, according to weight, with the most prevalent ingredient first and the least prevalent last. This won't tell you exactly how much of each ingredient there is in the product, only their relative proportions.

Most manufacturers will tell you the number and size of servings the product will provide—for example, *Two 12-ounce servings.* With lightweight, dried foods, much of that final weight is due to the water you put in. To find out how much food you're really getting, check the net weight of the package. Two products may claim the same serving size, but if one has a lower net weight, all you've been asked to do is add more water. All other things being equal, the product with the higher net weight will give you more food.

You'll need to learn by experience whether one serving of a given food really fills you up. Some hungry hikers have learned that it takes *two servings* to fill them up, so they buy accordingly.

Cross-Country Skis & Snowshoes 7

Most of North America gets snow for at least part of the winter. And for many outdoor enthusiasts, winter is the best time of year. The outdoors is quiet, crowds are non-existent, and the woods, streams and meadows take on a completely different look.

Snow is beautiful, but it presents challenges. Clothing and tents must be able to withstand a winter storm. Navigation can be more difficult, and you may need special knowledge of local weather patterns and avalanche safety.

Modern outdoor equipment has made winter sports easier and safer. Tents are lighter. Clothing is more effective. And packs and sleeping bags are available for nearly any winter demand.

If you're interested in exploring the outdoors in the winter, you'll probably need to use either cross-country skis or snowshoes.

Cross-Country Skis

Cross-country skiing is, basically, an uncomplicated sport. Its simplicity is one of its great attractions. The technique of moving across the snow on skis can be mastered in a few hours. Beginners can embark on day trips almost immediately. When you've learned the basics, you can work on perfecting technique in whatever specialty you choose—day touring, backpacking, backcountry skiing or racing.

You'll find that some skiing experts, authors and retail personnel have a very technical approach to cross-country skiing. They speak passionately about the pros and cons of different types of ski construction, boot design and waxes. Of course, technical information may play a part in your purchasing decisions, but it's best not to lose sight of the overall simplicity of the sport. The way equipment works for you is the important thing, ultimately more important than debating minor design differences in ski or pole construction.

In this section, we look at the major parts of a cross-country skiing package—skis, boots, bindings and poles. You'll find wide variations in different kinds of equipment, so to help you decide, ask these four questions before you go shopping:

1) What type of terrain will you be skiing over—prepared tracks, untracked snow or a little of both?

2) What type of snow conditions

A racer (left) needs different equipment from those heading into untracked backcountry snow (right). This racer trains in prepared tracks with low-cut racing boots on light, narrow and stiff skis.

are you likely to find in your area—cold and dry, or warm and wet? Is the temperature nearly constant or is there wide variation in air, and therefore snow, temperature?

3) How often do you ski, or plan to? Are you a weekend skier, a racer who trains several times a week, or someone who can only get away to ski three or four times a winter?

4) What's your level of skill and experience—beginner, intermediate or advanced? Are you a racer or experienced ski mountaineer wishing to try a different style? Your ability affects what kind of ski best meets your needs.

When you have answers to these questions, you should begin looking at skis from one of the following four categories—recreational, performance, backcountry or racing.

RECREATIONAL SKIS

Recreational, or *touring,* skis are designed for those who will be skiing both in and out of prepared tracks. There is no truly all-purpose or multi-purpose ski, but the recreational ski comes closest.

It is wide enough to hold you up on soft snow, yet narrow enough to move quickly in prepared tracks. Recreational skis are heavier than featherweight racing models but lighter than backcountry skis.

PERFORMANCE SKIS

Performance skis are designed for those who do nearly all their skiing in prepared tracks, but don't want the high-performance characteristics offered by racing skis. These skis are narrower and slightly lighter than recreational models. If you think you might try your hand in local public ski races, performance skis will serve you well.

For a first pair of skis, most beginners choose either recreational or performance. In the Western United States, where most skiing is through untracked snow, beginners usually start with a recreational ski. In the Midwest, East and Europe, where there are many more miles of prepared tracks, a performance ski is a good choice for a beginner.

BACKCOUNTRY SKIS

Backcountry skis are for the skier who pushes into deep, untracked snow. They are the widest and heaviest of all skis, characteristics which

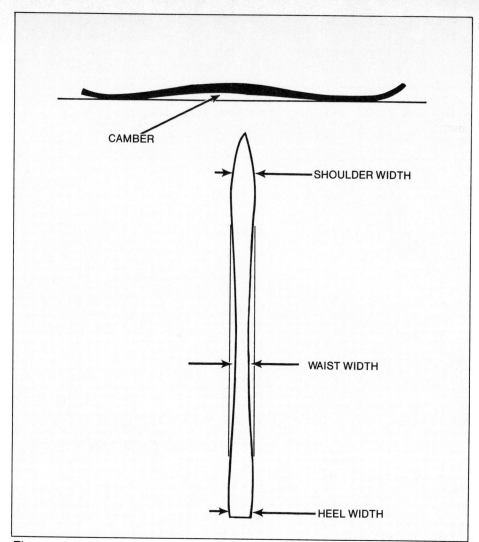

These are the important dimensions on cross-country skis. Sidecut, in conjunction with camber, enables the ski to turn in untracked snow and aids in the kick.

give them good flotation on soft snow and enough stability to support a skier wearing a heavy pack.

Most backcountry skis have metal edges to aid in turning. Because you can't rely on a track to guide your turn, you must master the art of turning.

RACING SKIS

Racing skis are the lightest, narrowest and stiffest of all models. They can be used only on the hard-packed tracks of racing courses. On unbroken snow, they sink in. And because of their narrow width, they offer minimal stability.

THE DOUBLE PYRAMID

If you're like most beginning skiers, you'll start off by touring, probably on recreational or performance skis. Your best plan is to start with day trips, then when you have a feel for skiing, move on to overnight outings. Stay on moderate terrain and master technique before you worry about setting any speed records.

Many skiers tour this way happily for the rest of their lives. But for those of you who desire a bigger challenge, you can go in one of two directions—backcountry skiing or racing. These are the most thrilling applications of cross-country skiing, but they are so different in terms of equipment and terrain that they are essentially opposite extremes. Therefore, it's valuable to think of cross-country skiing as a double pyramid, with racing as one peak and backcountry skiing as the other.

CONSTRUCTION AND DESIGN

The way a ski is built affects performance. Materials, design considerations and bases are the most important factors.

Materials—At one time, all cross-country skis were made of wood. Now, nearly all are made of fiberglass.

Fiberglass essentially displaced wood in the mid-1970s because it outperforms it in almost every way. In addition to being stronger, lighter and more flexible, fiberglass skis also require less maintenance.

Some authors, manufacturers and retail personnel can spend hours talking about different types of fiberglass construction, but we won't. Spending pages discussing it here ignores what we mentioned earlier—cross-country skiing is an uncomplicated sport. It's best to enjoy it with this in mind.

Fiberglass is dense, but so strong that very little is needed to give a ski the necessary strength. All fiberglass skis share the same basic construction method. Fiberglass is wrapped around or sandwiched on the top and bottom of a light core, made of either wood or foam. Three of the most common methods are the sandwich, torsion box and injection-molded. Unless you're a racer, you'll probably notice little difference in the performance of each.

Width—Ski widths vary considerably, from 44mm to over 80mm, as measured at the *waist,* the narrowest midpoint along a ski's length. Racing skis are narrowest; backcountry skis are widest.

Wider skis are heavier, more stable and float more effectively over soft snow. If you're skiing in packed tracks, you'll be able to use a narrow ski.

Lay a cross-country ski on its base and look at it from overhead. You'll see that it's cut in an hourglass shape. Skis are widest at the tip, narrow at the waist and wider again at the tail—a design called *sidecut.* The difference between the widest and narrowest parts of the ski is seldom more than 10%.

Sidecut helps a ski *track* a straight course and turn. Sidecut is useful only when you ski through untracked snow. When your ski moves sideways, as happens when you enter a turn, the wider tip bites into the snow, carving a turn. In prepared tracks, your ski doesn't have to carve the turn. It simply follows the prepared track. Because of this, racing skis have little or no sidecut. Backcountry skis have the most radical sidecut because you need to turn them on unpacked, downhill slopes.

Sidecut is not the only design feature affecting a ski's turning ability. A very flexible tip, for example, won't carve well.

Beginners should buy a reasonably wide ski for good stability. Ask for a ski with a *moderate* sidecut. As you gain skiing experience, you may move into racing or backcountry skiing, which require specialized designs.

Camber—If you hold two skis together, base to base, you'll see that the bases don't touch because the skis are arched. This arch is called *camber.*

Cross-country skis have a much greater camber than alpine skis for two reasons. First, when the ski is depressed and released during the skiing motion, the resulting spring gives you a little extra forward motion from the kick. Second, the high arch reduces the ski area touching the snow. This is good because cross-country skis glide best on tips and tails.

The center portion is the part that grips the snow when you kick for forward motion. This gripping action is provided by either a special kind of wax or by patterned "scales" cut into the base.

It's important to choose a ski with a camber appropriate to your skiing style, experience and the terrain you'll cover. Racing skis have the highest and stiffest camber. They are designed so the center of the ski touches the snow only during a powerful kick. If you can't punch your ski down hard enough, you'll slide backward.

Skis with too soft a camber flatten against the snow. The mid-section is built for gripping, not gliding, and if it touches the snow at the wrong time, you'll slow down.

Beginners should ask for a ski with *medium* or *soft* camber. If you buy a ski with too soft a camber, it may slow you down, but you'll still be able to make forward progress. You may not glide as well, but at least you'll have good traction for climbing. If you buy a ski with too stiff a camber, you may not be able to ski uphill.

The type of snow you encounter

When cross-country skis are held together, base to base, there'll be a gap equal to twice camber. Generally, racing skis have the highest camber and backcountry skis the lowest.

Skis are built to flex differently in the tip, mid-section and tail. If you're buying your first pair of skis, ask for the assistance of an expert who can match the skis' flex to your weight, ability and local terrain.

also determines the camber you need. The harder the snowpack, the stiffer the camber can be. Soft snow will compress and flatten under a hard-camber ski, putting the snow in contact with the base before the ski is fully compressed. If you ski mostly in soft snow, select a ski with a soft camber.

Flexibility—Skis are built to flex differently in the tip, mid-section and tail. The tips should be soft, so they don't dig in when you are skiing over bumps. The mid-section should be stiffer, and the tail more flexible, so it won't chatter over bumps.

If you are buying your first pair of skis, ask for the assistance of an expert who can match your weight, skiing ability, and the terrain you'll be covering to the proper camber, flex and sidecut.

Length—Ski length is determined by your weight and height. You can approximate correct ski length by your height.

If you're heavier than average for your height, buy a ski that's a few centimeters longer than indicated so you can get correct camber. If you weigh less than average, buy a ski just a few centimeters shorter.

Beginners may want a ski about 5cm to 10cm shorter until they get the feel of skiing. Backcountry skiers generally prefer longer skis that float better in soft snow. If you will be traveling through terrain with lots of trees and brush, shorter skis are easier to maneuver. A knowledgeable sales clerk will be able to help you weigh these different variables and choose the right length.

Bases—The popularity of the fiberglass ski has triggered the age of the synthetic base. Most bases are made from a polyethylene plastic, such as P-Tex or Fastex. They are more durable than old-fashioned wood bases and are totally waterproof.

Few cross-country skis have metal edges. The only time they are necessary is on rugged backcountry skis.

Waxable vs. Waxless Bases—Whether to buy a waxable or waxless ski is often the first question beginners ask. There is no clear-cut answer. You need to decide what your needs are and buy with them in mind.

Waxable bases are best for those who ski in prepared tracks, and in regions where the temperature is likely to stay consistently cold. For example, nearly all racers use waxable bases.

How Wax Works—Waxes work because microscopic snow particles grab the wax, digging in to hold the ski. When the ski is in motion, as in the glide phase and when going downhill, the snow cannot dig in, so the ski slides.

If a wax is too hard, the snow cannot penetrate it, and you slide backward. If you have applied a wax that is too soft, the snow grabs all the time, even when you are going downhill. This slows you down.

Some synthetic waxable bases are "brushed," a mechanical process that adds tiny grooves and ridges. This gives waxes a rough surface to adhere to.

To further improve performance, experienced skiers apply wax to only the middle of the ski—the part that comes in contact with the snow during a hard kick. The rest of the ski is left free to glide. To fully take advantage of this system, you need to develop a powerful kick.

It is generally agreed that a waxable ski, properly prepared, will outperform a waxless ski. But it isn't always easy to learn the skills of waxing, and waxing makes more sense in some parts of the country than in others.

Waxable skis work best in cold, dry snow. If you ski where the snow is likely to be wet and warm, waxless skis may be a better choice. When the temperature goes up or down, your wax may need changing, which can be a time-consuming process. Every experienced skier knows a waxing perfectionist, someone who stops every hour to change waxes, searching for the perfect combination.

The major advantage of waxless skis is convenience. They are always ready to use, and there is no reason to stop along the trail to apply a different wax. Typically, rental skis are waxless. So before buying waxless skis, rent some first.

What's Available—Waxless bases come in many different patterns, but they all work on the same principle—a projection sticks out into the snow in such a way that the ski can slide forward, but grips when it slides back. Because waxless ski bases are far from smooth, they make noise, especially when gliding over hard, icy snow.

Modern waxable bases have a "brushed" surface, which provides a rough surface for the wax to grip. Waxable skis are best for those who ski on prepared tracks and in regions where the temperature stays cold.

Waxless bases have a pattern that projects into the snow, allowing forward motion yet gripping when the ski slides back. Other no-wax bases are available.

THE HARD AND SOFT OF SKI WAXING

In many parts of North America, skiing on waxable skis is not only practical—it's also the best way to achieve high performance. Waxable skis work best in regions where the temperature is likely to stay consistently cold.

THE NATURE OF SNOW

Each snowflake is irregular, with many microscopic protrusions, barbs and edges. Newly fallen snow is the most irregular. As snow lies on the ground, thaws and refreezes, its sharp shapes change. Snowflakes become rounder, more like a lump of frozen water.

HOW WAX WORKS

Snow's microscopic irregularities dig into the ski wax just enough so that your ski grips on the uphill when you're moving slowly, but glides on flat and downhill terrain when you're moving too quickly for the snow to grip. New snow is sharper and more irregular, so it grips the wax more effectively. Old snow doesn't grab as easily, and you'll have to wax accordingly.

WAX SELECTION

Hard wax is for new snow or snow that has been on the ground for several days but hasn't melted or otherwise changed shape.

Klister wax is a sticky fluid, used for skiing over old snow that has gone through melting and refreezing. The lack of sharp edges on old snow means it won't grab in hard wax. Klister wax is soft and easier to penetrate.

Manufacturers produce several colors of hard and klister waxes, each designed for a certain temperature range. Waxes are coded with cool colors (green and blue) for sub-freezing temperatures, and with warmer colors (violet, red and yellow) for warmer temperatures.

Since conditions may change during the day, it's possible that you may have to change waxes during a ski trip. It's part of the challenge of waxing.

If you're just getting started and find yourself confused by the array of waxes, it may be simpler to use one of the two-wax systems now available. It's simple. Gold wax is used in subfreezing temperatures; silver for warmer weather.

Experienced two-wax users find that only a thin layer of gold wax is necessary in very cold temperatures. As the temperature warms, don't change waxes, just add more layers. A thin layer of gold wax, polished with your cork, works like a green hard wax. A thicker, unpolished gold layer works like a violet hard wax. A thin layer of silver wax works much the same as a hard red. Add more silver wax and you've got performance to match a red klister.

APPLYING WAX

First, make sure your ski is dry. It's best to wax your skis indoors before you go outside. If you have to carry your skis on a car-top rack, keep them dry in a waterproof bag. If neither is possible, wipe your skis thoroughly with a dry rag before applying wax. Then rub wax onto the ski much as you'd color with a large crayon.

You then use a waxing cork—available where you bought your waxes—to rub your hard wax into the ski and make the coating more durable.

Klister wax comes in a tube, so it's obviously going to be a little messier to apply than hard wax. Warm the tube with your hands, hot water or over a fire if the wax won't come out. Squeeze a thin ribbon down each side of your ski. Smooth it out with a spreader and wipe off any excess with a rag.

Remember, for optimum performance, apply wax only to the middle portions of your ski. Many skis have marks to show you where to apply wax in different conditions. It's often a good idea, however, for beginners to wax the entire ski. You won't glide as well, but you'll be able to climb hills without slipping.

CHANGING WAX AND TROUBLESHOOTING

First of all, give your wax a chance to work in. Many waxes slip for the first few hundred yards before they start working. If, after that point, your wax is still slipping, try another layer; don't go to a softer wax right away. It's easier to put wax on than take it off. Likewise, it's easy to put a soft wax over a hard one, but difficult to do it the other way around. If you do have to put a hard wax over a soft one, you first have to scrape off the soft wax before applying the new, harder layer.

WAXING CHART

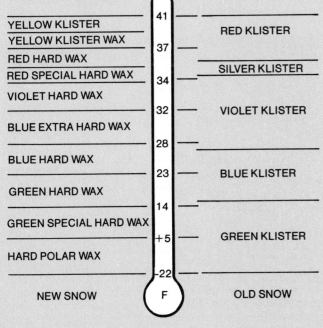

NEW SNOW	°F	OLD SNOW
YELLOW KLISTER	41	RED KLISTER
YELLOW KLISTER WAX	37	
RED HARD WAX		SILVER KLISTER
RED SPECIAL HARD WAX	34	
VIOLET HARD WAX	32	VIOLET KLISTER
BLUE EXTRA HARD WAX	28	
BLUE HARD WAX	23	BLUE KLISTER
GREEN HARD WAX	14	
GREEN SPECIAL HARD WAX	+5	GREEN KLISTER
HARD POLAR WAX	−22	

TWO-WAX CHART

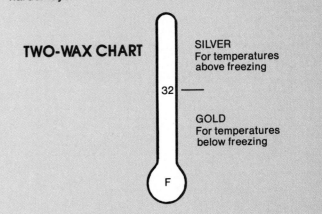

SILVER
For temperatures above freezing

32

GOLD
For temperatures below freezing

°F

Cross-country bindings hold only your toe, leaving your heel free to flex up for proper skiing techniques.

A different kind of waxless base is the mohair type. Strips of hair are laid down so the nap faces backward. They run quietly and perform well under some conditions, especially hard snow, where the more familiar patterned designs many not hold as well. But mohair bases can absorb water and freeze up, ending their good performance for that day.

You can improve the performance of any waxless base by applying a *glider wax* to the tips and tails. Glider wax increases the speed and distance of a glide by reducing friction on the parts of the ski that touch the snow during the gliding phase.

BOOTS

Cross-country ski boots connect your feet to the skis, allowing you to freely use the cross-country stride to move forward.

Boots should suit the type of skiing you will be doing, and just like any piece of footwear, they *must* fit well. A poorly fitted boot can give you blisters, cold feet and an altogether unpleasant skiing experience.

There are three kinds of boots—recreational or touring, backcountry and racing.

Recreational Boots—These are cut to ankle height. Most are made of leather, but fabric and rubber boots are becoming more and more popular.

Racing Boots—Compared to recreational boots, these are low-cut, light and likely to have the 7mm thick sole necessary to fit 38mm or 50mm racing bindings. They may be made of leather or fabric.

Backcountry Boots—This style resembles hiking boots because they are cut above the ankle and usually have lugged soles. They are most often made of leather and may also be padded or lined to ward off cold.

All cross-country boots have flexible soles. Their relative light weight would seem to be conducive to cold feet, but the nature of skiing provides some protection from the cold. Flexible soles allow good blood circulation to the feet, and skis offer good insulation from the snow. In addition, the active nature of the sport is the best safeguard against cold feet.

Until the last few years, the uppers and soles of most ski boots were stitched together with Norwegian welt construction, described in Chapter 2. Many backcountry boots still use this method. Most recreational and racing boots, however, now have molded soles of either injected or vulcanized rubber. Molded soles are less expensive and have good forward flex. To increase torsional and lateral stability, manufacturers add a steel, plastic or wooden shank.

Some ski boots have leather uppers. Leather is warm, durable, breathable and can be waterproofed. Less expensive boots may use split leather. Top-quality models should have full-grain leather. (See Chapter

Quality cross-country boots are made either of leather (left) or fabric and rubber (right). Here you can also see the two most common soles in cross-country boots—the stitched-down Norwegian welt (left) and the molded rubber sole (right).

Three types of cross-country boots: A racing boot (left) is cut low and has a thin sole for good flexibility. A recreational boot (center) has a heavier sole and upper than the racing model. A backcountry boot (right) is cut high and insulated for cold weather.

2 for an explanation of different kinds of leather.) Split leather has little natural water repellency, so it is usually treated with a plastic coating of polyurethane to improve its ability to shed water.

The lightest models may have uppers made of fabric, usually nylon. These boots must have leather at stress points—heels and toes—to provide abrasion-resistance. Fabric uppers breathe better than leather, but they are less waterproof. Once wet, though, they dry quickly. One way manufacturers increase water repellency is to laminate Gore-Tex to the upper fabric.

BINDINGS

Cross-country bindings are mechanically simple because they have only one purpose—to connect the toe of the boot to the ski. For proper skiing technique, the heel must be free.

The traditional toe binding uses

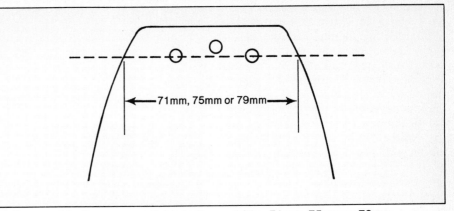

Nordic norm bindings are available in three widths, 71mm, 75mm or 79mm, measured in a line through the two outer pins.

three pins that fit into corresponding holes in the boot sole. The boot is held in place by a wire bail that clamps down over an extension of the boot's sole. Toe bindings are available in a wide range of designs, from light racing models, to heavy, sturdy designs suitable for backcountry skiing.

Nordic Norm Bindings—The boot and binding must be exactly the same size and design to match properly. In 1973, major cross-country ski manufacturers agreed to standardize bindings, so boots and bindings from different manufacturers could be interchanged. Called the *Nordic Norm,* this system established three widths—71mm, 75mm and 79mm—as measured in a line through the two outer pins. Most touring boots fit one of these sizes.

Racing Bindings—Until the 1976 Winter Olympics, the Nordic Norm

was the only binding system available. But with the progression toward even narrower racing skis, first Adidas then others began making new binding systems. These use thin nylon soles that offer excellent side-to-side control, while also having good forward flex. These systems have moved the pivot point ahead of the traditional placement, to a point in front of the boot toe. In addition, they have made the binding very small and narrow, eliminating any scraping against the side of the snow track.

Adidas, Rottefella, Salomon and others make these boot/binding combinations. All are lightweight. Be warned that elements of one brand are typically incompatible with other brands.

The same features that initially appealed to racers also attracted many ambitious recreational skiers. But racing bindings had some obvious

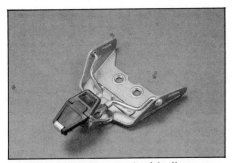

Traditional cross-country bindings use three pins that fit into corresponding holes in the boot sole. A wire bail clamps down to hold the boot in place.

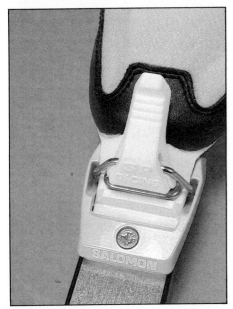

Notice the narrow profile and flexible connection between boot toe and a racing binding.

problems for recreational skiers. The 7mm boot sole was so thin that it offered little insulation, and the hard plastic soles used on racing shoes made for slippery walking.

Touring Norm Bindings—To solve these problems, a third kind of binding was developed—the *Touring Norm 50.* It combines the best features of the Nordic Norm and Racing Norm bindings. It has the same slim profile of the racing bindings but accepts boots with 12mm soles.

Heel Locators—If you are interested in backcountry skiing, you may want to use a heel locator. It is composed of two parts—a plastic stub attached to the heel of the boot and a V-shaped notch mounted on the ski.

When your heel is on the ski, the stub fits into the slot, holding your heel in place if your foot begins to move to either side. This does not interfere with the normal cross-country stride, but it does add lateral stability for turning in steep, untracked snow. Heel locators are unneccesary for racers and recreational skiers.

You can also use heel plates to keep your heel from sliding sideways while gliding. Some plates use pegs, as shown. Others use a wedge-shaped projection.

POLES

Cross-country poles must be flexible and springy to help you move forward. This is quite unlike downhill ski poles, which are characteristically stiff so you can plant the pole and pivot on it.

When choosing a cross-country pole, you'll need to consider two basic things—the material used in the shaft and the basket design.

Materials—Traditionally, ski poles were made of Tonkin cane, a bamboo-like grass. Even though Tonkin poles are fading from the scene, they're a good design. Their biggest advantages

The two most common types of cross-country ski poles are made of fiberglass (left) and aluminum (right).

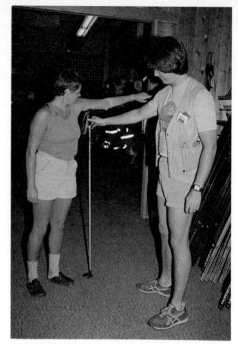
To find correct pole length, stand with your arm straight out. The correct pole fits under your arm, as shown.

are that they are relatively inexpensive, and if broken, can usually be repaired at home.

Ski poles of aluminum and fiberglass are replacing Tonkin poles. They're made in a wide range of strengths and flexes. They are more expensive than Tonkin and offer greater durability.

Racing poles of carbon-fiber shafts are usually too light and fragile for recreational skiing.

Baskets—You must choose the appropriate basket for the terrain you'll be covering. Small, angled, butterfly-shaped baskets work well on packed trails. But in deep snow, they penetrate too far. See below.

Choose your pole's basket shape by the snow conditions you'll be facing. The deeper the snow, the larger the basket you'll need.

Straps—Straps are made of either leather or plastic. It is important that they be adjustable. When you use the pole, the straps bear the pressure of downward arm force. An adjustable strap can be fitted to either the heavy gloves you would wear on a cold day, or to your bare hands on sunny spring days.

Because poles play such an important part in the skiing stride, they must be the correct size. To find proper length, stand with your arm extended straight out, parallel to the ground. A correctly sized pole should just fit under your arm.

Snowshoes

Snowshoes serve a valuable function for winter travelers. The techniques are easy. On gentle terrain, beginners can master "shoeing" within an hour. Learning to walk with a heavy pack, or over rough, steep ground may take longer, but seldom more than half a day.

Before buying a pair of snowshoes, decide what you will be using them for. If you're a winter mountaineer, you'll need snowshoes that can get you up steep, possibly icy, slopes. Forest walkers must buy a design that is large enough to keep them from sinking, but compact enough that it can be maneuvered through trees and in and out of gullies. Backpackers need a snowshoe large enough to support the extra weight of a pack.

You'll need to consider these seven factors in choosing a snowshoe—materials, flotation, size, traction, tracking ability, weight and design.

MATERIALS AND CONSTRUCTION METHODS

A snowshoe is a simple piece of equipment. It consists of a frame, webbing and some sort of binding. The materials and construction methods determine how well your snowshoe will perform in certain conditions and how durable it will be.

The Frame—Top-quality snowshoe frames are made of either wood or aluminum.

Wooden frames have been used for centuries by native Americans. The preferred wood is white ash that has been steamed and bent into the desired shape.

Since there are no hidden parts, it's relatively easy for a novice to inspect

Most beginning snowshoers quickly master basic walking techniques. Some people like the extra stability offered by cross-country ski poles. Others don't consider them necessary.

workmanship. The wood should have a straight grain and be free of knots. It should be varnished to keep it from absorbing water. Periodic varnishing may be necessary.

Wood-frame snowshoes usually have crossbars that are mortised into the frame. The front crossbar marks the front of the toe hole, so its place-

ment determines the location of the binding. The closer the binding is to the toe, the better the snowshoe will dig in when you climb steep slopes. Bindings set farther back are more comfortable for walking along gentle terrain or when descending. Most front crossbars are placed 1/4 to 1/3 of the way back from the toe.

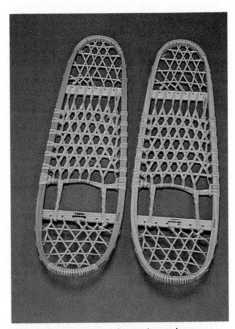

Wood-frame snowshoes have been used for centuries. Notice the two crossbars. The front one marks the front of the toe hole.

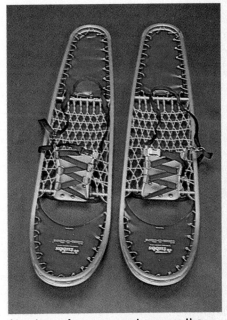

Aluminum-frame snowshoes are the most popular modern replacement for wood. Notice that the front crossbar is placed at the back of the toe hole.

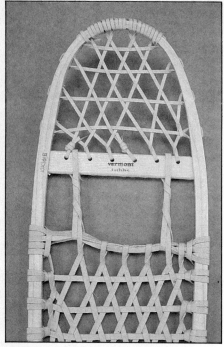

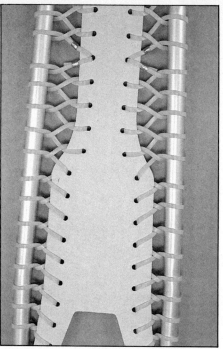

Neoprene-coated nylon webbing has almost completely replaced rawhide, the traditional webbing material.

Many aluminum-frame snowshoes use a solid deck of neoprene instead of lacing.

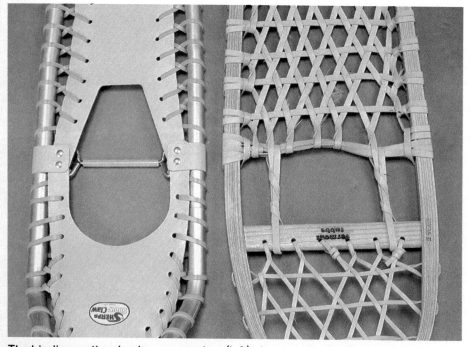

The binding on the aluminum snowshoe (left) pivots on an aluminum rod. On a wood-frame snowshoe (right) it pivots on the *toe cord,* the heavy bundle of webbing behind the toe hole.

Aluminum frames are the most popular replacement for wood. In alloy form, aluminum is stronger than wood. When anodized, it is resistant to corrosion and abrasion. Aluminum is also more expensive than wood.

Most aluminum frames have only one crossbar, usually placed at the back, rather than the front, of the toe hole. It serves as the bar on which the binding pivots.

Webbing—Quality snowshoes use webbing of neoprene-coated nylon. Rawhide is the traditional webbing material, but it has been almost completely replaced by neoprene webbing in both wood- and aluminum-frame snowshoes.

Neoprene is waterproof, so it can be used successfully in any kind of snow, including very wet snow. This makes it ideal for mountain treks where you may be using your snowshoes day after day with little chance to dry them out. Even though neoprene is very durable, it won't last forever. But if it does need replacing, the process is simple.

Many of the aluminum-frame, neoprene-laced snowshoes use a solid deck of neoprene, instead of lacing. The deck is attached to the frame with laces.

The most important section for flotation is the center third of the snowshoe. For this reason, many manufacturers use heavier and wider webbing in the center. Webbing in the center third is usually wrapped around the frame.

To protect against abrasion, webbing on the toe and tail should be threaded through countersunk holes drilled in the frame. Tailless snowshoes suffer from more webbing abrasion in the back since it is the webbing, not an extended tail, that drags across the snow. Most manufacturers wrap extra webbing around the back to protect against abrasion.

If you are considering wood-frame snowshoes, be sure to inspect the *toe cord,* the heavy bundle of webbing just behind the toe hole. This is where the binding attaches and pivots. The toe cord takes more punishment than any other part of the snowshoe, so make sure it is sturdy, tight and firmly attached to the frame.

Also inspect the toe hole. It must be large, offering plenty of room for your booted foot to pivot without catching on the forward crossbar or side lacing. Even the most secure binding allows some lateral flex. If you plan to wear heavy, insulated boots, you may need an extra-large toe hole. Bring your boots along when shopping.

A few snowshoes are laced with nylon cord. It has poor abrasion resistance, especially on crusty, icy snow. Another disadvantage is that it stretches and sags over time, necessitating frequent repairs.

Plastic Snowshoes—These have some specialized applications. They function well as children's snowshoes, but because of extreme flexibility are not suitable for use in soft snow or with a heavy pack. Plastic has an additional limitation—it may crack in very cold temperatures.

Some hikers use plastic snowshoes for spring hikes when the snowline is reached only after several miles of hiking. Their weight and cost—much less than either wood or aluminum—make them an attractive alternative for children or adults on a tight budget.

Wide snowshoes are the hardest for beginners to get used to. The Sherpa snowshoe, pictured here, is an easy size for those just starting out.

FLOTATION

You shouldn't sink more than a few inches when shoeing. The larger the snowshoe, the better it will float on top of the snow. A snowshoe with a rounded tail has better overall flotation than one with a pointed tail.

The more you weigh, the bigger snowshoes you'll need to provide adequate flotation. Ask a knowledgeable retail clerk to recommend the best size for you. Another good way to check proper sizing is to rent a pair of snowshoes and try them in the field. If you plan on carrying a very heavy pack, you'll need to increase your size estimate a bit.

The type of snow affects the flotation of the snowshoe, too. You may sink in twice as far in deep, new snow as you would on old, packed snow. Dry, powdery snow requires a larger snowshoe, too.

Don't assume that a snowshoe half the size will sink twice as far. It won't. If having a small, maneuverable, light snowshoe is important to you, rent a pair first. You may find that they don't sink as far as you expected. In the rugged mountains of the Western United States, where maneuverability is essential, many hikers are buying smaller snowshoes. In areas with plenty of wide open space and gentle terrains, large snowshoes are very comfortable.

SIZE

We've already mentioned that larger snowshoes float better on soft snow. There are other reasons, though, to do some thinking about which size is best for your needs.

Beginners often have trouble getting used to a wide snowshoe. These require a bow-legged walk that takes experience, fitness and long legs. Unless you meet these requirements, you'll do better with a snowshoe about 10 inches wide or less.

Mountain climbers and hikers, who occasionally have to carry snowshoes on their packs, prefer a small model. The same goes for those who hike in forests or bushy, rocky country. For them, the easy handling of a small snowshoe makes up for any loss of flotation.

TRACTION

All snowshoes offer some natural traction. Webbing digs into the snow well enough that, in soft snow, it's all the traction most hikers need. Look at the placement of the binding and toe

The Sherpa traction binding is a popular design for aluminum-frame snowshoes. It laces quickly, pivots easily for good tracking, and has aluminum teeth on the bottom for traction.

hole. The closer the binding is to the tip of the shoe, the better it climbs.

To cover steep, icy terrain, you'll probably need to add some additional traction to your snowshoes. You can outfit them with traction bindings that use aluminum teeth to grip the snow. Also available are aluminum traction bars that bolt to the crossbar of the snowshoe.

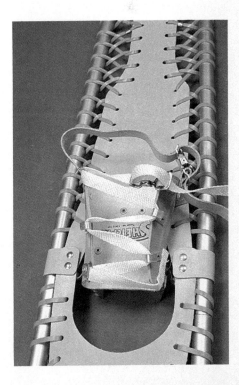

Proper tracking is essential for easy walking. A well-designed snowshoe should come forward with the toe up and the tail dragging. In these photos, the left shoe's tail is up and the toe down when the snowshoer steps forward. Such a tendency could lead to tracking problems in deeper snow.

TRACKING ABILITY

When you have selected a shoe with the proper size and flotation, you need to find out how well it *tracks*. This refers to how easy it is to walk with your snowshoes. Well-designed shoes follow your foot when you step forward. They ride out of the foot hole, with the tip up, and the tail or back dragging along the snow.

Tracking problems are among the most annoying you'll face. Two of the most common problems occur when the snowshoe's tip catches in the snow, and when a loose binding attachment causes the shoe to twist underfoot.

If your tip catches in the snow, it may be because the binding is placed too far back. The binding placement for snowshoes is non-adjustable. So be sure to test for this before you buy a pair. Hold the snowshoe by its binding—the tail should drop quickly. If it doesn't, you're likely to have tracking problems. The more rugged the country you'll be covering, the better the snowshoe has to track.

WEIGHT

Snowshoes that are too heavy are unwieldy. They'll sap your strength just like a heavy pack can. The general rule of thumb is that one pound on your feet equals about five on your back. Most snowshoes weigh at least three pounds per pair. Consider, too, that you'll almost always be carrying some snow that piles on top of the snowshoe. It's important, then, to buy the lightest model that meets your needs.

SNOWSHOE DESIGN

Snowshoes come in all sorts of shapes and sizes. For simplicity, we divide them into two basic groups—those without tails and those with.

Without Tails—The most common tailless snowshoe is the *bearpaw*. Bearpaws are available in a wide range of designs, but the true bearpaw is short and wide, often nearly as wide as it is long. Bearpaws are ideal for walking in tight places. But, because of their extreme width, they are not a good choice for beginners.

The *modified bearpaw* is easier to manage because it is longer and narrower than the true bearpaw. Modified bearpaws have nearly parallel sides. Another popular snowshoe, the aluminum *Sherpa snowshoe,* is an example of a modified bearpaw design that beginners can master in a few hours.

With Tails—Snowshoes with tails usually track better than those without. Regardless of the snowshoe design, the tail should be much heavier than the toe.

The *Maine* and *Michigan* types are long and wide. Because of this, they are difficult for beginners to handle. *Pickerel* and *Cross-Country* designs are long but much narrower than the Maine or Michigan. This makes them especially good for beginners.

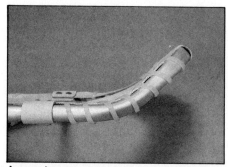

A prominent upturn in the toe will help keep it from catching in soft snow.

The largest of the tailed snowshoes is the *Yukon*. They're very long—up to about 60 inches—but only moderately wide. They usually have highly upturned toes, making them ideal for walking through deep snow in open terrain.

Which Shape Is Best?—Base your choice on your experience, the type of terrain and snow you'll be encountering, and other specific considerations, such as whether you'll have to carry your snowshoes on a pack. Beginners should look for a good all-around design that is neither too long nor too wide.

Another factor confusing the issue is that different manufacturers use different names for their models. In this book, we've used traditional names. However, not everyone goes by tradition, and a snowshoe one manufacturer calls a *bearpaw* may be called something else in another catalog. Always take a look at a snowshoe, either in person or in a catalog picture, before you buy.

BINDINGS

All snowshoe bindings work the same way. They are attached to either the toe cord in a wooden snowshoe or the metal crossbar in an aluminum model. Straps hold the boot across the toe, instep and heel. When you step forward, the binding pivots into the toe hole.

Good tracking requires a good binding. The binding should hold the boot firmly, allowing minimal lateral movement or forward shift. If the boot is allowed to slide from side to side, you may trip or slip when traversing steep hills, making turns or stepping on obstructions. If the boot crawls forward even a fraction of an inch, it will slip out of the heel strap, costing time and annoyance to readjust the binding.

Modern recreational bindings are made of either leather or neoprene nylon. Leather stretches when wet. Neoprene bindings hold their shape in any kind of weather.

Choosing the right kind of buckle may seem like a minor point in the warm comfort of a store, but the first time you have to adjust your snowshoes in the cold and wind, you'll appreciate having an efficient set.

Two kinds are common—the *spring-loaded-friction buckle* and the *belt-buckle* type with a stem that fits into

Pictured is a selection of modified bearpaw designs. They're popular among beginners because all are easy to handle.

holes punched in the strap. The latter is satisfactory for straps that can be set at home, but for straps that need field adjustment, a spring-loaded-friction type is easier to adjust with gloved hands.

Before you buy a binding, check how well it attaches to the snowshoe. No matter how firmly it holds your boot, you'll have poor performance if it fastens loosely to the snowshoe.

BOOTS

The boots you choose for snowshoeing should keep your feet warm, protect them from blisters and provide good ankle support. The boot must have a relatively stiff upper, so it will hold firm when you tighten the binding straps.

Most snowshoers use their hiking or backpacking boots for snowshoeing. These work best with a binding that protects the toe cord and webbing from the rubbing of lug soles.

For walking in extremely cold temperatures, winter boots, insulated with Ensolite or wool felt, will offer added warmth. Gaiters protect your boots and legs from snow and cold.

MAINTENANCE

Aluminum snowshoes and neoprene laces require very little maintenance. Check your webbing and binding straps periodically for frayed edges. It's better to replace a frayed strap at home than have it fail miles away from civilization.

Wooden snowshoes should be varnished at the factory. Once a year, reapply two or three coats of marine spar varnish.

A spring-loaded binding buckle is easy to operate with gloved hands.

A snowshoe binding pivots on a metal rod or toe cord and flexes forward into the toe hole. Straps hold your boot across the toe, instep and heel.

8

Mountaineering Equipment

The sport of mountaineering is as individual as each mountaineer. Some climbers are attracted to the glaciated peaks of the Cascade Mountains, Canadian Rockies and the Alaska Range. Others are rock climbers, drawn to the cliffs and ridges of the Schwangunks in New York, the Appalachians, Rocky Mountains, California Sierras, or innumerable smaller mountains, cliffs and outcroppings dotting the North American landscape.

Because mountaineering equipment is specialized, it's wise to decide exactly what kind of climbing you'll be doing. Snow and ice climbing? Rock climbing? Scrambling? A combination of all three?

Most mountaineers started out as hikers and backpackers. So if you're shopping for climbing gear for the first time, remember that you may already have some of the equipment you'll need for climbing—good boots, clothing, a warm sleeping bag and a tent. These were described in detail in previous chapters. Therefore, in this chapter we confine our discussion to equipment specifically designed for mountaineering.

If you are just getting started in the sport, it's wise to get only the equipment you'll need. As you gain experience and ability, and move into more difficult climbing, you'll see the need for more specialized equipment.

There's no need to buy a complete climbing "kit" before making your first trip. Proceed slowly, borrowing or renting to try out equipment, until you know exactly what you need.

By necessity, any discussion of mountaineering equipment must use some specialized terms. Some of these are explained in the text, others in a special mountaineering glossary on page 100.

A climbing class is a good place to learn mountaineering techniques and correct use of equipment. Check with your local outdoor-equipment store for a list of mountaineering classes.

CLIMBING EQUIPMENT AND SAFETY

Mountain climbing can be a dangerous activity, but with proper training and good equipment, your risks can be minimized. Each climber has the responsibility to learn how to use equipment properly. It's also your responsibility to know your limitations and avoid climbing routes that are too difficult. Additionally, it's imperative to know techniques of backcountry navigation, survival and first aid.

There are several ways to learn mountaineering techniques. Local climbing clubs usually offer both beginning and advanced classes. Some colleges have outdoor programs, and there are guide services in many national parks and wilderness areas offering mountaineering instruction.

Much can be learned from a good mountaineering book, and we have listed some of the best available in the bibliography on page 158. They are useful as an introduction and source of general information, but a book is never a substitute for qualified personal instruction and supervised practice.

WHERE TO PURCHASE MOUNTAINEERING EQUIPMENT

Mountaineering equipment is

available through both specialty outdoor stores and mail-order catalogs. Large cities usually have several shops that specialize in mountaineering supplies.

Typically, well-stocked stores hire knowledgeable retail personnel and may even sponsor clinics and slide shows to help you learn more about mountain climbing and mountaineering equipment. Even some cities and small towns hundreds of miles from the mountains have outdoor stores that carry a good selection of equipment for mountain climbers.

You may have a more difficult time getting expert help in a store that carries mountaineering gear "on the side." This makes it essential that you either take classes or do some research so you know exactly what you need.

If you are unable to find the equipment you need, or want a larger selection to shop from, you can shop by mail. In fact, mountaineering-equipment catalogs can be a gold mine of information on equipment specifications and technique. Some large retailers, including REI, carry only equipment that meets rigid quality-testing standards. You can confidently order by mail from such retailers.

The two major types of mountaineering require different techniques and equipment. Above is rock climbing. At left is ice and snow climbing.

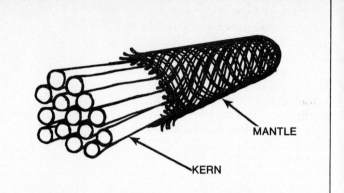

Ropecraft—the proper use and care of a climbing rope—is one of the most important things a climber learns. It includes how to coil and carry a rope, such as this kernmantle type. Kernmantle construction offers great strength and good handling characteristics.

Climbing Ropes

Climbing ropes are used for many things, but safety is the most important function. The rope must secure a climber in case of a fall. With a good climbing rope you can also haul loads and rappel.

A rope may be the single most important piece of safety equipment you will use. Therefore, it's important to know what kind of climbing you will be doing and buy an appropriate rope. It's just as important to know how to tie knots and how to tie the rope into your body harness. A rope improperly used may fail in an emergency. Again, taking a climbing class will help you learn ropecraft.

MATERIALS AND DESIGN

All modern climbing ropes are made of nylon. For many years, ropes were made of manila hemp, but nylon's superior strength, shock-absorbing ability and durability have made manila ropes obsolete.

There are two kinds of climbing ropes—*kernmantle* and *three-strand,* hard-lay ropes.

Kernmantle Ropes—These offer climbers the greatest strength and best handling characteristics. The *mantle* is a woven sheath of nylon over the *kern,* a core of twisted or braided strands of perlon—a type of nylon. The mantle contributes about 1/3 of the rope's strength and absorbs

This kernmantle rope has a bipattern sheath to help you find the middle of the rope. It's a useful feature for rappels.

abrasion that would otherwise damage the rope's core.

Kernmantle ropes vary in core construction, but all are more flexible than traditional three-strand ropes. They hold knots well, resist kinking and are easy to coil.

Some kernmantle ropes have a color or pattern that changes at the middle of the rope. This convenient feature helps you quickly find the middle of the rope for rappels. Bipattern and bicolor ropes have continuous strands throughout the rope's length.

Kernmantle ropes are sized in millimeters—9, 10.5 and 11mm are the most commonly used sizes for climbing.

Three-Strand Ropes—These are constructed of individual nylon fibers that are twisted into three main strands, which in turn are twisted around each other. Not all three-strand ropes are suitable for mountaineering. They must be of a mountaineering, or *hard,* lay to be used for climbing. Currently, only two brands of three-strand ropes are approved for climbing—Goldline II and Skyline.

Three-strand ropes are best for moderate glacier travel. Several characteristics make them a poor choice for rock climbers: The lack of a protective sheath means they are easily abraded. They kink and twist more easily than kernmantle ropes. And when subjected to a load, they stretch more than a kernmantle rope of the same diameter.

Even so, three-strand ropes are significantly less expensive than kernmantle ropes, and many climbers find them adequate.

Three-strand ropes are sized in inches, with 7/16 and 3/8 inch being most commonly used.

ROPE LENGTH

The proper length for a rope depends on your personal preference and the rope's intended use. For glacier travel, most climbers use either 120- or 150-foot lengths. The more technical the climb, the more useful a longer length will be.

Rock climbers use either 150- or 165-foot lengths, with the longer one becoming more popular. Longer ropes permit longer leads and give the *belayer* extra rope to work with. (See page 108.)

CARE AND MAINTENANCE

Your rope can be damaged by chemicals such as gasoline, battery acid and bleach. Stepping on a rope, especially while wearing crampons, can break some of the nylon fibers and weaken the rope.

Over time, dirt can work its way into the fibers of a rope and cause internal abrasion. It's a good idea to wash your rope about once a year. Run it through the washing machine, using a mild soap, gentle cycle and warm water. Hang it up to dry, out of direct sunlight because ultraviolet rays from sunlight deteriorate nylon fibers. However, dyes and the kernmantle construction protect climbing ropes from most normal exposure to the sun.

Ropes can soak up a great deal of water during normal use, either from precipitation or by being dragged across wet snow. A wet rope is very heavy and can freeze up. Some ropes are water-repellent. Their fibers are treated with a water-repellent substance before being braided.

Between periods of use, store your rope in a clean, cool place, out of direct sun. Remove all knots and coil it loosely, never under tension.

All climbing ropes should eventually be retired, but knowing when isn't always easy. Your rope will probably be good for between 100 and 400 hours of use, but much depends on its history. Technical rock climbing wears rope much more than snow and ice travel. Has the rope held any falls? Has it been put through especially rigorous usage—pendulums, jumaring, hauling equipment? Is the sheath abraded? Are there any cuts? Any time you have doubts about a rope's safety, replace it.

UIAA SAFETY STANDARDS

The UIAA (Union Internationale des Associations d'Alpinisme) is an independent group made up of representatives of climbing organizations of the alpine countries of the world. The group has developed technical standards for climbing ropes and some other equipment, including ice axes, carabiners and harnesses. Standards are revised periodically.

It's important to remember that not all mountaineering equipment goes through UIAA testing. Manufacturers may submit their equipment to the UIAA through the representatives of their country. Although the American Alpine Club is the U.S. representative, some top-quality American equipment is never tested by the UIAA. Nevertheless, the UIAA has done much to raise the safety standards of mountaineering gear, and it's valuable to look at some of the standards they have set.

UIAA STANDARDS FOR ROPES

Climbing ropes usually break because they have been previously damaged, stretched across sharp rocks or weakened by chemical contamination, ultraviolet rays or previous falls.

In reality, breakage is less of a concern than *impact force*. This measures the amount of energy transferred to your body when the rope catches your fall. If you are subjected to a high impact force, it's possible to be injured just from the shock of hitting the end of your rope.

The impact-force test is one of the most important UIAA tests: A weight of 90kg (198 pounds) is attached to one end of a 2.8m (9 feet) rope. To simulate a severe leader fall, the weight is positioned for a 5m fall and dropped. To pass, the rope must hold five such "falls" and the peak load on the first must not exceed 1200kg (2640 pounds). Lower impact forces mean that less stress is put on your body.

Climbing ropes are designed to stretch when subjected to a severe load, thus lessening the impact force on a falling climber. But when subjected to lesser loads, like hauling loads, rappelling or jumaring, it's desirable for the rope to hold its shape. The UIAA limit for low-load stretch is 8% of the rope's length when an 80kg static weight is attached to the rope.

Since 1978, UIAA standards apply only to kernmantle rope. Most kernmantle ropes designed specifically for climbing meet all UIAA standards. If you will be doing any technical climbing, it's important to buy a UIAA-approved rope. Reputable mountaineering-equipment retailers usually state whether their ropes meet UIAA standards.

A GLOSSARY OF MOUNTAINEERING TERMS

Anchor—A fixed point on the mountain into which the belayer is tied, using a nut, piton, ice screw or even a tree or rock horn. The anchor prevents the belayer from being pulled off his stance by the force of a falling climber.

Belay—One person providing security to another with a rope.

Boot-Axe Belay—A specialized type of belay used in snow climbing. The ice-axe shaft is driven deeply into the snow. The boot is planted in front of the axe for extra security, and the rope is wrapped around both.

Carabiner—An oval or D-shaped metal snap link used to connect various parts of the climbing system. The most important use is to clip the carabiner into a piton or nut so the rope can be passed through.

Chockstones—Also called *chocks* or *nuts*. Chocks are pieces of metal, available in different sizes, that are often wedged into cracks to anchor a belay or provide a point of protection for the leader.

Crampon—A set of metal spikes strapped to the boots to provide traction on snow and ice slopes.

Crevasse—A deep crack or fissure in glacial ice caused by the movement of the glacier.

Direct-Aid Climbing—Upward climbing in which the climber uses anything other than the natural features available. Usually done with etriers that are clipped into a nut or piton.

Etriers—Also called *aid slings* and *stirrups*. Etriers are short ladders, usually made of webbing, used in direct-aid climbing. When foot and hand holds are lacking, the climber stands in etriers, attached by means of a carabiner into a nut or piton.

Fluke—A shovel-shaped piece of aluminum that is driven into the snow in such a way that when exposed to a load, it buries itself deeper.

Harness—A network of webbing that wraps around your mid-section. It connects to the rope to distribute the force of a fall.

Ice Axe—A handheld snow- and ice-climbing tool that has many different functions. It provides stability for walking on steep slopes, a way to arrest falls by digging in the pick, and an aid to technical ice climbers by acting as a handhold and used to chop steps.

Ice Screws—Tubular or solid screws that are placed in ice to provide protection for the leader or anchor a belay.

Jumaring—Climbing up an anchored rope by means of a mechanical rope-climbing device that grips the rope when weight is applied, but releases and can be moved to a higher position when weight is taken off. Used in direct-aid climbing.

Nuts—See *chockstones*.

Pendulum—A rock-climbing move in which the leader swings on his rope to bypass a blank section and reach a crack or foothold.

Piton—Horizontal, vertical or angle-shaped metal spikes that are hammered into cracks to anchor a belay or provide protection for the leader.

Point Of Protection—A nut, piton, ice screw or fluke that is placed by the leader, into which the rope is clipped with a carabiner. Protection points shorten the distance the leader would fall.

Rappel—A means of descending by sliding down an anchored rope. Usually the rope is doubled, allowing it to be retrieved by pulling one end. Most climbers use a carabiner-braking system or some other specialized rope brake to control descent.

Self-Arrest—Using the pick of an ice axe to stop a sliding fall.

Traverse—To climb or descend across a slope, rather than go straight up or down.

Webbing—Flat, nylon "rope" used for a variety of functions. Webbing is used to make etriers, homemade harnesses, runners and slings to hold climbing hardware.

Ice Axes

Ice axes have changed considerably since the early days of mountaineering, when guides would equip their clients with long shepherd's staffs. The ice axe has evolved from a simple walking aid into a versatile and essential piece of equipment for any snow and ice travel.

Ice axes are divided into two groups:

1) The general-purpose axe is used by hikers in alpine terrain who may encounter an occasional snowfield. The axe is used primarily as a safeguard against falling.

It's also used on steep slopes by serious snow and ice climbers, who need to use their axe as both a protection against falling and as a climbing aid.

2) The ice-climbing tool is used by technical ice climbers on vertical and nearly vertical ice as a constant aid to climbing. They use it as a handhold and as a swinging and hooking tool to chop holds. You can also use it for stopping a fall—called a *self-arrest*—on moderate slopes.

Ice axes consist of a head, shaft, spike and an optional wrist strap or leash.

THE HEAD

This is the "business" end of the ice axe, and it's also the place where there's greatest design variation. The sharp, pointed end is called the *pick*. The broad, flat end is the *adze*. It's important to buy an ice axe with a head design that suits your type of climbing.

Materials—The traditional method of making ice-axe heads—drop forg-

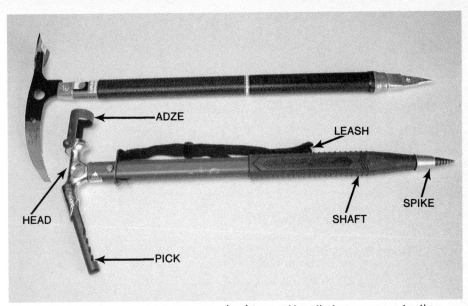

A general-purpose mountaineering axe (top) is used by climbers as a protection against falling and as an occasional technical tool on difficult slopes. The ice-climbing tool (bottom) is designed for climbing vertical and near-vertical ice slopes. The identified parts apply to both types of axes.

ing—isn't used much anymore. Forged heads are considered too heavy and expensive.

Most heads are now stamped from sheet steel. Sheet steel is uniform, cuts easily and can be heat-treated. The adze and pick can be stamped separately and then welded together. Or, the head can be stamped from a single piece of steel and twisted into shape.

The head is force-fitted and riveted to the shaft with two or more rivets.

The Pick—The pick is designed to grip into ice or snow for self-arresting and for driving the axe into ice for a handhold. To choose the pick design best-suited to your needs, look at three things—the *droop* (how far the

point drops down), the *angle* of the tip and the *teeth* along the bottom edge of the pick.

Most picks are drooped, which provides hooking action, helping the axe dig into the snow. The general-purpose axe has a moderate droop. Ice-climbing tools have the most radically drooped picks, designed to roughly equal the arc followed by the head when you swing the axe into a steep ice wall. Some very specialized tools have an even more severe droop for hooking placements.

Some ice-climbing tools are equipped with interchangeable picks that allow you to adapt the axe to a variety of climbing situations and ice conditions.

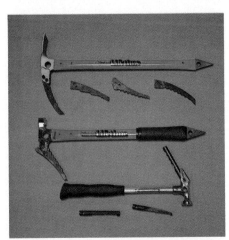

Some ice-climbing tools are equipped with interchangeable picks so you can adapt them to a wide range of ice conditions.

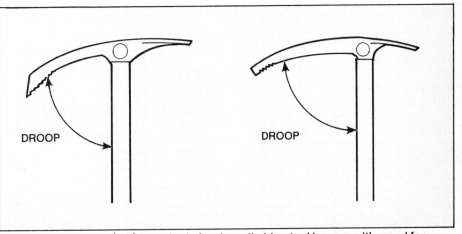

A radical pick droop (left) is typical of an ice-climbing tool because it's used for swinging and hooking. A moderate droop (right) is characteristic of general-purpose axes, which are useful for self-arrests.

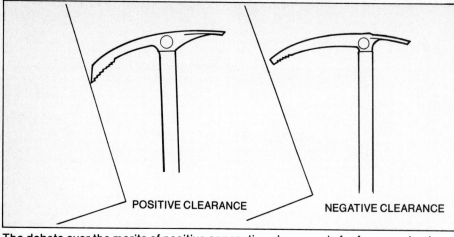

POSITIVE CLEARANCE   NEGATIVE CLEARANCE

The debate over the merits of positive or negative clearance is far from resolved. We advise beginners to avoid the extremes. An axe with a slight positive clearance should work well.

The angle of the tip, called *clearance,* has been the subject of much debate over the years. Picks can have either *positive* or *negative* clearance. In soft snow, either kind will penetrate, so the difference is unimportant. But, if you'll be encountering hard snow or ice, you'll need a pick that can grab effectively.

In a pick with positive clearance, the bottom point of the pick slants away from the shaft when the head and shaft are viewed in profile. In a negative-clearance pick, the tip of the pick slants toward the shaft.

An axe with positive clearance grabs quickly and effectively on hard ice, and the more pronounced the clearance, the quicker and harder it will bite.

This can be a problem, say some critics, who cite the danger in self-arresting of having the pick grab so quickly that the axe pulls out of your hands.

Conversely, a negative clearance may skate or drag along hard surfaces, and an axe that won't grab is of little use in a self-arrest. There is little consensus among climbing experts about which design works better. However, all experts would agree that the most important factor is *not* the design of the axe tip, but your skill and experience at self-arresting.

Most picks have teeth along the bottom edges starting just back of the point and running toward the shaft. Teeth provide additional gripping power for hard ice and snow. Axes designed as ice-climbing tools may have teeth the entire length of the pick to maximize gripping power.

The Adze—This is the broad cutting tool opposite the pick. It is used primarily for cutting steps and handholds in steep ice. The adze used to be a critical piece of ice-climbing hardware, but it's used less frequently now.

With the advent of the 12-point crampon for your boots, it's now possible to climb up steep ice slopes without cutting footsteps with an adze. Adzes may be flat or curved, straight or drooped, with either a smooth or scalloped edge.

Head Care And Maintenance—Occasionally, remove any rust that may have formed on the head. Keep the pick and adze sharpened. The sharper and thinner the points, the better they work. But very sharp points are dangerous, and they also wear down more quickly from abrasion. To achieve the best compromise between performance and durability, taper the edge smoothly to a width of a millimeter and then file it off abruptly to a

dull edge. Always sharpen with a small hand file since the heat from a grinding wheel may weaken the steel.

THE SHAFT

Until the early 1970s, most ice-axe shafts were made of hardwood, usually ash or hickory. But good wood became harder and harder to find, and its price eventually made it more expensive than stronger and more durable metal and fiberglass shafts.

Currently, most shafts are made of aluminum. They are lighter and stronger than wood, but tend to conduct more heat away from your hands. To solve this problem, manufacturers of aluminum shafts put a polyvinyl or rubber sheath over the gripping area of the shaft. This provides extra insulation and a better grip.

Aluminum's ability to conduct heat isn't a major problem if you're using your axe for hiking and general-purpose mountaineering. In these activities you use the axe to add stability on steep slopes, provide an anchor for boot-axe belays and help arrest a fall. These applications don't require you to grab the shaft for long periods. Only technical ice climbers, who use an axe to swing and hook, need to grip the shaft for a long time.

Some ice axes have fiberglass shafts, and at least one manufacturer offers a composite shaft—aluminum (for strength) wrapped with graphite (to reduce vibration) and an outer covering of fiberglass to insulate from the cold and protect from abrasion.

Care And Maintenance—Aluminum and fiberglass shafts require little or no maintenance. If your axe doesn't have a rubber grip, you may want to wrap the bottom few inches of the

Sharp, prominent teeth along the bottom edge of the pick provide additional gripping power in hard ice or snow.

This interchangeable adze of an ice-climbing tool is specifically designed to chop steps in very hard ice.

shaft with rubberized tape to protect against abrasion.

If you happen to have a wooden shaft, treat it once a year with boiled linseed oil and wrap the bottom of the shaft with tape. To store it, hang it by the head or lay it flat to prevent warping over time.

Occasionally, inspect the axe shaft to see if there are any major dents, holes or gouges that could reduce strength.

Safety Standards—To be approved by the UIAA, a shaft must be able to withstand a load of 990 pounds, have a head-to-shaft connection that holds 264 pounds, and a spike that doesn't break off under a 66-pound load. Most metal and fiberglass shafts meet UIAA standards.

THE SPIKE

A sharp spike is important when you need to drive your axe into the snow to execute a boot-axe belay or to probe for hidden crevasses. Most spikes are either riveted or glued to the shaft with epoxy. A flat blade provides the best anchoring.

FITTING AN ICE AXE

Choosing the proper length and weight of an axe depends on your height and the axe's intended use.

Axes are sized from 50cm to 90cm, measured from the end of the spike to the head, usually in 5cm increments. For walking-stick and general-purpose mountaineering uses, the axe should reach from your palm to the floor when held down at your side.

For steeper and more technical climbing, you'll need a shorter axe.

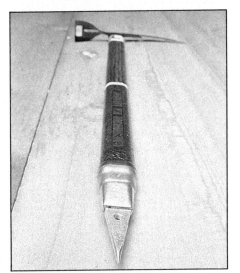

Flat-bladed spikes provide the best anchoring.

Your axe should reach from your palm to the ground when you hold it at your side.

This is because the axe is usually held on the uphill side of your body, and the steepness of the slope brings the surface of the snow closer. Under such conditions, a long axe is awkward. Similarly, long axes are difficult to swing and hook, so most technical ice climbers prefer a shorter one.

Just as it is easier to split wood with a heavy-headed splitting maul, an ice axe with a heavy head cuts and penetrates ice better than one with a lighter head. This is an important consideration for technical ice climbers, but of little concern for others. Ice climbers need an axe with an extra head mass of about 200 grams relative to general-purpose axes.

WRIST LOOPS AND LEASHES

Some axes are equipped with *wrist loops*—short loops of nylon webbing attached to a metal glide ring. Other axes come without a wrist strap, offering you a choice. You may add your own leash by tying a piece of webbing through the carabiner hole in the head, or climb without a leash or wrist strap.

A wrist loop offers protection against dropping your axe and watching it slide down the slope. In addition, the loop allows you to temporarily let the axe hang from your wrist, a real convenience in mixed snow and rock climbing, when you may need to reach up to grab rock holds.

Even so, some climbers prefer to climb without a wrist loop, citing the annoyance of having to change the strap from hand to hand every time

This ice climber prefers a long leash because he has to drive the axe into ice and hang onto the loop for support.

you change directions and traverse across a slope. Others say that if you lose your grip on your axe in a fall, the danger from the flailing axe may be greater than that from the fall.

Most climbers compromise by arranging the loop around the head and climbing without it on moderate terrain. They put in on when they reach more difficult climbing, where there is a greater risk of dropping the axe.

Some climbers prefer a long leash, made from a piece of 1/2-inch webbing, cut to about the same length as the axe's shaft, with a loop tied in the end. Others like a shorter wrist loop. Ice climbers need the long leash. But, if you will be using your axe for general-purpose mountaineering, the choice is largely a matter of personal preference.

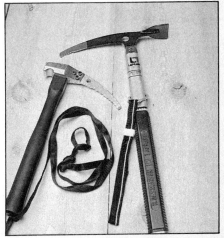

Ice-climbing tools (left) usually have a long leash. General-purpose mountaineering axes (right) typically use a short wrist loop.

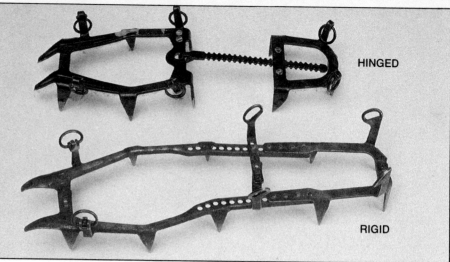

Crampons are spiked extensions of your climbing boots. They make climbing in snow and ice safer and easier. Two designs are available: Hinged crampons are best for general mountaineering. Rigid crampons are best for technical ice climbing in which long, steep ice must be surmounted with the crampons' front points.

HINGED

RIGID

Crampons

Crampons are metal spikes strapped to your boots to give traction on steep snow or ice slopes. Until the invention of crampons, climbers wore nailed boots. These provided some traction, but if the climbers wanted to ascend steep icy slopes, they had to cut hundreds, sometimes thousands, of steps in the ice.

The invention in 1908 of a 10-point crampon that strapped to the boot made it possible to climb previously unclimbable slopes without cutting steps.

The arrival in the 1930s of the 12-point crampon, with two forward-slanting points at the front, further widened the limits of the sport. These crampons allowed climbers to *front-point* up all but the steepest ice slopes. Nearly all modern crampons are 12-point models.

MATERIALS AND DESIGN

Most crampons are made from chrome-molybdenum steel, a strong alloy.

Crampons come in two basic designs—*rigid* and *hinged*. Rigid crampons are used primarily by technical ice climbers who appreciate the solid, stable platform that rigid crampons provide for front-pointing up steep, slippery slopes.

No leather mountaineering boot is absolutely stiff. There will always be a slight bend in the ball of the foot.

Rigid crampons, therefore, help stiffen the sole, allowing a lower heel profile and easing the strain on calf muscles. Rigid crampons also vibrate less than hinged ones when they are kicked into hard ice.

Hinged crampons are best for general-purpose mountaineering, where only occasional stretches of front-pointing are required. As long as you wear a stiff-soled mountaineering boot, hinged crampons provide an adequate platform for ice climbing. And they are more comfortable for long stretches of walking over moderately difficult terrain.

FITTING CRAMPONS

Always fit your crampons to the boots you'll be using with them. The crampon should fit snugly so that when you lift the boot up, the crampon stays attached without straps. Front points should protrude 1/2 to 3/4 of their length beyond the boot's

These crampons fit just right.

toe, and all points should be as close as possible to the edge of the sole.

Many modern crampons are adjustable, either in length or in both length and width. Never bend a point to fit your boot, as it can crack and break off under stress.

Crampon Straps—The most reliable and durable crampon straps are made of neoprene-reinforced nylon. They are strong, and lightweight and don't stretch or soak up water like traditional leather straps.

The most common strapping system uses two independent straps, one at the toe and a second that wraps around the ankle and instep from the two rear posts on the crampon. Belt-type buckles are the most secure. If using them, place the buckle on the outside of the boot so you don't hook it with your other crampon when walking.

It's a good idea to master putting on your crampons at home before you have to do it in cold, possibly dark, conditions in the field.

CARE AND MAINTENANCE

As with ice axes, keep your crampon points sharp by occasionally filing them with a hand file. Many snow and ice routes have unavoidable sections of rock or dirt. A well-made crampon will withstand such infrequent abuse without damage, but it pays to check for dull or bent points.

If one is seriously misaligned, don't

To provide a solid grip in hard ice, front points should protrude 1/2 to 3/4 of their length beyond your boot toe.

Use crampon straps made of neoprene nylon. The strapping system shown here is typical—independent straps on the toe and instep are secured with a belt-type buckle.

try to hammer it back. Take the crampon to a metal worker or reputable mountaineering-equipment shop so the point can be bent back into shape with heat to preserve strength.

Sharp crampon points can cause damage whether they are packed inside or outside your pack. It's best to buy rubber crampon protectors to keep the points from puncturing equipment in your pack or causing injury to anyone who inadvertently bumps into your pack.

Carabiners

A carabiner is a metal snap link used for both snow and rock climbing. Carabiners are used to connect ropes to protection points, attach the climber to belay anchors, clip directly into anchors for direct-aid climbing, and as a braking system for rappels.

MATERIALS AND DESIGN

Most carabiners are made of aluminum alloy, although some are still made of steel. The greatest force a carabiner must withstand is when holding a fall. The UIAA requires a carabiner to have a minimum strength of 2200 kilograms (4840 pounds) on the long axis with the gate closed. Used properly, it's unlikely that your carabiners will fail before other parts of your climbing system do.

There are two common shapes—oval and D-shaped. The weakest part of a carabiner is the *gate,* or opening. This means D-shaped carabiners are somewhat stronger than ovals because the shape concentrates the load on the solid side, across from the gate.

Forces on an oval carabiner are evenly distributed on both sides, one of which contains the gate. To boost the strength of oval carabiners, manufacturers add extra metal to the gate side, so the modern oval carabiner is strong enough to be used with confidence.

The gate has a pin that fits into a slanted or notched locking slot on the main body of the carabiner. Some carabiners have a slight protrusion at the opening end of the gate. By feeling for it you can tell which end of the gate opens.

A locking carabiner has a threaded sleeve on the gate that closes over the opening to guard against accidental opening.

CARE AND MAINTENANCE

Carabiners, especially those used for rock climbing, are subjected to tremendous abuse. They're banged against rocks. They get muddy. Dirty ropes abrade them. And dirt clogs the gate mechanism. Even so, well-made carabiners can stand up to it all and provide good service, if well cared for.

Sticking gates are usually caused by small burrs on the metal. Repair these by carefully filing them down. Clean

These are just three of the many jobs carabiners perform: Clipping your rope into a point of protection (top); as a braking system for rappelling (center); clipping etriers into a nut or piton (bottom).

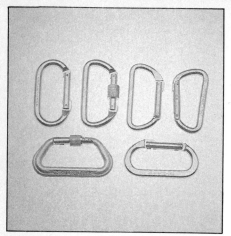

Carabiners are available in both oval and D-shaped, locking and unlocking models.

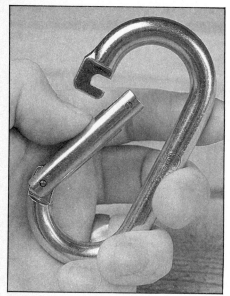

Carabiners are opened by a spring-loaded gate. Notice the slight protrusion that enables you to feel for the gate opening.

corroded or dirty gates by putting the carabiner under hot running water, or by applying a bit of spray lubricant such as WD-40 to the hinge spring. Always clean off the oil before using the carabiner, so it won't pick up more dirt and grit. Put the carabiner in boiling water for a few seconds to remove the oil. A dry, graphite or silicon lubricant won't attract dirt, but it discolors hands and clothing.

Webbing

Climbers use nylon webbing for a variety of purposes, including runners (loops of webbing tied to points of protection for technical rock and ice climbing), chock slings, slings to hold

hardware, etriers (aid slings), seat and chest harnesses, and other practical jobs around camp, like tying equipment to packs or cutting a makeshift belt.

For general climbing use, most climbers prefer tubular webbing because it is stronger and more flexibile than flat webbing. Flat webbing is often used for etriers because it is stiffer and causes the stirrups to stay open, making it easier to place your feet.

When cutting webbing, make sure you melt the ends with a match, fusing fibers together to prevent unraveling.

HARNESSES

In the early days of climbing, mountaineers simply tied the rope around their waist and set off. If they fell, they often faced severe discomfort and danger. The rope could ride up over the chest, restricting breathing and possibly causing internal injuries. There were cases in which climbers survived a bad fall, only to suffer injuries from an unsafe tying system.

To remedy the problem, climbers have started using harnesses that wrap around the waist, around the legs and through the crotch. Some also use chest harnesses. Harnesses distribute the force of a fall over a larger body area and keep you from twisting upside down. You can tie your own out of tubular webbing or purchase them commercially.

Homemade Harnesses—There are several variations of seat harnesses that you can tie yourself. All use loops through which you put your legs, followed by multiple wraps around the hips and waist. There are good directions in some climbing instruction books, and of course, a qualified instructor can also teach you how.

Commercially Made Harnesses—These are more expensive, but are usually worth the extra expense because they are easier to put on and take off. They have been carefully designed to provide maximum safety and comfort. We recommend them highly for any technical rock or ice climbing.

To meet UIAA specifications, a climbing harness must withstand a load of 1600 kilograms (3520 pounds) and support the body in an upright position. A seat harness must be used with a suitable chest harness to meet these requirements.

It's important to follow the manufacturer's directions on all aspects of harness use, including how to buckle the harness and tie in the rope.

Webbing is another piece of mountaineering equipment that has many uses. Etriers (left) for direct-aid climbing are usually made of webbing. Climbers use slings (right) to clip into points of protection.

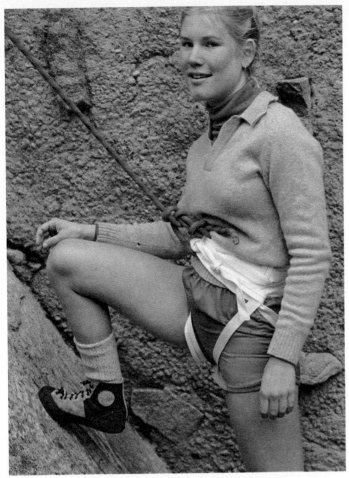

A nylon-webbing seat harness (above left) distributes the force of a fall over a larger area than if the rope were tied just around your waist. This model is homemade.

A chest harness is highly recommended for any technical rock or ice climbing. A commercially made harness like this one (above right) is more comfortable and easier to put on and take off than a homemade harness.

All beginning climbers (right) should wear a helmet. In addition, you should wear one on routes exposed to rock and ice fall, or on technical routes where there's a chance you may fall.

Helmets

Wearing a helmet is sensible, especially on routes exposed to rock or ice fall, when there's a good chance you may take a fall, and when the route is crowded with other climbers who may knock down rocks.

A climbing helmet *must* do five things:

1) The chin strap should be designed so that the helmet stays on your head, even in a tumbling fall.

2) The outer shell must be rigid enough to spread the load of an impacting object over the entire helmet.

3) The inner padding must be firm enough to absorb shocks, from both the top and sides.

4) The shell should resist penetration by pointed objects.

5) The helmet should not be so heavy, hot, bulky or restrictive of hearing that you want to leave it home instead of wearing it.

Most climbing helmets are made of fiberglass, polymer, polycarbonite or polymid shell, and a special high-density, slow-return foam lining. Protection comes from both the shell and the lining.

Some European helmets will accommodate a head lamp. They're a good choice for climbs that begin or end in darkness.

A proper climbing helmet has a chin strap to secure the helmet even in a tumbling fall.

TECHNICAL CLIMBING—BELAYING THE LEADER

On easy and moderately difficult snow and rock routes, the leader and following climbers ascend simultaneously, connected by the rope. If someone falls, there is usually enough time for other party members to brace themselves to stop the slide. But when the route becomes difficult enough that a fall is expected, or when the consequences of a fall would be serious, the method changes.

TACTICS

On difficult routes, climbers *belay* each other. In this technique, one climber is always stationary, braced and anchored into the mountain by means of hardware—a nut, piton, ice screw or fluke. The other climber, called the *leader,* moves ahead, while the stationary *belayer* plays out rope.

At certain points, the leader may place points of protection—on rock, nuts or pitons; on snow, flukes, pickets or ice screws—and clip the rope into them with a carabiner. This shortens the distance the leader would fall. On very difficult routes, he may place protection every few feet.

When the leader nears the limit of the rope, he finds a secure belay stance, places an anchor and clips it into his harness. The following climber then traces the leader's route, retrieving the protection hardware along the way. If the following climber falls, the consequences are relatively minor because he's belayed from above by the leader.

BELAYING

Climbers can belay one another by several different methods, but the most common is the *hip belay.* To give a hip belay, the belayer runs the rope around the back of his hips. If the other climber falls, the belayer uses his outside hand—the *braking hand*—to wrap the rope around his body to help stop the follower's fall. Because the belayer is anchored to the mountain, he can't be pulled off his stance.

Belaying and using rock and snow hardware on technical routes requires much practice. Well-trained, practiced and disciplined climbers know their limitations and equipment. The best way to get the most out of your mountaineering equipment is to know how to use it properly. Again, we recommend that you enroll in a reputable mountaineering class to learn proper belaying techniques.

1) On difficult places, climbers secure each other by belaying. The climber at the right climbs ahead, secured by the climber at the left.

2) As he climbs up the crack, he places two points of protection to shorten the distance he would fall.

3) Here, the leader has reached a ledge and is belaying his partner from above as the partner climbs up to join him.

The hip belay is the most common type. As the leader moves higher, the belayer plays the rope out from around his hips. If the leader were to fall, the belayer would brake the rope with his right hand by wrapping it around his hips. He'd use the friction of the rope passing around his body to help brake the rope.

Technical Rock & Ice-Climbing Hardware

Technical climbing is distinguished from general mountaineering by its difficulty, sophisticated techniques and the specialized equipment it requires. We make only a brief survey of the equipment required for technical mountaineering. To learn more about the equipment and how to use it, read one of the books recommended on page 158. And register for a climbing class with a qualified instructor.

SNOW AND ICE HARDWARE

Specialized snow and ice equipment is used to anchor belays and rappels and to protect the leader in case of a fall. The specific use and effectiveness of this equipment often depends on the condition of the snow and the quality of placement. Pickets and flukes are used in soft snow. Ice screws are used in hard ice.

Pickets—These are T-shaped, aluminum stakes from 18 inches to more than 3 feet long. They have a hole in the end to clip in a carabiner so the rope can be attached. Because of their narrow profile, they are best used in very hard snow, where they can't be pulled out.

Flukes—Snow flukes have largely replaced pickets because of the increased safety they offer. A fluke is a piece of shovel-shaped aluminum attached to a metal cable. You drive the fluke into the snow at about a 45° angle to the direction of the load and dig a slot for the cable. When exposed to a load, the fluke digs deeper into the snow.

Ice Screws—Although available in several different styles, all ice screws

Modern climbers are concerned about the rock damage caused by metal climbing hardware. They now carry equipment designed to minimize the impact of their sport.

do essentially the same thing—anchor belays and protect the leader on hard ice. They have an eye in the end into which you slip a carabiner. You place an ice screw by either driving it in with a hammer or pounding it in far enough for the threads to catch, and then twisting it with your hammer or ice-axe pick until fully set.

The tubular screw has the greatest holding power of all ice screws. As it is placed, chips of ice are extruded out the center, thus reducing the tendency to shatter hard ice.

ROCK-CLIMBING HARDWARE

Rock-climbing hardware serves the same function as ice equipment. It anchors belays and rappels, and protects the leader in case of a fall.

There has been tremendous innovation in rock-climbing hardware, allowing climbers to successfully finish previously "unclimbable" routes, and even changing the ethics of the sport.

The first rock-climbing hardware

was developed in Europe. Early European *pitons*—which you place into cracks in the rock—were made of soft metal. They conformed to the shape of the crack, and were often difficult to remove. Thus, it became common in Europe for the first ascent party to leave in some pitons.

The invention of the chrome-molybdenum steel piton in California in the late 1950s revolutionized technical rock climbing. "Chrome-moly" pitons are very hard, so they could be put in difficult placements that had turned back climbers before. Because the pitons didn't bend, they could be removed from cracks by pounding them from side to side. But the metal was so strong—usually stronger than the surrounding rock—that small pieces of rock were chipped off every time a piton was pounded in and removed.

Soon, climbers became concerned about the scars and holes chrome-moly pitons were leaving in rock

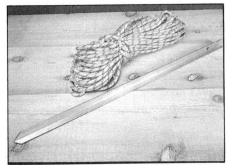

You drive a snow picket into hard snow to anchor belays or provide a point of protection for the lead climber.

A snow fluke is a shovel-shaped piece of aluminum. You clip a rope into its metal cable or webbing loop.

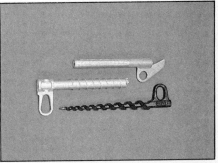

Ice screws hold effectively in hard ice. The two top screws are tubular models. The bottom screw is driven in, twisting itself into place with each blow.

Pitons are hammered into rock cracks. When the rope is clipped in, the point is secure for the leader or acts an anchor for the belayer.

Modern chrome-moly pitons are harder than the surrounding rock. When pounded in, they chip off small pieces of rock. On popular routes, piton scars have resulted, as shown.

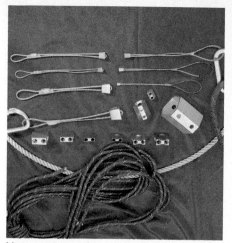

Nuts and chocks are available in sizes from 5/32 inch to 3 inches, fitting the wide variety of placements you'll find in climbing. The smallest chocks are wired. The larger ones must be rigged with nylon rope.

This asymmetrical, hexagonally shaped chock is placed in the crack so that it twists into a more secure placement when subjected to a load. It doesn't scar rock.

A spring-loaded cam device is best for smooth-sided parallel cracks.

faces. Following the lead of British climbers, many North Americans started climbing with *nuts* and *chockstones,* also called *chocks.* Instead of pounding them into cracks, you fit them into natural openings in the cracks. Early nuts had limited applications, but as more innovative designs came out, climbers found that nuts could be used in nearly every situation that previously required a piton.

Pitons aren't yet completely obsolete. But most modern climbers subscribe to the doctrine that it's better to place nuts, if possible, because they don't damage the rock.

Pitons—Basically, these are metal spikes with an eye. You pound them into a crack to anchor a belay, rappel or provide protection for the leader. They come in a wide variety of sizes, from tiny knife blades that fit into cracks less than 1/16 inch wide, to large-angle pitons for cracks up to three inches wide. Large pitons are sometimes called *bongs,* named after the sound they produce when hammered into cracks.

A correctly placed piton provides a very sound, secure anchor. You hammer in a piton with a special piton hammer carried in a belt holster.

Nuts And Chockstones—These are pieces of metal in various shapes and sizes that are attached to either webbing, rope loops or small pieces of wire cable. The nut is wedged into a crack in such a way that when subject-

ed to a load, it wedges harder into the crack. You clip a carabiner into the perlon or wire loop so you can attach the rope to the secured nut.

Nuts first became popular in Britain. There, pitons caused too much rock damage and were not considered "sporting." Climbers picked up small pebbles and wedged them into the cracks instead. Soon, they started using machine nuts with webbing tied through the hole. The practice spread, and nuts designed specifically for climbing began to be manufactured.

Now, you can find a wide variety of sizes and shapes to fit nearly any climbing situation. Tiny *stoppers* are as small as 5/32 inch wide, and some of the largest sizes fit into cracks three inches wide. Asymmetrical, hexagonal-shaped nuts twist into a secure placement when loaded. Spring-loaded cam devices called *Friends* can grab on smooth, parallel-sided cracks.

Generally, the smallest nuts come pre-wired from the factory because they would require such thin webbing or rope that they wouldn't be strong enough. Large chocks and nuts must be rigged with rope or webbing. Usually, the manufacturer recommends the best rope size to provide maximum strength.

You can place nuts and chocks without a hammer. Their removal is usually easier if you use a thin *nut pick* to pry them out of cracks.

Bicycles & Bicycling Accessories

9

Bicycling is one of the most popular, versatile and practical of all recreational sports. Bicycles are used for fun, racing, commuting and tours ranging from a few to thousands of miles. No matter what kind of cycling you enjoy—and most cyclists combine different kinds—you should know some basic things about bicycling equipment.

Basic bicycle design has changed little over the past few decades. Certainly, there have been many technological advancements in metallurgy, aerodynamics and manufacturing. But the bicycle itself is little different.

Frame shape has remained relatively constant. Wheels and tires have become lighter and stronger, but they still perform the same function. The bike is still powered by a *drive train* made up of pedals, a crank set, the chain and gears. With this in mind, it's fair to repeat the adage that the bicycle is "The last thing man invented that he understood."

Bicycles are designed for specific functions. Some are set up to climb hills easily. Others ride best along flat terrain.

Consider this extreme example. Some racers change bikes several times during the course of a race. If their route traverses rough roadway, they ride a sturdy frame designed to absorb shocks. For long mountain ascents, they may change to a light bike with frame dimensions that make hill climbing easier. And when the race nears its conclusion, they may change to an ultra-light machine with gearing that helps them sprint to the finish.

Of course, such tactics are impractical for touring cyclists and too expensive for all but the most ardent racers. Still, it states the facts of bicycle

life—the way a bike frame is built and the components on it determine the way it will ride.

Although bikes look alike, as you shop around you'll find astonishing differences. One bicycle is most comfortable for long-distance touring. Another is best for riding city streets, turning and climbing short hills. Some adapt well to heavy loads.

Others ride best without luggage.

The key to finding the best bicycle for your needs is to decide what kind of cycling you'll be doing most. Before you go shopping, ask yourself these questions:

1) What kind of riding do you do or plan to do? Short commutes? Longer day rides without luggage? Multi-day camping trips?

Bicycling is incredibly versatile. You can do long-distance tours, city commuting or racing.

2) What is your local terrain like? Hills? Flat ground? Will you be doing much riding over rough roads?

3) How fast do you like to ride? Are you a leisurely rider, or do you like to push yourself hard?

4) Are there special features you'll need, such as fenders, lights or attachments for luggage racks?

5) How much are you willing to spend?

The Bicycle

Main bicycle parts are the frame, wheels (including the tires) and components, such as brakes, gears, seat and pedals. You need to consider each when buying a bike.

THE FRAME

This is the heart of the bicycle. If you are short of money and have to pick and choose where to invest your funds, don't be cheap on the frame. You can always put less expensive components on a good frame and then upgrade them as your budget and cycling expertise grow. But a substandard or poorly selected frame means a poor bicycle. It's that simple.

The Tubing—Low-priced bicycle frames are made from straight-gauge, *low-carbon steel* welded from a steel strip. This produces a seam along the tube, which reduces durability. Low-carbon steel frames are nearly always welded together.

Some frames are made of *high-carbon steel*. They are stronger and less malleable. But, the higher percentage of carbon means that manufacturers can't weld the tubes together. They braze them instead. Brazing is similar to soldering and is more expensive than welding.

If you're planning on using your bike for serious commuting or tours of more than a few miles, it's better to move up another step and buy a frame made from chrome-molybdenum steel—commonly called *chrome-moly*. Chrome-moly tubing is lighter and stronger than carbon steel. A few manufacturers use "high-tech" alloys of manganese-molybdenum steel or chrome-vanadium steel, but such frames are reserved primarily for racers.

The bikes we discuss in this chapter use the standard diamond frame. Learn the names of different parts of the frame before you shop for a quality bike.

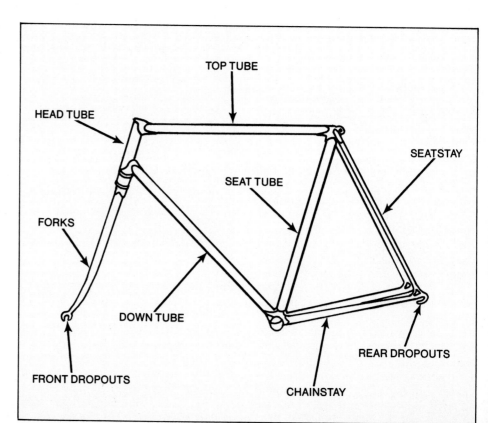

TOP TUBE

HEAD TUBE

SEATSTAY

SEAT TUBE

FORKS

DOWN TUBE

REAR DROPOUTS

FRONT DROPOUTS

CHAINSTAY

Tube construction is also a factor. *Double-butted* tubes offer the most strength for the least weight. In this design, the tube is thicker at the ends than in the middle. There's an increase in outside strength at the joints, where it's needed, and less weight along the middle of the tube. Double-butted frames also offer a comfortable ride by absorbing road shock well.

Frame Size—It's critical to find a bike that fits you well. If your bike is too small, you'll fatigue quickly. If it's too big, you'll waste energy reaching for the pedals, and lose power. Since nearly all adult bicycles have the same size wheels—27-inch diameter—manufacturers vary bicycle size by making frames of different sizes.

Most bicycle models come in several frame sizes. A common selection is 19, 21, 23, and 25 inch. This is measured along the frame's *seat tube*—the tube running from the seat down to the center of the cranks. European frames are measured in metric units. Frames are commonly available in sizes from 48cm to 64cm, usually in 2cm increments.

There are several ways to determine the frame size that fits you best. An easy way is to straddle the bike as

1) To determine proper frame size, straddle the frame with your feet on the floor. There should be about an inch clearance between your crotch and the top tube.

2) Set your saddle height so that your knees are slightly bent at the bottom of the pedal stroke.

3) The saddle can be adjusted forward or backward so you can reach the handlebar grips and brake levers comfortably.

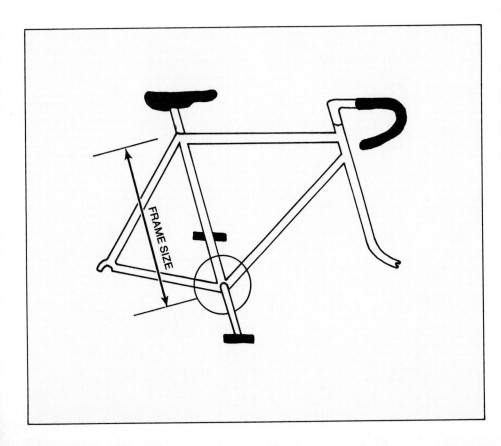

FRAME SIZE

Bicycle frames are measured along the seat tube from the top down to the center of the cranks.

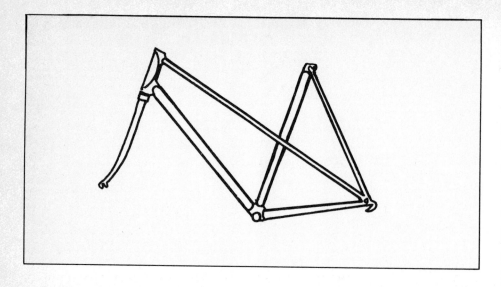

The most durable women's frame is the mixte frame. The two narrow tubes that run from the head tube to the rear dropouts add stiffness.

shown. There should be about one inch clearance between your crotch and the top tube.

If you can't find an exact fit, buy the next smaller size. Then adjust seat and handlebar height to get a good fit. You can't adjust a frame that is too big. You just have to live with it.

Fitting Children—Many times, parents buy children a "too big" frame, expecting them to grow into it. This is bad because a bike that's too big causes problems. It's harder to control and takes more energy to climb hills. In addition, it's no fun for a child to ride a bike he can barely straddle.

"Women's" Frame—The standard man's frame, called a *diamond frame,* has a horizontal tube at top running from the seat to the front handlebars.

To accommodate skirts, women's frames are built without the horizontal top tube. This makes the women's frame less durable and more flexible than a standard diamond frame. A women's frame isn't stiff enough for long-distance riding or carrying heavy loads, but it's adequate for riding short distances.

Now that it's socially acceptable for women to ride a bike while wearing pants, there's no overwhelming reason for a woman not to get a diamond frame. However, if you plan to cycle with a skirt, you'll need to buy a women's frame.

Another reason for considering a women's frame is size. It's difficult to build a standard bicycle frame smaller than 19 inches. If you are too short for

a regular frame, a women's frame may be the best option for you.

The best and most durable women's frame design is called the *mixte* frame. It uses two narrow tubes that run from the top of the head tube to the back corner of the frame, passing on either side of the seat tube. The frame can be made in small sizes, is relatively stiff and offers good riding characteristics.

Frame Dimension—Manufacturers produce two different kinds of frames, depending on the angle at which the *down* and *seat* tubes (the non-horizontal ones) are connected.

In a *steep* frame the tubes are relatively more upright. This produces a frame with a firm, stiff ride and quick handling—ideal for delivering all of your pedaling power to the bike. These are the best choice for racers and serious riders who like to ride fast with little or no luggage on their bikes. We'll call this design a *racing* frame.

A racing frame (left) gives a stiff, firm ride and quick handling. This is because certain tube angles are greater. A touring frame (right) absorbs road shocks better, producing a softer, more comfortable ride for long distances.

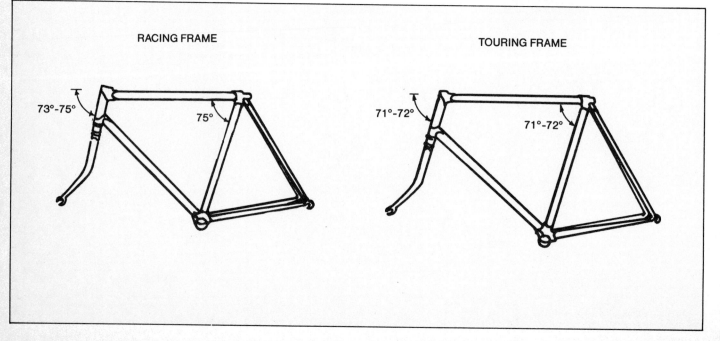

RACING FRAME   TOURING FRAME

73°-75°   75°   71°-72°   71°-72°

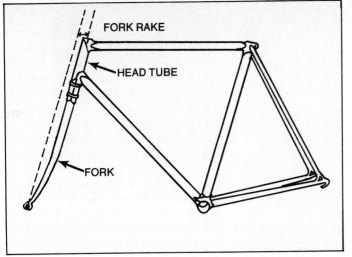

Fork rake is the distance from the front axle to the center line of the fork and head tube. The greater the fork rake, the softer the ride. Touring frames have more fork rake than racing frames.

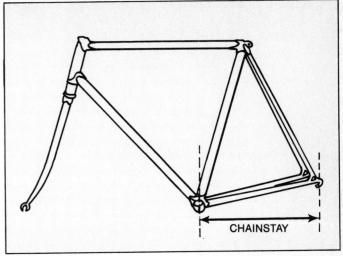

Racing bikes usually have shorter chainstays than touring bikes. A long chainstay provides enough room for carrying luggage on a rear rack.

Many riders prefer a more relaxing *touring* frame, which has down and seat tubes connected at a smaller angle. This produces a "softer," more absorbent ride—a real advantage for long tours, or when you carry luggage on your bike. The touring frame is more comfortable than the racing design, but a bit less efficient in terms of pedaling power.

Most recreational riders choose a bike with frame angles somewhere in the middle. Some manufacturers and cyclists call these *sport* frames. If you're going to be doing long-distance touring or carrying heavy loads, buy a sport or touring frame.

Another way frame builders manipulate a bike's riding characteristics is through the *head-tube angle* and *fork rake*. The head tube is the short vertical tube in which the handlebar assembly pivots. Touring frames have a shallow head-tube angle and greater fork rake—the distance between the front axle and the center line running down the fork and head tube. This contributes to the softer ride preferred by long-distance cyclists. Racing frames have a steep head-tube angle and little fork rake.

The final frame dimension to consider is *chainstay length*. The chainstay is a set of horizontal tubes running from the crank to the rear axle. Racing bikes have short chainstays, from 16 to 17 inches. Chainstays on touring bikes are longer, usually between 17 and 18 inches. Longer chainstays are helpful for carrying luggage because you can place the load in front of the rear axle.

All of these variations in frame dimensions contribute to a basic measure called *wheelbase*. It's the distance between axles, measured horizontally. A bike with a long wheelbase—41 inches or more—is good for touring with heavy loads. A 40-inch wheelbase is a good all-around size for general touring. Bikes with wheelbases shorter than 40 inches are designed for racing and fast rides without loads.

Racing frames also have a shorter wheelbase than touring frames. Wheelbase is a byproduct of the frame's angles, fork rake and chainstay length.

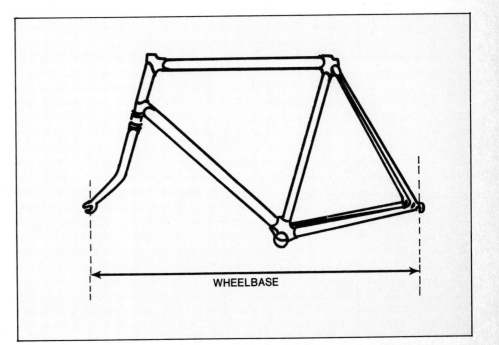

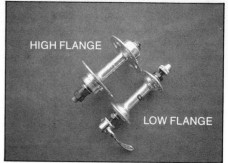

High-flange hubs offer a slightly stiffer ride than the low-flange design because the wheel's spokes are shorter. The touring bike shown at left has low-flange hubs.

WHEELS

If you want to save weight, a good place to start is the wheel. Because of centrifugal force, weight on a spinning part is multiplied. This is why racers spend lots of effort in getting light wheels and tires for their bikes.

If you will be carrying loads with the bike, good wheels are essential. They should be as light as possible, but still sturdy enough to support the added weight.

Rims—Aluminum-alloy rims, as opposed to steel rims, are a must for serious cyclists: They are superior in three ways—weight, strength and braking.

An aluminum rim is at least a half pound lighter than a steel rim of the same size. Remember, that's a half pound saved where you need it most, on a spinning part.

Aluminum rims are more dent-resistant than steel. And when aluminum does dent, it's easy to repair. All bicycle wheels eventually go out of alignment and will need to be *trued* periodically.

Quick-release hubs allow you to take your wheel off with a quick twist of a lever. It's a convenient feature if you have to change a flat tire or remove your wheels to load your bike in a car.

Aluminum rims offer superior braking, especially in wet weather.

Rim width depends on the riding you do most. For fast, unloaded biking, you can get narrow rims 1 inch wide or smaller! For bike touring, choose rims either 1-1/4 or 1-1/8 inches wide. They are a compromise between light weight and comfort.

Hubs—Aluminum-alloy hubs are lighter and more durable than steel hubs. Hubs come in either high- or low-flange models, but differences are minor. High-flange hubs give a slightly stiffer ride because the spokes are shorter. Low-flange hubs give a softer ride.

Better-quality hubs have a quick-release mechanism that allows you to take off your wheel with a simple twist of a lever. This offers immeasurable convenience for loading your bike in a car or making on-road repairs. But remember, it can also make a thief's life easier, too.

Tires—Your choice of rims will determine what kind of tires you can use. It's best to think of rims and tires as a package. Choose them together.

There are two kinds of tires—*clinchers* and *tubulars*. The latter are also called *sew-ups*. Nearly all tourers use clinchers because they are relatively inexpensive, resistant to punctures, and after some practice, easy to repair.

For carrying loads, choose 27x1-1/4 inch or 27x1-1/8 inch sizes. The first dimension is wheel diameter, the second rim width. These sizes provide good cushioning and durability. If you rarely carry loads and want a lighter tire with a more responsive feel, a 27x1 inch tire offers less rolling resistance. The 27x1 clincher offers such good rolling characteristics that it's being used by some racers.

Most racers and a few serious touring riders use sew-ups. Because they have a very narrow profile and can be inflated to very high pressure, sew-ups offer superior handling and rolling characteristics. However, good ones are expensive, subject to frequent flats, and a hassle to put on because they must be glued to the rims. Sew-ups are not suitable for long-distance touring with luggage.

Inner tubes are dimensioned like clincher tires. For infrequent city riding, regular inner tubes are OK. But if you tour or do a lot of commuting, consider getting *thorn-resistant* tires. The rubber is cut differentially,

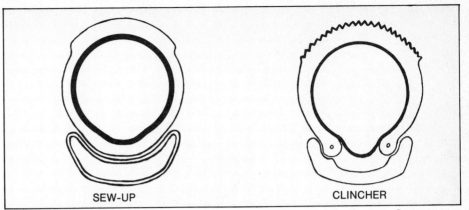

SEW-UP   CLINCHER

In a sew-up tire the tube is sewn into the casing and tread at the factory. Sew-up tires are glued to special sew-up rims. A clincher tire uses separate tubes. The tire is held to the rim by air pressure pushing the tire's wire bead against the rim.

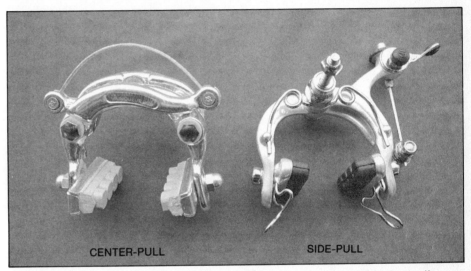

CENTER-PULL   SIDE-PULL

On center-pull brakes, the brake cable attaches to a transverse cable that pulls each of the brake arms. On side-pull brakes, the brake cable is mounted to the side and pulls brake arms directly. Below is a mounted side-pull brake.

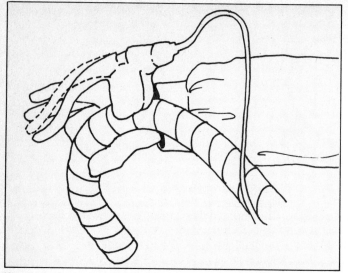

If your brakes are adjusted correctly, the pads will grab when you pull the levers only a few millimeters.

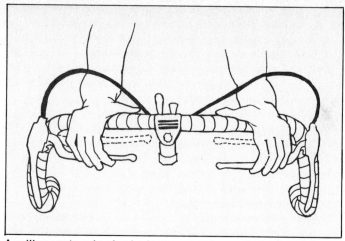

Auxiliary extension brake levers enable you to brake while holding your hands on the top of the handlebars. The main problem with such levers is that even when flexed to the limit, they don't grab as securely as standard levers. Also, you have less steering control when braking this way.

so the tube is thicker on the outside. They weigh a bit more than regular tubes, but are much more puncture-proof. Tire patching will become an infrequent problem.

COMPONENTS

Components are the various pieces of equipment that go on the frame—brakes, derailleurs, gears, seat, chain, cranks and pedals. Unless you are buying a custom bike, you'll probably get a bike outfitted with a set of components chosen by the manufacturer or retailer. But the components on nearly all bikes are partially interchangeable. As you gain more cycling experience you may want to buy better components to replace those that came with the bike.

If you want your bike set up with specific components, don't be afraid to ask. If you're buying an inexpensive bike, you'll probably have to take what comes on the bike. But on many better bikes, the retailer may be willing to change some of the components so that the bike is better suited to your needs. This is another good reason to know what kind of riding you'll be doing before you go shopping.

BRAKES

Consider your brakes the most important safety items on your bike. It doesn't pay to get cheap ones.

Types—There are two basic types of brakes—*coaster* and *caliper.* Caliper brakes may also be called *hand-pull.*

Coaster brakes are usually on one-speed bikes. You stop the bike by pushing backward on the pedals. This is a good design for children whose hands may not be big or strong enough to pull a hand-brake lever. However, for serious riders, and most adults, coaster brakes are not suitable. They don't stop the bike fast enough, and there is a tendency for the back wheel to skid.

Your bike will probably come equipped with caliper brakes. You'll find two types—*center-pull* and *side-pull.* Each has a handle that pulls a cable, operating a mechanism that presses brake pads against the wheel rims.

Center-pulls are a little slower to grab than side-pulls. Racers need brakes that grab immediately, so they almost always use side-pulls. However, some very important races have been won by riders using center-pull brakes. In the final analysis, either type is adequate for most riders if the brake mechanism is high-quality and properly maintained.

Maintenance—Any brake must be properly adjusted to work correctly. The brake pads wear down over time and should be periodically replaced to keep your brakes working properly.

If you plan on using your bike for touring with luggage, take extra care in selecting and maintaining your brakes. A fully loaded bike is difficult to stop, particularly when you're going fast.

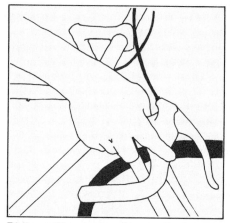

Riding with your hands near the brake is safe and comfortable.

When the brake pads just touch the rim, you should be able to flex the levers only a few more millimeters. A characteristic of a lesser-quality brake is that the levers have too much play and flexibility, giving a "spongy" feel.

Extension Levers—Many 10-speed bikes come with auxiliary extension brake levers. These are parallel to the handlebars and are designed to allow you to brake while holding the top of the bars and sitting upright. It's best not to rely on these brake levers. Usually, you have to pull them quite a distance before the brakes grab, and when they do, they don't stop you as quickly as conventional levers.

If you think you need auxiliary brake levers, we recommend that you change your handlebar grip instead.

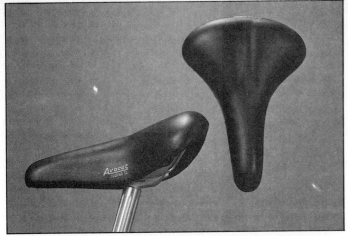

A racing saddle is smooth and contoured to minimize leg rubbing. Shown here are two views of a women's saddle. It's wider than standard to better fit the female pelvis.

This wide, padded, spring-cushioned saddle is comfortable for short, leisurely riding. We recommend it if your bike has upright handlebars.

Experienced riders place their hands on the "pocket" on top of the brakes. In this position, you can sit relaxed and still effectively grab the regular brake levers with your fingers.

HANDLEBARS

10-speed bikes usually come with *drop,* or *racing,* bars. One- or three-speed bikes usually have upright bars.

Drop bars are best for racing, climbing hills, long-distance touring and general-purpose fast riding. When you use them correctly on a good-fitting bike, you are in a relaxed, bent-over position. It's the most efficient position for pedalling hard and cutting wind resistance. For long rides, it protects your back from road shocks.

Upright handlebars are OK for leisurely riding and short-distance touring.

SEAT

There are few components that have more effect on your cycling enjoyment than the seat, or *saddle.* No matter how well your frame fits, you'll have a painful experience if your seat is uncomfortable.

As with most components, you can find many different styles and sizes. One- and three-speed bikes often come with wide, padded seats equipped with springs. These are very

A sheepskin seat may make riding more comfortable for you.

comfortable when you sit upright for slow, short rides. But if you plan on doing longer touring or want to ride fast, a wide seat eventually chafes and rubs. The springs also absorb much of your energy that should be going to the pedals.

Serious cyclists prefer narrow "racing" saddles made of vinyl, plastic or leather. Some have a bit of padding. Others are hard. Try out your

saddle by going on a few day rides. A saddle has to be broken in, just like a pair of hiking boots. However, if you've taken several rides and your saddle still feels uncomfortable, it may not be fitting you right and you may have to try a different style. It pays to invest some time and energy in finding a saddle that fits.

Women usually prefer a specially designed women's saddle. It's built for the female pelvis, which is wider than the male pelvis most saddles are designed to fit.

A sheepskin seat cover can be added to provide extra ventilation and protect against rubbing and soreness.

CRANKS AND PEDALS

Inexpensive bikes have a one-piece crankset made of a solid piece of steel. These are heavy and limit you to using just the chain rings that come with the crankset.

The next step up in quality is a cot-

Basically, crank design depends on how the crank arm attaches to the center of the chain ring. High-quality, cotterless cranks are best because they're easy to disassemble and service.

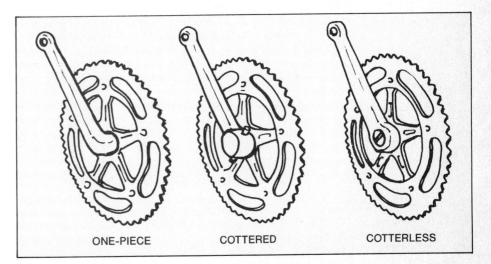

ONE-PIECE   COTTERED   COTTERLESS

tered crank—the crank arms are held on the axle with a secured, metal pin. It functions well for leisurely riding, but durability is a problem. If the pin breaks—and it can happen—you may be left stranded with an unrideable bike.

Most quality bikes are equipped with cotterless cranks—the crank arms are bolted to the axle. These are very durable and are the best choice for any sort of serious cycling—especially long-distance touring—because durability is important.

Sizes—Crank arms come in different sizes, with 170mm as standard. If you are short, or have short legs, 165mm cranks might be more comfortable. Similarly, long-legged riders sometimes prefer 172.5mm or 175mm cranks.

Pedals—It's a good idea to closely inspect the pedals that come on your bike. Exchange them for a better pair if you're not satisfied. Low-quality pedals often wear out and may break along the road, leaving you stranded.

To hold your feet securely in the pedals, be sure that the pedals come with *toe clips*. Many beginning riders shy away from toe clips, thinking that they are designed for racers only. In fact, they make riding easier for everyone, novices included. With your feet clipped into the pedals, you can pull up on the pedals as well as push down. This circular pedaling motion is by far the most comfortable and efficient. You have to feel the difference to believe it.

Another common misconception is that toe clips are dangerous because

Toe clips hold your feet securely in the pedals and allow you to pull up on the pedals as well as push down.

you won't be able to pull your feet out of the pedals if you start to fall. Actually, the opposite is true. In any high-speed fall, your feet are better off strapped into the pedals. You may end up with abrasions, but that's far better than the broken leg that could result if your feet flail around.

Gearing—Most serious riders eventually buy a multi-speed bicycle. One- and three-speed bikes are fine for leisurely riding along flat and rolling terrain. But if you are headed for hills of any sort, or if you want to ride fast or go on long tours, you'll need a 10-speed bike, or perhaps one with more than 10 speeds.

Gearing is a ratio between the number of teeth on the front chain ring and the rear sprocket, or cog. Most multi-speed bikes have two or three front chain rings and a *cluster* of five or more rear cogs. You change gears by using front and rear *derailleurs* to move the chain from chain

ring to chain ring and cog to cog.

The greater the difference between the number of teeth on the front chain ring and the rear cog, the higher is the gear. For example, a gear ratio of 52 (teeth on front chain ring) x22 (teeth on the rear cog) is higher than a 42x22 gear ratio.

The higher the gear, the more roadway is covered by each pedal rotation. This makes high gears harder to pedal. Low gears are usually easy to pedal, but you don't cover as much ground per pedal revolution.

Gear selection has a lot to do with your riding style and experience. It's common for beginners to choose gearing that is too high, on the assumption that it's more efficient to pedal more slowly, even if you have to struggle to get the pedals around.

With experience, though, you'll probably find it's most comfortable and efficient to choose a gear in which you can maintain a cadence of 80 to 100 pedal revolutions per minute (rpm). Racers call this *spinning*.

Your style of riding determines what range of gears you'll need. If you live where there are lots of hills, or if you plan on carrying luggage, you'll need a good selection of low, easy-to-pedal gears. If most of your riding is done on flat or rolling roads, with little or no load, you'll be better off having more gears in the middle range.

Recreational riders seldom use their highest gears. These are best left to road racers. It's better to make sure that you have enough gears in the middle and low range.

This bike has three front chain rings. You change gears by moving the chain from ring to ring with the front derailleur. Most quality bikes let you install different-size chain rings by means of the five bolts near the crank arm.

Your lowest gearing occurs when the chain is on the smallest front chain ring (right side) and the largest rear cog (left side). Low gears are easy to pedal, but you cover less ground with each pedal revolution. The reverse is true for high gears.

SINKING YOUR TEETH INTO BICYCLE GEARING

The best way to express a bicycle gear ratio is with the Equivalent Wheel Diameter (EWD) system. Understanding this system is easier if you think back to the days of high-wheeled bikes. On those machines, the pedals were attached directly to the front wheel. One revolution of the pedals produced one wheel revolution. The larger the wheel, the more ground was covered with each pedal motion. Basically, the larger the wheel, the higher the gear the cyclist used.

When chain drives were invented, the EWD system was used to compare different chain ring/rear cog combinations. Use this formula:

$$EWD = \frac{\text{\# teeth on chain ring}}{\text{\# teeth on rear cog}} \times \text{wheel diameter (in.)}$$

For example, if your chain is on a 42-tooth chain ring and an 18-tooth rear cog, and the bike has 27-inch diameter wheels, then:

$$EWD = (42/18) \times 27 \text{ inches}$$
$$= 63 \text{ inches}$$

You'd cover the same amount of roadway with each pedal revolution as if you were riding a high-wheeled bike with a 63-inch-diameter front wheel. EWD doesn't tell you how far each pedal revolution will take you. To figure that, multiply EWD by 3.14.

The EWD system allows you to compare different gear settings. For example, 40 (teeth on chain ring) x17 (teeth on rear cog), 42x18, 52x22 and 54x23 all produce about the same gear ratio—an EWD of 63 inches. You can also use the table below to get EWD values for bikes with 27-inch wheels.

Use the following guidelines to choose the best gear ratios for your bike:
Low Gears—EWD less than 65 inches.
Middle Gears—EWD 65 to 85 inches.
High Gears—EWD more than 85 inches.

The exact gear setting you need for comfortable pedaling depends on the terrain, your fitness and the load you're carrying. A racer in top condition may be able to climb a given hill with a 63-inch gear. An experienced recreational rider might need a lower gear, such as 54 inches. A bikepacker with loaded panniers may have to shift down to a 40-inch gear to maintain a convenient uphill cadence.

EQUIVALENT WHEEL DIAMETER (inches)

 # TEETH ON CHAINWHEEL

# TEETH ON REAR COG	28	32	34	36	38	39	40	42	44	45	46	47	48	49	50	51	52	53	54	
14	54	61.7	65.5	69.4	73.2	75.2	77.1	81	84.8	86.7	88.7	90.6	92.5	94.5	96.4	98.3	100.2	102.2	104.1	14
15	50.4	57.6	61.2	64.8	68.4	70.2	72	75.6	79.2	81	82.8	84.6	86.4	88.2	90	91.8	93.6	95.4	97.2	15
16	47.2	54	57.3	60.7	64.1	65.8	67.5	70.8	74.2	75.9	77.6	79.3	81	82.6	84.3	86	87.7	89.4	91.1	16
17	44.4	50.8	54	57.1	60.3	61.9	63.5	66.7	69.8	71.4	73	74.6	76.2	77.8	79.4	81	82.5	84.1	85.7	17
18	42	48	51	54	57	58.5	60	63	66	67.5	69	70.5	72	73.5	75	76.5	78	79.5	81	18
19	36.7	45.4	48.3	51.1	54	55.4	56.8	59.6	62.5	63.9	65.3	66.7	68.2	69.6	71	72.4	73.8	75.3	76.7	19
20	37.8	43.2	45.9	48.6	51.3	52.6	54	56.7	59.4	60.7	62.1	63.4	64.8	66.1	67.5	68.8	70.2	71.5	72.9	20
21	36	41.1	43.7	46.2	48.8	50.1	51.4	54	56.5	57.8	59.1	60.4	61.7	63	64.2	65.5	66.8	68.1	69.4	21
22	34.3	39.2	41.7	44.1	46.6	47.8	49	51.5	54	55.2	56.4	57.7	58.9	60.1	61.3	62.5	63.8	65	66.2	22
23	32.8	37.5	39.9	42.2	44.6	45.7	46.9	49.3	51.6	52.8	54	55.1	56.3	57.5	58.6	59.8	61	62.2	63.3	23
24	31.5	36	38.2	40.5	42.7	43.8	45	47.2	49.5	50.6	51.7	52.8	54	55.1	56.2	57.3	58.5	59.6	60.7	24
25	30.2	34.5	36.7	38.8	41	42.1	43.2	45.3	47.5	48.6	49.6	50.7	51.8	52.9	54	55	56.1	57.2	58.3	25
26	29	33.2	35.3	37.3	39.4	40.5	41.5	43.6	45.6	46.7	47.7	48.8	49.8	50.8	51.9	52.9	54	55	56	26
28	27	30.8	32.7	34.7	36.6	37.6	38.5	40.5	42.4	43.3	44.3	45.3	46.2	47.2	48.2	49.1	50.1	51.1	52	28
30	25.2	28.8	30.6	32.4	34.2	35.1	36	37.8	39.6	40.5	41.4	42.3	43.2	44.1	45	45.9	46.8	47.7	48.6	30
32	23.6	27	28.7	30.4	32.1	32.9	33.8	35.4	37.1	38	38.8	39.7	40.5	41.3	42.2	43	43.9	44.7	45.6	32
34	22.2	25.4	27	28.5	30.1	30.9	31.7	33.3	34.9	35.7	36.5	37.3	38.1	38.9	39.7	40.5	41.2	42	42.8	34
	28	32	34	36	38	39	40	42	44	45	46	47	48	49	50	51	52	53	54	

If you live in a rainy climate, lightweight fenders are essential.

A frame pump fits along the seat tube of your frame. A pump and a patch kit are necessary for commuting and long-distance touring.

It's customary to attach the bottle cage to the down tube, low enough so it won't upset the bike's center of gravity. For very hot days, some riders carry two bottles, the second attached to the seat tube.

Fenders—If you live in a rainy climate, or do lots of winter riding, fenders can greatly reduce the soaking effects of road spray.

Most fenders are made of lightweight plastic or aluminum, so they don't add a lot of weight. They do catch the wind, which is the reason many people put them on only during rainy seasons.

Pump—This is a necessity for any long-distance or rural touring far from a gas station. Changing a flat tire is a simple, quick procedure once you get the hang of it, but it's impossible without a pump to fill the new or patched tube.

Pumps fit either into brackets that you clamp to your frame, or, if properly sized, directly onto your frame without brackets.

Make sure that the pump you buy will fit the tube's valves. There are two types—*Schrader* and *Presta*. Sew-ups and light clincher tubes use Presta valves. Most other tubes for touring use Schrader valves, the same type found on auto tires.

Unless you have a pressure gauge and experience, avoid using a gas station pump to fill your bicycle tires. It's hard to judge exactly how much pressure you're putting in. Blown tires are the result of miscalculation.

Lights And Reflectors—Night riding requires a headlight and taillight. If you plan on doing a lot of night riding,

If you're just getting started in cycling, the best plan is to buy a crankset that gives you the option of changing chain rings and a rear freewheel that allows you to buy additional cogs. Go for a few rides and try out your gears. If they aren't quite right, you can exchange your cogs for more appropriate ones at minor expense.

Not all rear derailleurs fit every freewheel cluster. If you have some large cogs, you may need a *long-arm* rear derailleur. The manufacturer's guidelines will tell you if your derailleur will fit.

BICYCLE ACCESSORIES

Because there are dozens of bicycle accessories, it's a good idea to be frugal in selecting them. Choose only those that will contribute to your safety or significantly add to your cycling enjoyment. Everything you put on your bike adds weight—the cyclist's greatest enemy.

Water Bottle—This is essential if you plan on doing any long-distance touring. *Bottle cages* are made of either steel or aluminum alloy. Steel is probably the better choice for touring riders. It's nearly as light as alloy and a good deal cheaper.

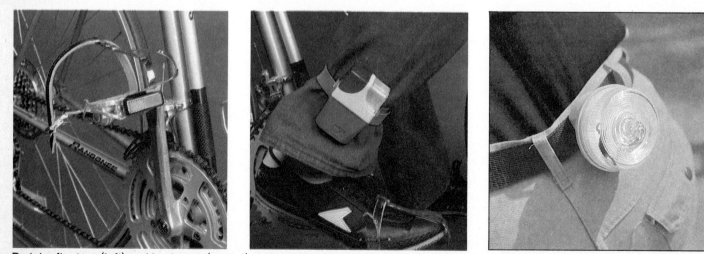
Pedal reflectors (left) and leg lamps (center) are among the most effective nighttime biking devices. The up-and-down motion of your pedaling tells drivers that you are a cyclist. A flashing beacon (right) is also effective. It can be mounted nearly anywhere on your bike or clothing to alert drivers.

it pays to find out how to light your bicycle thoroughly. Much has been written in cycling magazines about this topic. Your local police department may have guidelines, too. Some lights are very effective. Others don't do the job and aren't worth the expense.

It's most important that you be effectively lit from the back so approaching motorists not only see your lights, but also *recognize you as a cyclist*. This is why pedal reflectors and leg lights that strap to your ankle are so effective. The up and down motion of your pedaling tells approaching drivers that a cyclist is ahead.

Lights are powered by batteries or generators. Battery-powered lights are a little heavier, and of course, the batteries need to be replaced occasionally.

Generators will power your lights as long as you're moving, but they create extra drag. If you're going slow, they won't supply much power.

Reflectors alone *are not* adequate for night riding. Properly placed, they can help alert cars, but you should always use them in conjunction with lights.

Kickstands—Most serious riders don't use a kickstand, claiming they aren't very useful and they add a lot of extra weight. Others say that kickstands are handy for holding up a heavily loaded bike. Consider both arguments and decide for yourself.

An alternative is the *Flickstand,* a clip that attaches to your frame. You flip it into position to hold your front tire rigid. This makes it easier to prop your bike up against walls and posts.

A properly equipped touring cyclist can carry everything he needs and still have a ride that's fun, safe and comfortable.

The Flickstand is a lightweight alternative to a kickstand.

Bicycle Touring

Bicycle riders take trips ranging from short jaunts of a few hours to multi-day tours thousands of miles long. One of the attractive features of cycling long distances is that you can cover so much ground in a day. Only the strongest hikers can manage more than 20 miles per day. But even novice cyclists can cover daily distances in excess of 50 miles. It's not uncommon for transcontinental cyclists to average more than 100 miles a day.

For day tours, it usually isn't necessary to outfit your bike with any special equipment. A few tools, a bit of food, and a raincoat can be carried in your jersey pockets, in a fanny pack, or strapped under your saddle.

For longer day tours along remote roads, or for bicycle-camping expeditions, you'll need to outfit your bike with racks and *panniers*—bicycle

packs that attach to a rack.

"Bikepacking" differs from backpacking in several important ways. The most important is that you will be carrying the load on the bicycle rather than on your back. It's impractical and unsafe to carry heavy loads on your back while cycling. It raises your center of gravity too high, so a shift of weight or a gust of wind from a passing truck can send you tumbling.

A second major difference is the amount of equipment touring cyclists need to carry. Because many backpacking trips are taken in remote areas where food and shelter aren't available, backpackers need to carry everything for the entire trip.

Cyclists can get by with less—most touring cyclists carry much less weight than they do when backpacking. Unless you're pedaling to Alaska or other remote regions, you'll be able to restock food and other supplies at stores along the way.

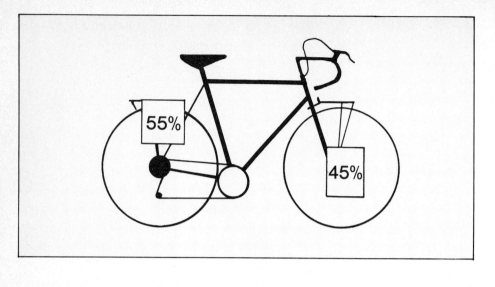

Be sure to load your bike so there's weight over both the front and rear wheels, as described in the text. Keeping the weight close to the axles is also recommended.

LOADING YOUR BICYCLE

When touring, you should load your bicycle so stability and handling characteristics aren't compromised. One of the most comprehensive studies shows that it's best to split your load over the front and rear wheels.

An unloaded bike distributes 55% of the rider's weight on the rear wheel and 45% on the front. Ideally, you should maintain this ratio when you load your bike with touring gear.

In fact, it's tough. But if you can place about 30% of the weight over the front wheel, your bike will handle relatively well. Under no circumstances should you put all of the weight over the rear wheel.

A medium-size pannier should be mounted as far forward as possible on the rear rack. Another set of medium-size bags should be mounted on a front rack so they are low on the front forks. You'll find that a heavily loaded handlebar bag causes the front wheel to wobble. Similarly, rear panniers that are mounted behind the rear axle make the front wheel unstable.

RACKS

Front and rear racks are available in a wide variety of styles. The most important things to look for in any rack are rigidity and strength. A bike rack must not break during use. If it does, it will likely fall into the wheel, breaking spokes and perhaps causing a crash.

Quality racks are made of either steel or aluminum alloy. Steel racks are heavier and can withstand more abuse. You can also bend them back into shape if necessary. Aluminum-alloy racks are lighter and sturdy enough for all but the most rugged roads. If they bend, the metal may snap.

Make sure you understand how a rack attaches to your bike before you buy it. Some require you to disassemble your brakes. Unless you feel totally confident doing this, it's better to choose a different model or have a bike mechanic do the job. Make sure that all bolts are tightened fully and checked frequently against loosening.

Rear Racks—All rear racks consist of a platform attached to the frame dropouts by at least one strut, and to the seatstays by clamps, plates or eyelets.

The simplest rear racks are single-strut models. They are suitable for carrying light loads. If burdened with more weight, they have a tendency to sway back and forth, disrupting your pedaling motion and stressing the frame unnecessarily.

Single-strut racks must have a secure attachment to the seatstays. The attachment carries much of the weight from the panniers, and if it isn't tight, the rack can slide down the seatstay tubes until it comes to rest on your brake cable, taking the paint with it.

The most reliable racks attach to

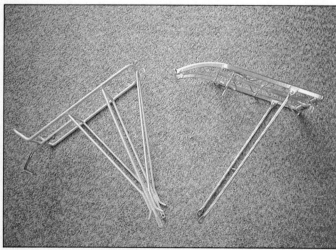

A single-strut rack (right) is OK for light loads only—under 15 pounds. Multiple-strut racks (left) offer more side-to-side stability for heavier loads.

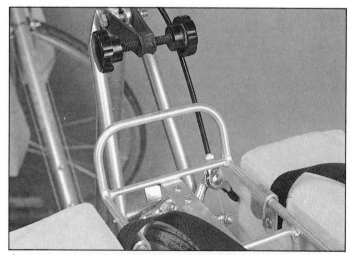

An upturn on the front of a rear rack keeps things from sliding forward into the brake cable.

Front panniers mount to a special front rack that holds the panniers low so they don't adversely affect steering.

This large-capacity rear pannier is yellow for high visibility and has outside pockets for convenience. Notice the cut-out section for heel clearance.

the brake bolt, eliminating the slippage problem.

On custom touring bikes, there may be a brazed-on eyelet to which the rear rack is attached. This is the most secure method of all.

If you're planning to carry heavy loads, a multiple-strut rack is a much more reliable choice. It comes with either two or three struts. The extra struts offer more stability and reduce pressure on the seatstay attachment. The other great advantage of the multiple-strut rack is that the extra struts help keep the packs from getting tangled in your spokes.

Another handy feature to look for in rear racks is an upturn of the tubes in front of the platform, just behind the brake. This keeps your luggage from sliding forward into your brake cable and possibly engaging the brakes.

Front Racks—More and more people are putting some of their baggage on a front rack. This enables you to use front panniers and place the weight down low, radically improving handling.

A good front rack has the same qualities as a rear rack—rigidity and strength. Most attach to the dropouts of the front fork and to the front brake bolt.

PANNIERS

Panniers, saddlebags and handlebar bags used to be made of canvas with leather straps. Now, nearly all panniers are made of colorful nylon fabric with nylon zippers and Velcro closures.

Nylon pannier bags are usually waterproofed, but it's unlikely that seams are sealed. To make your panniers completely waterproof, you'll need to seal the seams with a commercially available seam sealer. Or, buy a waterproof cover to go over your bags.

Make color choice with safety in mind. Panniers should be as bright and visible as possible. Yellow is good on both counts, and some manufacturers offer panniers made of reflective material. They cost more, but the additional safety for night riding may be worth it.

Sizes—When shopping for panniers, the most important decision to make is how much room you need. It's unwise to buy them too big. Panniers don't work well unless packed nearly full. The extra fabric flaps in the wind, causing unnecessary wind resistance and annoyance. In addition, why pay for space you don't need?

If you are planning on taking weekend tours, you will need a *total* pannier capacity of 1500 to 2000 cubic

inches. Only tours in remote regions require more than 2000 cubic inches of capacity.

Designs—Front and rear panniers attach to racks by straps and buckles or, more permanently, by a piece of fabric that sits across the rack. They are also secured by a strap set at the bottom.

Most panniers have some sort of rigid or semi-rigid material—usually aluminum, plastic or hard foam—to stiffen the pannier and help keep it from rubbing against the spokes.

Panniers come in various shapes and designs. Some are square; others are tapered. And some have a beveled, aerodynamic front. It's possible to buy panniers with internal compartments and outside pockets to help you organize your gear.

Rear panniers must have a generous cut-out section to allow plenty of clearance for your heels during pedaling. Even slight heel nicking against the bag will eventually wear a hole through the material. Some models seem to work fine until you pack them full of heavy gear. Make sure you test for this before starting a long tour.

Also, it's best to avoid panniers that stick up above the level of the rack. A pannier system makes sense only if you can place the weight as low as possible. High-riding panniers defeat that purpose and cause problems when you try to tie a sleeping bag or tent to the top of the rack.

If you plan on combining public transportation with your cycling trips, it may be wise to invest in panniers that you can strap together and carry like a suitcase. This may be required if you need to check your bags on an airplane. It's also a handy feature for those cycling in Europe, where it's easy to combine cycling with train travel.

HANDLEBAR BAGS, SEAT PACKS AND FRAME PACKS

Handlebar bags, seat packs and frame packs offer an alternative to panniers. They are ideal for day touring or as a way to add a little storage capacity to your panniers for long tours.

Handlebar Bags—Most modern handlebar bags attach to the bars by means of their own frame, usually a simple metal bar that wraps around the bars and stem. This holds the bag away from the bars so you can hold on wherever you like.

Handlebar bags usually hold about 500 cubic inches. Since anything tied to the handlebars will affect steering, pack only light items. It's a good place for maps, small food items, sun screen and perhaps a *small* camera.

Some manufacturers include an elastic stretch cord that stretches from the bottom of the bag to the front forks to keep the bag from bouncing

You can hook up your bike to a trailer for carrying children, groceries and extra baggage. Most experts say that children are safer traveling in a trailer such as this, rather than on a high-mounted child's seat.

around on rough roads. Because some cyclists find this feature unnecessary, it's designed to be removable.

A bag that opens toward you is much easier to use while you're riding. It also helps keep rain from leaking through the zipper.

Seat Packs—These go by all sorts of names—*seat bags* and *saddlebags,* among others. They are suspended under the back of the seat. With a capacity of about 200 cubic inches, seat packs are best for small things.

Frame Packs—Frame packs fit into the inside triangle of your frame. Their major drawback is that if they are too heavily loaded, they bulge out, interfering with pedaling.

Bicycle Clothing

Bicycling has some specialized clothing requirements, and because of this, an entire line of cycling clothing has evolved to meet these needs. Though novices look at cleated cycling shoes, black shorts and fingerless gloves with suspicion, these accessories *are* useful features for practically all cyclists.

SHOES

Whether you're a commuter, long-distance tourer, racer or just a casual, sometimes rider, your shoes must do three things—fit well, be rigid and adhere to the pedals.

Racing Shoes—Racers wear the most efficient cycling shoes. They have a very stiff sole, usually made of leather or nylon. Heels are narrow so the shoe will clear the crank arm during pedaling. The soles have an aluminum or plastic cleat fitted with a slot that clips into the pedal. When you tighten the toe strap, your foot is locked into the pedal. This makes it easy to pull up and push down on the pedals.

Racing shoes, however, are made for riding, not walking. Their stiff, slippery soles are tricky to walk in. And the cleats force you to stride forward in an awkward toe-in-the-air manner.

Touring Shoes—For long-distance touring, in which you may need to use the same shoes for riding and walking, it's better to buy a pair of special touring shoes.

They have a rubber sole for easier walking and a steel shank to keep the

A seat bag is the best place to carry a patch kit, tools and extra clothing.

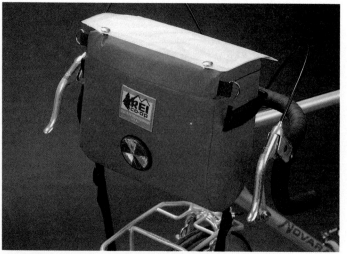

A handlebar bag is a good place to keep small items you may need while riding—raingear, maps, food, sunglasses or sunscreen.

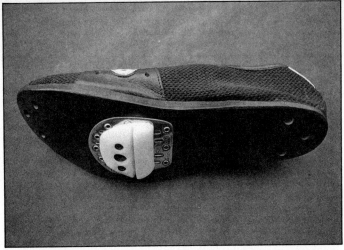

A racing shoe is most efficient because of the cleat attached to the sole. The cleat clips into the pedal, allowing you to effectively pull up and push down the pedals.

These touring shoes have light fabric uppers and steel shanks for stiffness. A textured rubber sole replaces the cleat and makes for easier walking.

soles stiff. They don't have a cleat that fits into the pedal, so they won't adhere to the pedals as well as racing shoes. But these shoes aren't made for racers. They're designed for those who must compromise in order to walk comfortably.

Some touring shoes have a rippled or ribbed sole that grips the pedals. One brand has a simulated cleat molded into the rubber sole. It doesn't work as well as a real cleat, but does a better job than regular sneakers.

Other Shoes—Many experienced cyclists ride happily in tennis or running shoes. The knobby soles act much like cleats, keeping your feet attached to the pedals. Before you assume that your jogging shoes will work, though, try them out. Some running shoes have wide heels that will hit the crank arms every time you downpedal. Also, over time the edge of your pedals may wear holes in the soles of your expensive running or tennis shoes.

Running shoes must have a fairly stiff sole, or they won't work for pedaling. Soft-soled shoes mush around the pedal. This is both uncomfortable and inefficient.

SHORTS

Your shorts are the most important item of cycling clothing. Several kinds are designed specifically for cycling.

Knit cycling shorts are made of wool or synthetic stretch material. The crotch is lined with chamois.

These are the most comfortable cycling shorts you can buy. The chamois is seamless to cut down on rubbing. It also absorbs sweat, and some even have a very thin layer of foam under the chamois for a bit of extra cushioning.

With a chamois lining, there's no need to wear underwear. In fact, most experienced cyclists find that underwear does little more than bunch up and cause chafing. The legs are cut long, so your legs won't rub on the edge of your saddle. Instead, the shorts' material rubs, with very little friction.

Chamois-lined shorts are ideal for all cycling except long-distance touring, when you are on the road day

Touring shorts look a little different from black racing shorts. They're lined with soft, absorbent terrycloth, not chamois.

after day. To keep the chamois clean—a must to avoid infection—it needs to be washed every day or two and allowed to air dry. At home, you can keep two pairs of shorts and rotate their use, but that's impractical during a long tour when washing and thorough drying are difficult.

A more practical solution for the long-distance cyclist is to buy a pair of touring shorts made of woven material. These have long-cut legs like knit shorts, but are lined with terrycloth instead of chamois. Terrycloth isn't as comfortable, but it can be machine washed and dried.

You can also get ankle-length versions of both types of cycling shorts.

Cut-off jeans and jogging shorts are widely used for cycling. They're OK for short rides, but for longer distances, the exposed seams and short legs cause uncomfortable chafing and rubbing.

JERSEYS AND SHIRTS

The best upper-body apparel for any cyclist is the cycling jersey. For touring, buy a wool-blend jersey that has pockets in the back. (Synthetic, pocketless jerseys are designed for track racing.) Pockets in most cycling jerseys are large enough to carry some extra food, a small rain jacket, a few tools and even an extra water bottle—all at once! In fact, many riders don't bother with panniers during one-day tours. They find that jersey pockets do the job well.

Don't wear a cotton T-shirt under a

Above: The wool-blend cycling jersey (left) is the most practical choice for long-distance touring and all-weather riding. The cotton T-shirt (right) is OK for warm-weather pedaling.

Right: The rear pockets of cycling jerseys are handy for carrying extra food, tools, raingear or maps.

jersey. The T-shirt quickly gets soaked with perspiration, and if you head into a long downhill run, the wet shirt can give you quite a chill. A better solution is to wear a wool blend or polypropylene long underwear top that wicks away perspiration from your skin. Special wool/acrylic-blend cycling tops are made for wearing under jerseys.

A T-shirt worn alone isn't nearly as bad as layering with one under a jersey because the constant wind dries the T-shirt and keeps it from getting soaked.

Never do any serious touring bare-chested, in a runner's singlet or halter top. The wind you produce while riding doubles the burning effect of the sun. And if you happen to fall, a jersey with sleeves offers quite a bit more protection from abrasions than does bare skin.

RAINGEAR

Preparing to bicycle in the rain is much the same as for any outdoor sport. Gore-Tex rain suits have become very popular because they keep out the rain fairly well and still allow your perspiration to escape.

If you can afford only one piece of a Gore-Tex suit, take along a parka. It's more important to keep the trunk of your body warm and dry. Wet legs are annoying but not overly dangerous if the rest of you is warm. A Gore-Tex rain suit or parka is just as useful in camp as it is on the bicycle.

Cycling ponchos and capes have been traditional wet-weather gear for years, but don't work nearly as well as a Gore-Tex rain suit. They don't protect you from water spraying up underneath from the road. And they have an annoying habit of flapping all around, sometimes into your face.

GLOVES

Fingerless cycling gloves with a padded leather palm and mesh back

Waterproof and breathable Gore-Tex rainsuits are great for cycling. Riding in wet weather demands extra care, so be sure to use a helmet.

Fingerless cycling gloves make riding safer and more comfortable.

add to long-distance cycling comfort. The padding helps absorb the inevitable shocks that come with long-distance riding. The leather helps you grip the handlebars.

Another good reason to wear gloves is to protect your hands in case of a fall. Even in a minor spill, your palms can be painfully skinned, which could stop your riding for a while. Cycling gloves help!

For cold-weather riding, you may need gloves that cover your whole hand. Many riders use wool gloves or specially designed, fully insulated cycling gloves with leather palms.

HELMETS

There is no more important piece of bicycle safety equipment. Accidents do occasionally happen, sometimes through no fault of your own, and it's just common sense to be prepared.

Be selective when shopping for a helmet. Some designs are excellent, others ineffective. The leather-strap style worn by some racers may look stylish, but offers only minimal protection.

The most effective helmets are full, hard-shell models, offering protection against both impact and penetration by sharp objects. There are two basic designs. One cushions impact through a lining of nearly solid foam, and the other does it with a system of suspension straps. Quality helmets are made in both styles. Avoid helmets designed for other sports.

Bicycle Care & Maintenance

Bicycles, thankfully, are relatively simple machines. This makes it easy for most owners to perform at least some of their own maintenance and repairs. Even if you're not interested in doing your own repairs, it helps to know a few easy maintenance checks.

MAINTENANCE

Check four places regularly—brakes, cables, wheels, and nuts and bolts. This is especially important on the bolts that hold luggage racks. These have a tendency to loosen over time, and if they do, your rack will fall off, usually into your spokes. At home, check these things every few rides. If you are on a tour, check them every morning and again at lunch.

Get in the habit of performing four quick maintenance checks on your bike: 1) Check your brakes for proper adjustment and make sure the brake pads have plenty of rubber left.

3) Spin the wheels to see if they are true. Also check for broken spokes.

2) All cables should be tight. Look for frayed wire. It's a signal that your cable should be replaced.

4) Make sure all screws and bolts are tight, especially those securing racks.

If you're embarking on a long-distance tour, it's important that at least one member of the group has some bicycle-repair experience. You can share tools, but someone obviously needs to know how to use them. Following is a list of repairs that frequently have to be made on the road.

1) Repairing flat tires, including wheel removal and re-inflating the tube to the correct pressure.

2) Adjusting the brakes and replacing worn brake pads.

3) Adjusting derailleurs.

4) Replacing or adjusting brake and derailleur cables.

5) Replacing broken spokes and doing some on-the-road wheel truing.

6) Adjusting the seat post, stem and handlebars.

TOOLS

It's not necessary to fill a tool box with specialized bicycling tools. The beauty of bicycle maintenance is that you can do the easy jobs with a few simple household tools. If you enjoy working on your bike, you'll probably decide to invest in some specialized tools, but it's not necessary. Many riders never go beyond doing just the simple jobs and enjoy cycling just as much as the mechanical wizards.

The first specialized tools you should buy are a patch kit for repairing flat tires, two tire irons for getting clincher tires off the rim, and a freewheel remover and spoke wrench for changing broken spokes on the road. If many of your components use Allen screws, get Allen wrenches.

10 Canoes, Kayaks & Inflatable Rafts

Traveling the waters of North America offers a unique perspective of both history and the natural world. The rivers, lakes and sea coasts were once the prime routes for transportation and commerce. Steamboats and barges plied most of the navigable waterways of the continent.

With advances in rail and automobile transportation, much of the commercial traffic left the water. Even so, there will always be a romance associated with water travel that's difficult to duplicate in any other kind of outdoor endeavor.

Some water enthusiasts enjoy tackling whitewater rivers. Theirs is a rigorous and exciting sport. Others prefer to paddle along quiet lakes and slow-moving rivers—a great way to observe wildlife, scenery and do a little fishing. A growing number are setting off on trips along the shores of some of our larger freshwater lakes.

Canoeing is a relaxing way to travel along rivers or lakes.

You'll find kayak enthusiasts on all kinds of water from whitewater rivers to salt water.

And in the Northwest and other coastal areas, saltwater kayaking and canoeing have become popular for campers and others who want to observe marine animals up close.

In this chapter, we concentrate on the three major vessels used in these pursuits—canoes, kayaks and inflatable rafts. As with all outdoor activities, there are specific techniques to learn so you can safely and effectively handle your vessel. We strongly recommend that you get instruction in the skills of whatever water sport interests you.

There are many good books about paddling techniques, safety manuevers and trip planning. Personal instruction is often available through a local college, water-sports club or outdoor-equipment shop. In some areas, local guides may provide instruction programs, too.

Before deciding what kind of boat to buy, ask these questions:

1) What kind of boating interests you? Whitewater? Flat-water boating in lakes and rivers? Touring in large bodies of water subject to winds, tides and possible storms?

2) Do you prefer to paddle your own boat? Work in tandem with another person? Or would you rather share a boat with a group of three or more?

3) Do you plan to take primarily one-day trips, or would you like to tackle multi-day excursions?

4) How much experience do you have in the specific skills of kayaking, canoeing or rafting?

5) How much money are you willing to spend?

Your answers to these questions will largely determine what kind of boat and accessories will best suit your needs.

Canoes

The canoe is one of the most enduring elements of American history. American Indians of the East and Middle West paddled rivers and lakes in birch-bark canoes. West Coast Indians hunted whales in ocean-going canoes hollowed out of huge cedar logs. For these people, the canoe was essential to hunting and food gathering.

Canoes are still popular, but nearly everything about them has changed. Most people use canoes for recreation. And, although there are still a few craftsmen making canoes in the old style, new materials and designs have revolutionized methods.

WHAT THE CANOE DOES BEST

Canoes can be used in both flat water and moderate whitewater. If you will be heading into the roughest grades of whitewater—sometimes called *wildwater*—a kayak or raft will probably be better than an open canoe.

Canoes are very roomy. It's easy to fit in enough gear for a multi-day trip.

Covered, decked canoes—called *C-1* or *C-2,* depending on whether they carry one or two people—can handle whitewater admirably. To the uninitiated, a C-1 looks much like a kayak, but with one important exception—you paddle it like a canoe rather than a kayak. Covered canoes are popular in some areas, but in this book, we discuss only the more common open canoes.

Depending on its size and design, a canoe can carry one, two, three or more people, making canoes ideal for families and groups. Typically, they're also roomy enough for the packs and luggage of multi-day trips.

There's a wide variety of canoe designs to choose from. Decide what you need based on the type of canoeing you'll be doing.

Open canoes handle well in light-to-moderate whitewater. If you're interested in tackling rough whitewater, a kayak or inflatable raft is more seaworthy.

DESIGN

Every canoe design is a compromise. A boat built to turn easily won't *track* in a straight line quite as well. A canoe with high sides—called *freeboard*—will keep whitewater from splashing inside, but stands higher and catches the wind. This makes it difficult to paddle in a cross wind. Canoes built large enough to carry lots of equipment are unwieldy to maneuver. The strongest and lightest materials may be too expensive for most recreational canoeists.

The list goes on. It's important to realize that your canoe won't do everything perfectly. You have to decide what characteristics are most important and buy a canoe that provides them.

Length—Most canoes are from 16 to 19 feet long, except for a few shorter models designed for solo use. The longer your canoe, the better it tracks and the more equipment and people it can hold.

Longer canoes provide more stability on whitewater and wind-whipped lake water, but they don't turn as easily in tight situations.

The longer the vessel, of course, the heavier it will be. Most canoeists have to carry the canoe from time to time. For those facing frequent *portages*—carries from one body of water to another—light weight is an important feature.

The most popular length for general day touring with up to two people is

For lake touring, choose a long canoe with a keel for good tracking.

about 16 feet. If you plan on doing multi-day touring or will be facing rough conditions, buy a canoe at least 17 feet long.

Depth—A deep canoe, with plenty of freeboard, deflects waves and increases the amount of cargo you can carry. But it has the disadvantage of catching the wind—a real problem on large bodies of water. A highly upturned bow or stern offers similar trade-offs. Waves won't be as likely to spill inside the boat, but there's more

surface area to catch the wind.

Hull Shape—Some canoes have *keels*—a protrusion beneath the hull. Others don't. A smooth-bottomed boat turns easily, but a keel is needed for effective tracking. Consequently, whitewater canoeists prefer a keelless model. Flat-water paddlers, especially those who may be facing strong winds, find a keel essential.

If you'll be paddling in both kinds of water, a *shoe keel*—a shallow, wide keel—may be a good compromise.

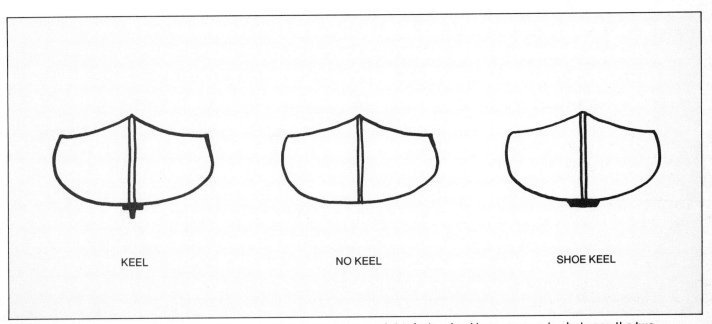

KEEL   NO KEEL   SHOE KEEL

A smooth-bottom canoe turns easily, while one with a keel tracks straight. A shoe keel is a compromise between the two designs.

The *rocker* has a similar effect on turning. This is the upsweep of the bottom line from the middle toward the ends of the canoe. To determine what kind of rocker a boat has, put it on a flat floor. If the boat can be rocked end-to-end, it has a high rocker. Boats with little or no rocker lie practically flat on the floor.

The greater the rocker, the easier the boat will turn. Boats designed for flat water have little or no rocker.

Canoes have either flat, round or V-shaped bottoms. Flat-bottom canoes are stable, but when heavily loaded they move slowly through the water. Round bottoms look more unstable, but when properly loaded they are just as stable as flat-bottom canoes. Also, the round-bottom canoe moves through the water more easily than a flat-bottom model. A V-shaped bottom has many of the same handling characteristics as a round bottom. Its shape also adds tracking ability.

The Entire Design Picture—If you've done any comparison shopping, you probably know that canoe designers often combine seemingly contradictory features in an effort to build a boat that can do several things well. For example, all factors of hull shape—keel, rocker, profile and length—can be combined in such a way that, theoretically at least, the canoe offers a compromise in handling characteristics.

In the final analysis, there are no absolute rules in canoe design. The best way to find out how a given canoe will function is to try it. Perhaps you can talk to others who own the same kind of canoe and get their experienced advice. It may be possible to borrow or rent different designs and give them a try on the water.

MATERIALS

The materials a canoe is made from largely determine its weight, durability and price. Materials can also affect a boat's handling ability. Canoes are priced from a couple of hundred dollars to well over a thousand.

Traditionally, canoes were built of birch bark, animal skins or carved from logs. Next came boats of canvas and cedar strips. These designs can still be found if you look hard enough—or are willing to pay the price—but most consumers prefer one of the new, lighter, more reasonably priced materials—aluminum, fiberglass, plastic or composite.

Aluminum—Although once very popular, aluminum canoes have claimed a smaller and smaller part of the market in recent years. They were once among the most reasonably priced models. But, with the rising cost of making aluminum, the price of aluminum canoes has also jumped. Public interest is now shifting to other materials. Even so, aluminum models are readily available, and it's a material that merits consideration.

These canoes are very durable, and if they get dented, you can usually pound them back out. If an aluminum canoe is somehow punctured, you can make temporary repairs at the site by bolting a piece of aluminum over the hole. Permanent repairs, however, require heliarc welding, a process beyond the capabilities of most recreational boaters.

Aluminum is noisy—waves slap against the bottom, creating an annoying accompaniment to your paddling. When you hit a rock, aluminum tends to stick rather than slide over. Also, it transmits heat and cold. If you're paddling in very cold water, you'll need to use insulating knee or seat pads. The same is true for hot days, when aluminum absorbs the heat of the sun and gets uncomfortably hot.

Fiberglass—Most fiberglass canoes are made by bonding a fiberglass mat and cloth with epoxy or polyester resin. Because fiberglass is relatively easy to work with, many people build their own fiberglass canoes in home workshops. Plans and materials can be purchased at a specialized watersports shop or by mail.

Minor repairs are easy, even in the middle of a trip. Fiberglass canoes can be found in all price categories.

Although technically not a fiberglass, *Kevlar* is a highly specialized and expensive fiber material that looks much like fiberglass. But Kevlar has some different properties that are important. It has a tensile strength about 40% higher than fiberglass. A Kevlar canoe may weigh less than half

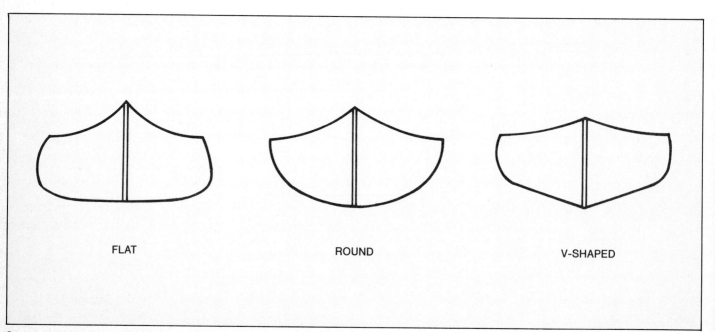

FLAT   ROUND   V-SHAPED

Canoe bottoms vary. These are the designs you'll see most often.

Above: Occasionally, you may need to portage your canoe overland between lakes and streams or around rough rapids. A portage yoke installed in your canoe cushions the load on your shoulders.

Left: In rough water, you'll want to paddle kneeling down. Special knee pads or a boat cushion will protect your knees.

an equivalent-size fiberglass canoe. Its light weight makes it suitable for racing and for those who need to carry their canoes over long portages. You can repair Kevlar with a fiberglass-repair kit.

Plastic—Plastic canoes have become very popular, primarily due to their durability and reasonable cost—often less than $500. Most plastic canoes are made of polyethylene or polyvinyl chloride (PVC).

Repairs can be difficult and may be impossible to perform in the field. But field testing has proven plastic to be virtually indestructible, so the situation rarely occurs.

Plastic is more flexible than fiberglass. This makes it a little more difficult to maneuver in whitewater because it won't *edge* quite as well as a stiffer boat.

Composite—These boats—made of a vinyl, foam and acrylonitrile butadiene styrene (ABS) sandwich—have combined many of the best features of other materials into one. The ABS sandwich was developed by the U.S. Rubber Company and has been most heavily marketed under the trade name *Royalex*.

The ABS sandwich is exceedingly strong and insulates well. Weight is about the same as fiberglass, and durability is at least as good as plastic. You can make temporary repairs with a fiberglass-repair kit. Perhaps the best news is that composite canoes are usually moderately priced. Models can be found for about $500.

CANOE ACCESSORIES

There's more to a canoe than materials and hull design. No matter what you'll be using your canoe for, you need to know about seats, painters and bailers. If you plan on tackling whitewater or windswept lakes, it's a good idea to look into buying a deck cover and knee pads. And, for long carries, you'll need a portage yoke.

Seats—Typically, there are two seats in a canoe. They may be made of wood, fiberglass, plastic or aluminum. As mentioned, aluminum seats can get very hot or cold, so you may need to pad them in hot or cold weather.

In whitewater and in rough, windy conditions, it's practical to paddle kneeling down to lower your center of gravity. A boat cushion will suffice in an emergency, but for any prolonged kneeling, you should buy special kneeling pads that strap in place. They're cup-shaped to hold your knees comfortably.

Painter—This is simply a rope that is attached to the bow or stern of the canoe. All canoeists need some sort of painter to tie up the canoe to the shore or docks. Nylon and polypropylene ropes are the best.

Whitewater canoeists need longer painters—perhaps over 100 feet long—to *line* their boats down (or up) dangerous rapids. Lining is a procedure you use with rope from shore to carefully guide your unloaded boat through dangerous rapids.

Bailer—It seems that some water always gets into your canoe. A bailer is a scoop you use to throw water out. The simplest is a plastic milk or bleach bottle cut to make a scoop. It also helps to have a sponge in the canoe.

Splash Cover—This is a fitted, waterproof fabric that fits over the canoe to keep out rain, spray and waves. Some canoeists buy commercially made splash covers, usually made of coated nylon. Others prefer to make their own.

Portage Yoke—Occasionally you may need to carry your canoe overland between lakes and streams, or along a river to avoid a dangerous set of rapids. It's possible to carry a canoe on your shoulders for short distances without any special equipment. But if you're planning long portages, it's best to buy a portage yoke. It's a padded crosspiece that either clamps or bolts into your canoe and rests on your shoulder. Yokes are made of either aluminum or wood.

CANOE PADDLES

The paddle is one of your most important pieces of equipment. Just ask someone who has broken one halfway down a river! In choosing your paddle, you should know what kind of canoeing you'll be doing.

Shape—Paddle blades come in two basic shapes—oval and square. If you'll be doing any high-performance canoeing—whitewater river running or racing—you'll probably choose the square blade. It compensates for not being able to get your entire paddle into the water. River rocks can take their toll on the paddle's corners, but you'll still need the extra bite offered by a square-blade paddle.

Oval-blade paddles are satisfactory for flat-water touring in which speed and maneuverability aren't as important. Paddles with a bent shaft are also popular for flat-water paddling. They provide more power because at the peak of the power stroke, your hands are ahead of the blade, a more efficient position.

There are two popular types of grips—oval and T-grip. It's best to buy the kind you find more comforta-

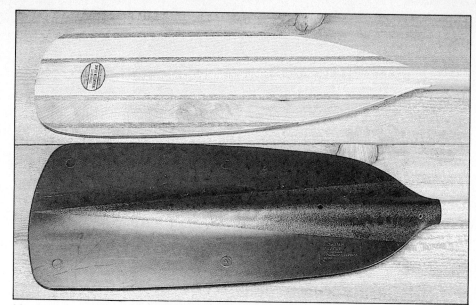

Most canoe paddles are still made of wood (top), but paddles with plastic blades (bottom) or fiberglass are becoming more popular. If you buy a wooden paddle, make sure it's made of laminated wood, like the one shown.

ble. Most serious canoeists prefer the T-grip because it's easier to grip for stroking and steering.

Size—Here's the best way to accurately determine the best paddle length for you: Sit in a canoe and take a few strokes. You should be able to comfortably dip the entire blade into the water. If the paddle is too short, you'll have to reach. If it's too long, several inches of the blade will be left out of the water.

Blade widths range from about 5 to 10 inches. A narrower blade will be

easier to draw through the water, but gives less push, and you'll end up making more strokes per mile. A wide blade provides more propulsion, but each stroke is more tiring.

Materials—Most canoe paddles are made from wood. Some are cut from a solid piece of wood. Others are laminated. A quality laminated paddle is much stronger than one cut from a single piece of wood. Paddles with fiberglass blades and aluminum handles are becoming more popular, especially among whitewater enthusiasts.

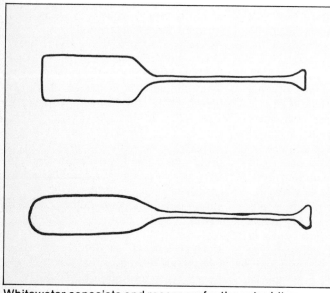

Whitewater canoeists and racers prefer the extra bite provided by the square paddle. Flat-water canoeists can use either design.

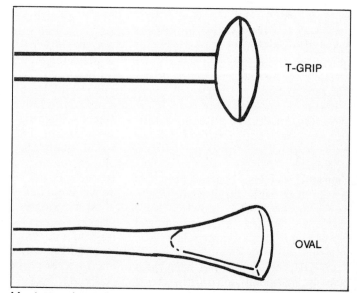

T-GRIP

OVAL

Most experienced canoeists choose the T-grip paddle because it's easier to control the blade when executing advanced strokes.

Kayaks are more maneuverable than most canoes, so they're a good choice for difficult whitewater.

Kayaks

No doubt about it, the kayak is an exotic water craft. Our historical image is one of Eskimos paddling their seal-skin kayaks through frigid Arctic waters, dodging icebergs and swells in search of their prey. The Eskimos of Alaska and Canada used kayaks primarily for hunting. Most of the development of recreational kayaking took place in Europe.

Today, the seal-skin boats of the Eskimos have given way to more modern designs and materials, yielding kayaks that meet an amazing variety of water conditions.

WHAT THE
KAYAK DOES BEST

Kayaks are used for both whitewater and flat-water paddling. They are more maneuverable than most canoes, so they're a good choice for difficult whitewater.

Kayaks hold only one or two people, so they lend themselves better to individual boating than do canoes. Unless you purchase a special sea-going kayak, you won't be able to pack along as much equipment as you can in a canoe. Finally, because of the low center of gravity and the tippy nature of kayaks, most novice boaters take a little longer getting used to a kayak. If you get some personal in-

struction and practice a bit, you'll quickly gain confidence and find that kayaks are actually *easier* to paddle than canoes.

There are a wide variety of designs and materials to choose from. Before purchasing one, decide on the kind of kayaking you'll be doing.

Most kayaks are manufactured by small "cottage industries" and individual custom builders. This means that retailers may not have the same wide selection of kayaks they may offer in canoes. It also means that you may have the opportunity to meet and talk to the person who built your kayak—a potentially rewarding experience. Also, when you gain more experience, you may have the oppor-

tunity to work with a custom builder and have him make a boat just for you. The novice, however, will probably find more than enough choices in standard retail lines.

DESIGN

Nearly all factors of hull design discussed with respect to canoes apply to kayaks. It's an often-repeated saying that a boat hull is a boat hull, be it canoe or kayak.

As with canoes, kayaks are built mainly for either straight tracking or easy turning. Whether you need a boat that can turn on a dime or will maintain a straight compass bearing depends on whether you're interested in whitewater or flat-water kayaking.

Many people take a while to get used to a kayak's low center of gravity. However, after a little practice, most agree that a kayak is easier to paddle alone than a canoe.

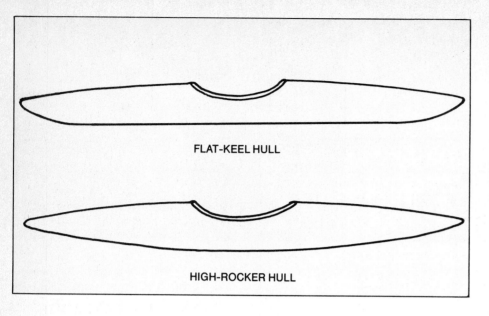

FLAT-KEEL HULL

HIGH-ROCKER HULL

Flat-keeled kayaks are designed for straight tracking. The more rocker a kayak has, the easier it turns and the harder it is to paddle in a straight line.

Length—Flat-water kayaks are longer, wider and higher than white-water boats. Experts recommend buying a flat-water boat between 14 and 17 feet long. To compare, most whitewater kayaks are 13 feet long or shorter. Longer boats track better and, of course, offer more storage space for equipment. Some flat-water boats are equipped with foot-controlled rudders, or *skegs*—fixed fins—on the stern to aid control.

Volume—Generally speaking, the greater the volume of the kayak, the more buoyant it will be, and the more storage space it will have.

Some complex whitewater designs, however, achieve relatively good buoyancy with low volume by manipulating hull shape and deck-to-hull distances. Kayakers running big whitewater rivers need the extra buoyancy of a high-volume kayak.

Hull Shape—Whitewater kayaks have more rocker than the straight-keeled, flat-water touring kayaks. The more rocker a boat has, the easier it turns and the harder it is to paddle in a straight line. A flat-water kayak should lie flat on the ground, with the hull curving up only at the ends.

When viewed in profile from the end, kayak hulls can range from flat to V-shape. When you first get into kayaking, it's best to buy a boat that falls somewhere in the middle, with a round or slightly arched hull. When you gain more experience, you'll know better what kind of hull design exactly fits your needs. Also, it's good to remember that even within a given kayak discipline, such as flat-water

touring or whitewater slalom competition, there's considerable room for personal preference. What works for one person may not work for another.

KAYAK MATERIALS

Traditional, skin-covered kayaks have long since been replaced by several modern materials—primarily fiberglass and plastic. The type of material a kayak is made from partially determines its weight, durability and—especially on whitewater—some of its performance characteristics.

Fiberglass—There are numerous fiberglass designs available. All share the same basic technology—fiberglass cloth is combined with resin and "laid up" to form the shape of the kayak. Some manufacturers lay up extra layers of fiberglass in hull areas they think need extra reinforcement.

Essentially, fiberglass kayaks are light and rigid. They're easy to repair, even along the side of the river if need be.

Kevlar, the fiber that makes the lightest, strongest canoes is also used in the lightest, strongest and most expensive kayaks. Light weight is undeniably important. After all, a light kayak paddles easier, and easier paddling means that you use less energy.

Most kayakers, however, are content with a fiberglass or plastic boat. Only those with very specialized needs choose Kevlar crafts.

Plastic—Plastic hulls are usually made of *rotationally molded* polyethylene. A mold is rotated and covered by progressively thicker layers of plastic. Plastic is heavier than fiberglass, but for many kayakers its durability more than compensates. Plastic boats rarely need to be repaired. They are slightly less expensive and more flexible than a fiberglass kayak of the same size.

Kayak hulls can range from flat to V-shape to round. Beginners should get a kayak with a slightly rounded hull. It's a design that offers a compromise between absolute tracking and turning ability.

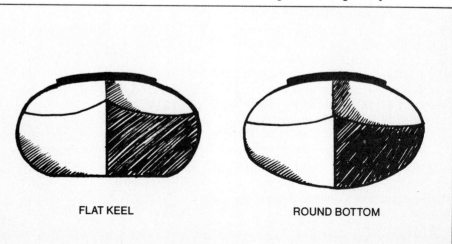

FLAT KEEL

ROUND BOTTOM

Wood Frame And Fabric—This type of construction is often used in folding kayaks. The fabric shell isn't durable enough for whitewater use, but it is adequate for flat-water touring. Folding kayaks are very handy if space is limited, or if you have to pack your kayak into a small car or ship it on a bus or plane.

FEATURES AND ACCESSORIES

When you've found a kayak of the design and materials to meet your needs, you should look at accessories. Some will be built into your kayak, others are purchased separately.

Foot Braces—Every kayak should have foot pegs so you can brace yourself for efficient paddling. These are adjustable, either by pins or screws, or with a spring-loaded lever.

Old-style kayaks sometimes had a bar running across the width of the boat. This method is now considered dangerous, especially for whitewater paddling. It's possible to get your feet trapped under the bar. In whitewater kayaking especially, you always want to be able to get out of your boat in an emergency.

Knee And Hip Braces—It's been said that you don't sit in a kayak as much as you wear it. To this end, various types of plastic, fiberglass and foam braces are incorporated into kayaks to provide the boater with a secure fit. If

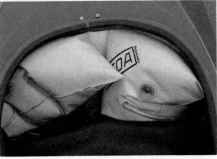

Usually, you have to buy flotation bags separately. They keep your kayak high in the water in case it swamps. Notice the foam pillar in the middle of the kayak.

A spray skirt fits around your waist and attaches to the rim of the cockpit, sealing the cockpit against water. If you need to escape, you pull the white ball to release the spray skirt.

your kayak doesn't fit quite right, you can glue in extra foam padding to improve fit.

Seats—Most kayak seats are made of molded plastic or fiberglass suspended from the cockpit rim. If your seat is too low, you can glue down closed-cell foam—such as the type used in sleeping-bag pads—to lift you up a bit.

Flotation Bags—A kayak must have flotation added to keep the boat high in the water and to avoid rock damage in case of swamping. Flotation bags are usually made of vinyl. They come in various sizes, and some have an opening into which you can stuff equipment. This way the bag can serve two functions.

Foam Pillars—Most production kayaks come with three- to four-inch plastic or ethafoam pillars that keep the boat's deck from collapsing on your knees. This also adds rigidity for whitewater rivers.

Spray Skirts—A spray skirt fits around your waist and attaches to the rim of the cockpit, effectively making the cockpit watertight. Most commercially made skirts are of neoprene, but it's possible to sew your own of waterproof nylon.

The skirt should always be equipped with a strap or cord on the outside so you can release the skirt if you need to get out of the boat in an emergency.

The anatomy of a fully equipped kayak: Foot braces are adjustable. If the seat and knee pads don't fit quite right, you can glue on extra closed-cell foam until they fit.

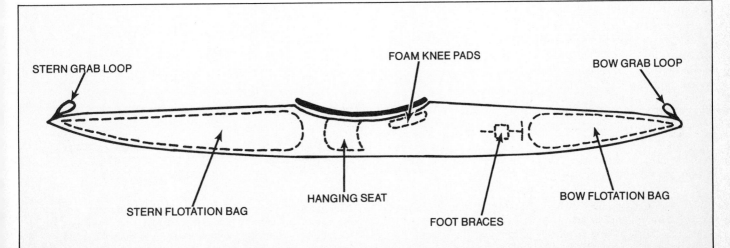

STERN GRAB LOOP

FOAM KNEE PADS

BOW GRAB LOOP

STERN FLOTATION BAG

HANGING SEAT

FOOT BRACES

BOW FLOTATION BAG

Most kayak paddles are built with the blades set at 90° to each other. As one paddle bites into the water, the other is feathered into the wind.

KAYAK PADDLES

Kayak paddles are built with a blade at each end, set at 90° to each other. You rotate the paddle with each stroke. As one side bites into the water, the other is *feathered,* set sideways to the wind. This is an important energy-saving feature when you're paddling into a strong headwind.

Shape—Blades are either flat or curved. Curved-blade paddles are either *right-handed* or *left-handed.*

You'll find that as you rotate the paddle to feather each stroke, you automatically and consistently rotate the paddle with the same hand. If you use your right hand to rotate the paddle, you need a right-handed paddle. If you do the rotation with your left, buy a left-handed paddle. You'll need to work a paddle to find out which way you do it. Just because you are right- or left-handed in other activities doesn't necessarily mean you'll rotate your paddle with the same hand.

Some paddles have an adjustable connection at the midpoint of the shaft, so you can line up your blades in the same direction if you want to. But since a feathered paddle is so efficient, it's best to set your blades at a 90° angle.

Shafts are either round or oval-shaped. An oval shaft is generally easier to hold, and you always know which way your blades are oriented. But again, let personal taste dictate your choice.

Length—Correct paddle length is determined by the kind of paddling you'll be doing, your height and personal preference.

Flat-water paddles are generally longer than whitewater paddles. Tall people usually need a longer paddle, but the key statistic is torso size and arm length, not overall height. In the final analysis, the best way to find correct paddle length is to try out several different sizes and buy one that feels most comfortable.

Materials—As with canoe paddles, the two major choices are wood and fiberglass with aluminum handles. Both materials are durable. Let experience be your guide.

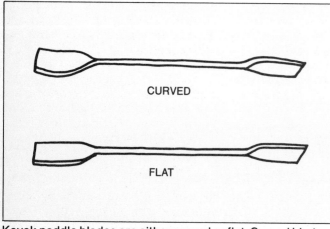

Kayak paddle blades are either curved or flat. Curved blades may also be called *spooned.*

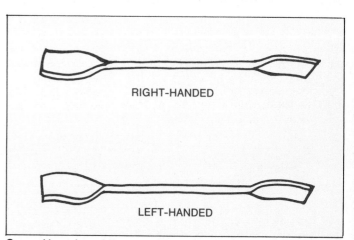

Curved kayak paddles are either right- or left-handed. If you use your right hand to rotate the paddle, you'll need a right-handed paddle. Be sure to try out a paddle before buying it.

Inflatable Rafts

Rafts also have an historical link, although the connection isn't quite as direct as with kayaks and canoes. In the late 1860s Major John Wesley Powell and his party of eight became the first to run the Colorado River through the Grand Canyon. Powell's expedition mapped one of the last remaining unknown areas of the Continental United States. He battled the Colorado's fearsome rapids in three 21-foot oak boats and a 16-foot pine boat, each powered by oars. The so-called rubber rafts that are now found on Western rivers are a direct outgrowth of Powell's wooden boats.

Today, rafts are manufactured in dozens of shapes and sizes, suitable for every kind of water sport from running the roughest rivers to fishing on quiet lakes. In addition to inflatable rafts, you can buy inflatable kayaks. We discuss them after the section on rafts.

Inflatable rafts are well-suited to family and group activities.

WHAT RAFTS DO BEST

Properly used, inflatable rafts can handle the roughest grades of white-water. Although they are considerably less maneuverable than either canoes or kayaks, they are more "forgiving." You can bring a raft through a tough set of rapids with less skill than required by a kayak.

Rafts are ideal for families and large groups of people. As long as you have a knowledgeable and experienced boater in charge, rafts offer a safe way to give children and paddling novices a taste of moderate whitewater. Also, they are capable of carrying plenty of gear, making them perfect for multi-day excursions.

But you can do more with a raft than take it into whitewater. They provide a comfortable alternative to canoes and kayaks on gentle rivers, and small rafts provide the only way for backpacking fishermen to get onto mountain lakes. Because they can be deflated and folded up, rafts can be carried in a car trunk.

For long-distance touring on flat water, you'll be better off with a canoe or kayak. Rafts move ponderously and don't track as well as the other kinds of boats.

DESIGN

The design, materials and special features of a raft determine its capacity, how quickly it will turn, and how safe it will be on specific kinds of water. It's possible to find rafts of all sizes, from individual backpacking models designed for lake use, to large multi-person river rafts used by guides on exciting whitewater trips.

Oars vs. Paddles—Rafts can be either rowed or paddled. Some of the largest river rafts have wood or metal *rowing frames* mounted on the side tubes to provide a solid platform for rowing, and possibly a *sweep oar* on the back to aid in steering.

Paddling is a way to get everyone involved. If the river is small with many tight passages, it may be the only way to get the raft through. Rowing is most practical on lakes and big, wide rivers where there is plenty of space for the oars. The choice of whether to row or paddle your raft may come down to the personal preference of the people handling the boat.

Size—Most non-commercial whitewater rafts are from 11 to 20 feet long. Flat-water fishing rafts are typically smaller. Individual models may consist of only a simple inflatable tube with a floor.

Manufacturers often rate rafts according to the total amount of weight they are designed to carry or the number of people that can fit in.

You'll probably find that most manufacturers exaggerate the number of people a raft can comfortably hold. Such figures are based on top load-carrying capacity, but if you load a raft to capacity, there will probably be little room left for equipment, moving around and general comfort.

Most people find that a "four-man raft" will comfortably hold only three. A "three-man raft" holds only two. And a "two-man raft" is best used solo.

The best size should be determined by the number of people and amount of equipment you plan to carry and the kind of water you'll be navigating. Bigger rafts are harder to control, but you'll need one if you want to face rugged whitewater rivers.

Width also affects how a raft handles. The wider it is, the more stable it will be in rough water. A narrower raft, however, will maneuver better through tight passages.

Tubes—All inflatable rafts are made of tubes. In addition to the tubes around the edge, some rafts have inflatable floors that increase buoyancy and make kneeling more comfortable. The larger the diameter of the tubes, the better the raft floats, the easier it turns and the more equipment it can carry. However, larger tubes cut down

You can row small rafts with their built-in oarlocks. Larger, multi-person rafts are usually outfitted with a wooden or metal rowing frame.

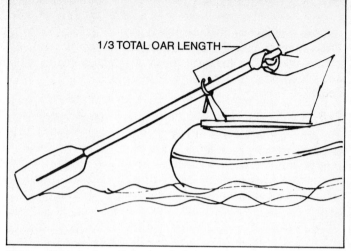

1/3 TOTAL OAR LENGTH

The correct oar length for a raft depends on its width. One-third of total oar length should fall between your hand and the oarlock.

on interior space and make it harder to reach the water for paddling or rowing.

If you are planning to use your raft for whitewater, make sure that your tubes are divided into at least two, and preferably more, chambers. If one chamber is punctured, you'll still have some buoyancy left.

Some rafts are designed so the tubes turn up at the ends. This is a good design for whitewater. Because less of it contacts the water, the raft pivots faster. Also, an upturned bow deflects splashing water and rides over waves, instead of digging into them.

Materials—Inflatable rafts are commonly called *rubber rafts,* but actually most are made of a strong base fabric such as nylon or Dacron coated with waterproof material such as neoprene or Hypalon. So-called plastic rafts are made of polyvinyl chloride (PVC).

Inflating The Raft—Only the smallest rafts can be inflated by blowing them up by yourself. Therefore, you should carry some sort of pump.

A foot-bellows pump requires little energy, since you use your leg muscles. The barrel pump moves a greater volume of air, but it's more tiring to use because you pump it with your arms and shoulders. Either pump comes in small models that can be stowed in your raft for on-river use.

PADDLES AND OARS FOR RAFTING

Oars and paddles are available in both wood and fiberglass. Wooden oars are generally made of straight-grain ash or similar wood. The best paddles are made of laminated woods.

As in canoe and kayak paddles, fiberglass raft paddles and oars are made with a fiberglass blade mounted to a metal shaft. Plastic, injection-molded paddles are adequate for flat-water paddling, but they may not have enough durability for whitewater.

Choosing the correct paddle length depends on your height and the width of the raft's tubes. One expert provides this method: Sit on the side tube of the raft and paddle. The top of the paddle should be level with your nose when the blade is totally immersed.

Oar length is generally determined by raft width. The most often-repeated formula is that one-third of the oar's length should fall between your hand and the oarlock. The best way to find the proper length paddle or oar, though, is to try several different sizes in the water and then make your decision.

INFLATABLE KAYAKS

There are several different models of inflatable kayaks, all of which are surprisingly maneuverable and seaworthy. They may or may not have decking. Covered models can be used much like standard kayaks.

Inflatable kayaks should never be used in rugged whitewater rivers, though, because they aren't rigid enough to stand up to the stress of heavy water. But, they're ideal if you need to pack a kayak into a mountain lake or if you're being flown to a remote lake or river.

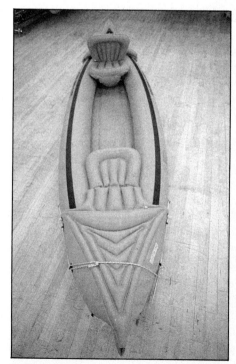

Inflatable kayaks are relatively inexpensive, compact and surprisingly seaworthy.

Boating Accessories

Some accessories are essential. These include a life jacket and helmet. Others are optional, but very useful, depending on your experience and needs.

LIFE JACKETS

Carrying life jackets while boating is required by law. To be safe, you should wear one at all times.

The U.S. Coast Guard inspects and approves life-jacket designs, but the Coast Guard stamp of approval doesn't mean that a certain life jacket works for everyone. The ratings are determined by the life jacket's ability to hold up a certain amount of dead weight. If you happen to weigh more than that, the life jacket won't keep you floating, even in quiet water.

Rather than depend on Coast Guard ratings as a measure of quality, it's better to rely on the expert advice of a knowledgeable store clerk or river guide.

Here's a summary of the different types of life jackets, with their Coast Guard designations.

Type-I Jackets—Commonly known as *Mae West jackets,* these bulky devices offer the best flotation of any jacket. If you are submerged, a Type-I will lift you into a vertical position. They may be too big for strenuous whitewater paddling, but they're ideal for children or adults who are along for the ride in a canoe or raft.

Type-II Jackets—Also called *horse collars,* these models are rectangular with a vertical split. There's a hole for your head and straps that tie the ends around your middle. A Type-II jacket is suitable for flat-water boating but should never be used for whitewater. It has a tendency to slip over your head.

Type-III Jackets—These are the most commonly used for whitewater. They look like vests and completely enclose your upper body and zip shut at the front. Flotation comes from foam sewn into the fabric. Type-III jackets leave you free to paddle and won't pull off, even if you capsize in heavy water.

Type-IV Jackets—Basically, these are seat cushions and ring buoys. They provide adequate protection if you capsize in calm lake water, but are completely inadequate for any sort of river boating. They may float away

This is a selection of Type-III jackets—the best design for whitewater kayakers.

before you have the chance to grab them.

Type-V Jackets—These are similar to Type-III vests, except that they are usually snapped closed with horizontal straps. They are very buoyant but won't lift you into a vertical position if you become submerged. Type-V jackets are most often used by whitewater rafters.

HELMETS

Helmets are a must for any whitewater kayaking. If your kayak turns over, your head may bump against river rocks until you can get yourself righted again.

Specially designed kayaking helmets are available. Other choices used by kayakers are hockey, rock-climbing and even motorcycle or football helmets. Of these, kayaking helmets are lightest.

Look for the following things in a kayaking helmet:

1) It should have padded, crushable foam, much like a good rock-climbing helmet.

2) The helmet should protect your forehead, temples, ears and back of the head. A blow to the side of the head is just as likely as one to the top.

3) It must be comfortable enough so that you'll wear it at all times.

WATERPROOF BAGS

The nature of your trip determines whether you'll need to pack your equipment in waterproof bags or boxes.

Certainly, for short fishing expeditions on a calm lake, you won't be carrying much equipment, and it's unlikely to get very wet. But for any sort of river running, especially overnight trips, you'll need to pack your gear in waterproof containers because at least part of it will probably get wet.

If you are using a large raft with plenty of storage room, you can use wooden boxes, fiberglass and plastic coolers, and heavy metal boxes.

But if you are kayaking or canoeing, you'll need to save space and weight. Waterproof bags of heavy-duty plastic or PVC-coated fabric are the best. If a bag is going to leak, it will probably happen at the closure. To test how waterproof a closure is, fill the bag with air and check for leaks.

11 Outdoor Accessories

So far, we've covered a wide range of outdoor equipment for specific activities. In this chapter, we discuss the many important accessories that will add to your safety and enjoyment in the outdoors.

THE 10 ESSENTIALS

In the 1930s the Seattle Mountaineers, a Northwest climbing club, started teaching classes about outdoor activities such as hiking, backpacking and mountaineering. They created a list of 10 essential items you should have when in the backcountry.

Since that time, the concept of the 10 Essentials has become familiar to experienced campers, hikers, climbers and canoeists all over the world. Here they are:

1) Map of the area.
2) Compass.
3) Flashlight with extra batteries and bulbs.
4) Extra food.
5) Extra clothing.
6) Sunglasses.
7) First-aid kit.
8) Pocket knife.
9) Matches kept waterproof.
10) Firestarter to help get a fire going in wet wood.

We've already discussed most of these items. For example, you can find out about clothing in Chapter 1. Food is discussed in Chapter 6. In this final chapter, we discuss the rest of the 10 Essentials and cover many other commonly used outdoor accessories. Some are shown in the accompanying photo.

Maps

No matter which outdoor activity you do, you'll be able to find an appropriate map. Several kinds are commonly available. Some can be used by themselves, without a compass. But for complex outdoor navigation, you'll need to use a compass and should therefore know how to navigate with one.

Learning to use a map and compass is easy, partly because there are many books on the topic. Also, youth organizations such as Scouts have been teaching map-reading and compass work for decades. If you sign up for a mountaineering or canoeing course, as recommended earlier in this book, there's a good chance that map and compass work are part of the curriculum.

Outdoor-navigation classes, designed primarily for adults, are becoming more popular, too. Often these classes are designed to teach the skills of competitive *orienteering,* a sport combining hiking and running with map and compass navigation.

Whether or not you're interested in pursuing the competitive aspects of orienteering, navigation skills are useful in all outdoor pursuits. Also, don't overlook resources close to you. Many people learn from their friends and family members. It's an old way that's tried and true.

TOPOGRAPHIC MAPS

Topographic maps are the most useful type for hikers, climbers and whitewater boaters. They are published by the United States Geological Survey—among others—so are often called *USGS maps,* or *topo maps.*

The maps show three things—horizontal distance, vertical terrain and vegetation cover. Horizontal distance is indicated by a ratio of map inches to actual inches, vertical distance by means of contour lines at prescribed intervals. Vegetation is reproduced as shaded green areas.

They are available in a variety of scales—often called a *series.*

United States Series—These are drawn to a scale of 1:250,000—meaning one inch in the map represents 250,000 inches, or about four miles. This series is best for broad orienting, such as planning a long hiking, cycling or boating trip, identifying peaks from a mountain summit or just studying the lay of the land. The scale is far too wide for actual navigation.

The maps are issued for all states. For some areas they are the only topographical maps available.

15-Minute Series—As the name suggests, these maps cover an area of 15 minutes of longitude by 15 minutes of latitude, about 12 by 18 miles. Scale is 1:62,500—about one inch to the mile. This provides enough topographic information for navigation and route selection.

7-1/2-Minute Series—These cover 7-1/2 minutes of latitude by 7-1/2 minutes of longitude, roughly 6 by 9 miles. Scale is 1:24,000, or about 2-1/2 inches per mile. Because this series is four times more detailed than the 15-minute series, these maps are ideal for cross-country navigation. But because they cover a relatively small area of land, you need more maps to cover the same land area a 15-minute map does. The USGS is slowly replacing 15-minute maps with 7-1/2-minute coverage.

A 7-1/2-minute topographic map is great for wilderness navigation. The map reproduced here is four times as detailed as a 15-minute map of the same region.

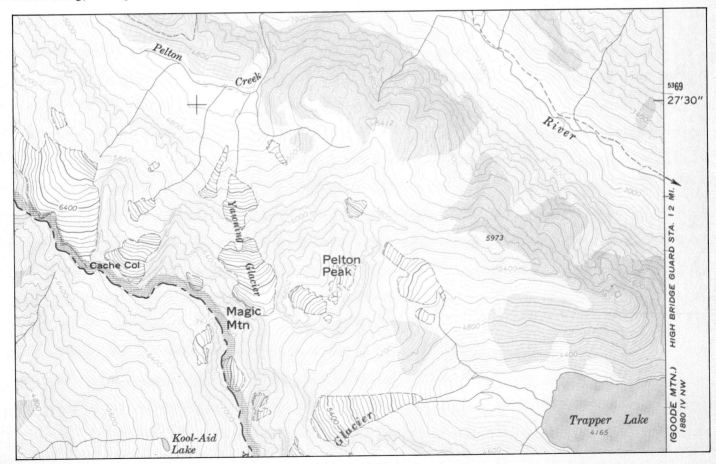

Purchasing Topographic Maps—Topographic maps for a local area are usually available in outdoor and sporting-goods stores. If you can't find the ones you need, or you need maps for another state, order them directly from the USGS.

For maps west of the Mississippi River, write to U.S. Geological Survey, Federal Center, Denver, CO 80225. For areas east of the Mississippi, order from the U.S. Geological Survey, Washington, D.C. 20242.

Indexes for each state are available free. You'll need an index to order the maps you need. Each topographic map is titled, usually by the name of a notable geographic feature within the area it covers.

Topographic maps are also available for Canada. Order indexes and maps from the Map Distribution Office, 615 Booth Street, Ottawa, Ontario, Canada K1A 0E9.

FOREST SERVICE MAPS

U.S. Forest Service maps are much different from USGS topographic maps, but they are still an invaluable tool for trip planning and sometimes navigation, too.

Generally, they don't show land elevations although a few have primitive contour lines. Forest Service maps are valuable because they depict up-to-date road and trail conditions and any new buildings that may have been erected. They are updated more often than USGS topographic maps.

These maps can usually be obtained for a small charge from ranger stations and larger Forest Service offices in large cities.

OTHER MAPS

Other specialized maps may be available, published by local government agencies, outdoor clubs and private companies. USGS topographic maps are in the public domain, so it's legal to reproduce them for other kinds of maps. That's why you'll find privately produced hiking maps drawn over USGS topographic maps. It's also common to see them reproduced in guide books.

Cycling and boating clubs often publish maps and guides showing popular touring areas. Sketch maps of mountaineering and cross-country routes are often available in book form or from local climbing clubs.

Forest Service maps are valuable for showing up-to-date road and trail conditions and any buildings in the national forest featured in the map. However, they usually lack contour lines.

Cycling clubs and government agencies often publish special cycling maps that show scenic and lightly traveled roads well-suited to riding.

Compasses

The Earth is a giant magnet, with magnetic poles located near the North and South poles. The magnetic pole in the Northern Hemisphere is located on Bathurst Island in the Canadian Arctic, 1400 miles from the true North Pole. Your compass points toward this magnetic pole, not the true North Pole. The difference has a real effect on navigation. This is all the more reason to learn proper orienteering techniques before you have to depend on your compass in an emergency.

Because it always points toward the magnetic North Pole, a compass is the most accurate way to determine direction. Inexpensive, round compasses that aren't marked with degrees are actually toys. Don't use one in the field. Backpackers and boaters who use a compass for serious navigation usually buy an *orienteering compass.* The needle pivots inside a housing, which is mounted on a plastic baseplate. There are also many kinds of

Backpackers and mountaineers often use an orienteering compass. On it is an azimuth scale marked in black, a red magnetic needle and a plastic base marked with the direction-of-travel arrow. It measures rules in millimeters and inches.

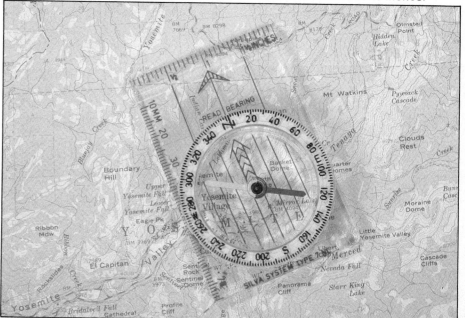

specialized compasses designed primarily for professional use. The *cruiser compass* used by foresters and surveyors is one example.

Unless you're interested only in finding approximate directions, your compass isn't usable without a map. Topographic maps are best for navigation because they show the lay of the land.

THE HOUSING

Most compass housings are made of either plastic, aluminum or brass. The housing contains three basic things—the needle, a system to damp the needle and a dial marked on the outside of the housing to show degrees.

The Needle—It is suspended on a synthetic sapphire or ruby bearing, making it free to rotate toward north. The north end of the needle is usually marked with red to prevent confusion about which way the needle is pointing.

Damping—Your compass should have some sort of damping mechanism to slow down the needle and halt its quivering. The most common method is to fill the housing with a fluid—usually kerosene. Less frequently used is the *needle lock.* By alternately locking and unlocking the needle, you can bring its swinging and vibration to a halt.

The Dial—Marked around the outside of the housing are the 360° of a circle. You use these degree designa-tions, called an *azimuth scale,* to determine your direction of travel. Most housings are marked in either 2° or 5° increments. Obviously, the more precise the marking, the easier it is to set a precise course.

One degree of compass error equals 92.4 feet per mile. For most backpackers and boaters, that's close enough, especially considering that rough terrain, winds and currents can do more to throw you off course than a compass error of a few degrees.

THE BASEPLATE

The baseplate is normally made of a transparent material, usually plastic, with orienteering lines and arrows. You use these for lining up the compass on your map and determining direction of travel. It's also common to find various scales marked along the side of the baseplate. These may be a simple ruler, usually marked in millimeters or inches, or a map scale.

Elaborate orienteering compasses may have a set of map scales set to the standard topographic map scales (1:250,000, 1:62,500 or 1:24,000) that can be snapped onto the edge of the baseplate.

Some models have a folding cover with a sighting mirror and sighting line. These make it easier for accurate measurement and field sighting. A magnifying lens in the baseplate aids in deciphering tiny map symbols and lines.

Flashlights & Candle Lanterns

A flashlight or headlamp is a necessity for *all* backcountry travel. Campers and backpackers not planning to travel after dark usually prefer a handheld light. Headlamps are popular among campers and hikers who do nighttime tasks and want to keep their hands free, and also among mountaineers who have to climb in darkness.

BATTERY-POWERED LIGHTS

These are the most practical for hikers, climbers and canoeists who don't want to pack in gas- or butane-powered lanterns. Flashlights come in different sizes, from small penlight styles that can be put in your pocket to larger models that are carried with handles. Headlamps function the same way as flashlights, except that the battery pack is separate from the light, connected to it by wires.

The major differences between lights involve the number, size and kind of batteries they use, the size of the bulb and the materials used in the casing.

Batteries—The D size is usually considered the standard for flashlights, although many flashlights actually use smaller sizes. In descending order of size are D, C, A and AA. Size AA batteries are commonly used in portable recorders and calculators, in addition to small flashlights.

Flashlights use either carbon-zinc or alkaline batteries. Alkaline batteries weigh about 50% more than standard carbon-zinc models and may cost three times as much. But, because they have a useful life two to four times as long as carbon-zinc batteries, alkaline batteries are preferred by many.

Low temperatures drastically reduce the energy output of alkaline and carbon-zinc cells. Rewarming the battery may increase its output temporarily, and even a "dead" battery can be temporarily revived by being warmed up. However, you should

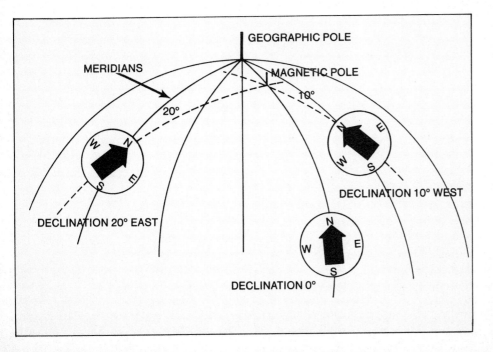

Compass needles point to the magnetic North Pole, not the true, geographic pole. The actual difference—called *declination*—depends on your location in the Northern Hemisphere.

We recommend alkaline batteries for your flashlight. Left to right—C, 9-volt, AA and D.

never heat up a battery over a stove or open flame because it may explode. Batteries will last longer if stored in a cold place.

Nickel-Cadmium (NiCad) rechargeable batteries are commonly used in calculators and other home devices. Although they can be recharged as many as 1000 times, the charge may last for only an hour. This is the main drawback for outdoor use. This means that unless new developments are made, NiCad batteries are best used for emergencies only.

Lithium batteries weigh less than half of comparable alkaline batteries, produce twice the power, last much longer (perhaps years) and are unaffected by cold temperatures. Their use has been promoted by some experts, but at the moment they are so costly that they may be even more expensive to use than shorter-lived batteries. A single lithium cell produces 2.8 volts, a bit less than that produced by two standard 1.5 volt batteries. Therefore, you can't use two lithium batteries in a standard flashlight. The voltage would be too high.

The energy produced by lithium batteries is provided by pressurized sulfur dioxide gas. If short-circuited, a cell may rupture and release the noxious gas, which smells like rotten eggs. Each cell contains only a small amount of gas that dissipates quickly. The greater danger comes from the corrosive nature of the gas. It can quickly damage battery contacts. Lithium batteries are commonly used in smoke detectors and burglar alarms.

Bulbs—The type of bulb you use greatly affects battery life. A brighter bulb uses more energy and decreases battery life.

Two types of bulbs are common in flashlights—PR2 and PR4. A PR2 bulb is the brighter, rated at 0.8 candlepower, drawing 0.5 amperes from a fresh battery. A PR4 bulb is rated at 0.4 candlepower and draws 0.27 amperes. At 70F, a PR2 bulb powered by two alkaline D-cells will burn about 11.8 hours, a PR4 bulb about 30.3 hours, before the batteries are drained.

The *PR* designation means that the bulb attaches to the flashlight by inserting and twisting. A bulb labeled with an *S* means that it screws in.

The Switch—It's wise to take precautions to ensure your flashlight doesn't turn on inside your pack and exhaust your batteries before you reach camp. The two most common methods are to tape the switch in the off position, or take out one of the batteries and reverse it.

Some flashlights are designed to avoid these problems. You turn them on by twisting the head of the light a quarter turn. It's a good system for backpackers because it eliminates any chance that your flashlight will turn on accidentally.

The Casing—Most flashlights are now made of plastic. It's lighter than metal, and if properly cared for, strong enough for most outdoor uses. When inspecting a flashlight, look at the battery connections to see that they are riveted and that wires are well-soldered.

CANDLE LANTERNS

Candle lanterns are best used to hang in your camp or tent to illuminate a small area for reading or cooking. They're especially effective inside an igloo or snowcave because the shelter's walls reflect light. A candle lantern even provides a bit of warmth. Be sure to use candle lanterns with caution, especially inside tents.

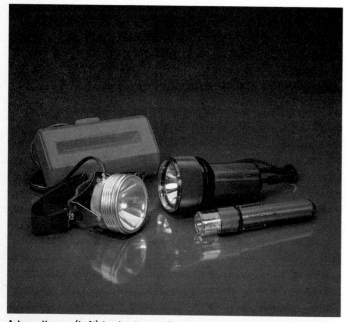

A headlamp (left) is designed for campers and mountaineers who need to keep their hands free. These handheld flashlights (right) show the wide variety of sizes you can buy.

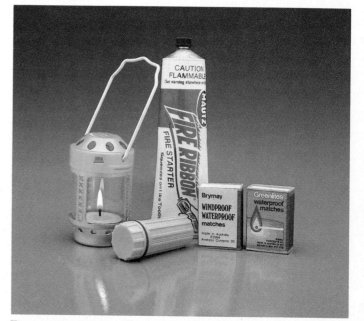

These accessories will help you light up your camp and start your stove or fire. Left to right—candle lantern, waterproof match container, jelly fire starter and wind- and waterproof matches.

Plastic frames (left) are generally more durable than metal (right), but metal frames can usually be bent a bit to improve fit.

The side panels of mountaineering glasses block potentially dangerous side glare.

Sunglasses

Sunglasses are necessary for mountaineering, cross-country skiing or any sport that may take you over snow. Boaters often need sunglasses, too. And even if you won't be facing the glare of snow or water, you may need sunglasses for visual comfort.

LENS CONSIDERATIONS

For general use, your glasses should filter out 65% of available light. At high altitudes or if you travel over snow, the glasses should cut out 85% of available light.

Here's a good guide: Stand in front of a mirror in an average-lit room. If you can't see your eyes through the glasses, they're probably dark enough to use on snow or at high altitudes.

Mirror coatings on lenses do not improve the light-blocking ability of the lens although they may help reduce glare. Gray or gray-green lenses are best for general use because they do not radically alter the color balance of available light. Yellow, green and red lenses are best for fog and haze because they filter out the blue light scattered by water droplets, thereby improving contrast.

There are two major kinds of invisible radiation that affect your eyes—*ultraviolet* and *infrared*. You feel infrared rays as heat. They cause more discomfort than actual damage. Ultraviolet rays, however, can be very dangerous. Too much can cause *snow blindness*—a painful burning of your eyes caused by wearing inadequate eye protection. If you are going to high altitudes or hiking over snow, you must wear sunglasses that block at least 95% of the ultraviolet.

Glass lenses offer an effective block to both ultraviolet and infrared rays. The best glass lenses are ground to their shape. A less expensive method is to heat the glass and cast it over a mold. You can tell the difference by holding the lens under a light, such as a fluorescent tube, and moving the lens back and forth. If the light appears wavy, the lens has probably been heated. If there's no distortion, the lens has been ground.

Dark plastic lenses effectively cut out ultraviolet but not infrared rays. They are generally lighter and more shatterproof than glass lenses, but they are also more subject to scratching.

Ski goggles are not recommended for mountaineering use. The plastic used in most of these lenses is too thin to provide adequate protection in bright sun.

If you wear regular eyeglasses, there are a couple of alternatives to prescription sunglasses. You can wear clip-on sunglasses or ski goggles over your regular glasses. Neither clip-on glasses nor goggles alone provide adequate protection for mountain use, but when worn with your regular glasses for other uses, they work fine. The best, although most expensive, solution is to have sunglasses ground to your own prescription.

FRAMES

Frames are made of either metal or plastic. Thin metal frames are less durable than plastic. Many metal frames are designed so that you can bend them to fit just right.

Glasses designed for mountaineers, skiers, boaters and others in high-glare situations often have side panels to cut the glare from the side. The panels should have small holes punched in the sides to allow ventilation and prevent fogging.

First-Aid Kits

A first-aid kit should be available at all times, whether you're on a canoe trip, day hike, car-camping trip or an extended hiking expedition. It can be purchased commercially as a packaged unit, or you can put together a kit designed exactly for your health needs.

Obviously, the most important part of first aid is not the kit, but your knowledge and experience in first-aid techniques. To that end, we strongly recommend taking a first-aid course. Courses are offered regularly from the Red Cross, in college evening classes, and through hiking, climbing and skiing clubs. If you're unable to find a course to take, read one of the books recommended on page 158.

When you've learned some basic first aid, be sure to frequently review your skills. It's easy to get rusty. We recommend that, if possible, you take refresher courses every few years. The more you know, the better you'll be able to use a well-stocked kit.

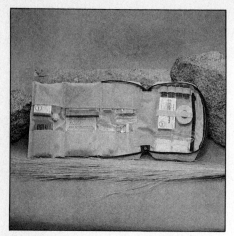

Compact, commercially packaged first-aid kits contain most of the necessary items listed. You should customize your kit to fit your needs.

KIT CONTENTS

There are different kinds of kits for different activities. Most basic is the personal kit, designed to meet minimal and common outdoor injuries—blisters, scrapes, cuts and burns. As your skill improves, you may want to include more equipment to deal with more serious injuries—broken bones, sprains and serious lacerations. If you are headed into remote country, it's wise to make sure your kit is well-stocked.

The Basic Kit—Here's a list of items to be included in your personal kit:

1) Bandages of various sizes for minor cuts and scrapes.

2) Gauze pads in sterile envelopes for larger wounds.

3) Adhesive tape to hold on bandages, cover blisters or tape an injured ankle.

4) Moleskin or molefoam pads to cushion your feet and prevent blisters.

5) Elastic bandage to wrap an injured ankle, knee or wrist.

6) Razor blade to cut tape, shave before taping or for general purposes.

7) Aspirin or aspirin substitute to relieve pain and treat a fever.

8) Antacid, antihistamine, salt tablets, laxatives, pain relievers or other over-the-counter medication to deal with minor ailments such as headaches, upset stomach, allergic reaction to insect stings, heat exhaustion and constipation.

9) Triangular bandage to bind a large wound.

10) Safety pins to secure bandages, slings and splints.

11) Soap to clean out a wound before bandaging it.

12) A first-aid book that includes step-by-step instructions for treating common outdoor injuries.

13) Any prescription medicine you are taking.

Knives

Pocket knives are no longer simple two-bladed models. Now you can get elaborate, multi-use tools that may include a corkscrew, screwdriver, scissors and even a fork and spoon. The heart of any knife, however, is the blade. If you can't cut with it, it's unlikely you'll use it. Therefore, it's best to find a knife with a good blade and *then* look at the other accessories.

THE BLADE

Most knife blades are made of either carbon or stainless steel. Both are iron alloys that are proven to hold an edge well. Although carbon steel will gradually turn from a bright shiny finish to a dull gray, performance isn't affected by this color change. Stainless steel has chromium added to preserve its bright finish and resist rusting.

The harder the steel in the blade, the harder it will be to sharpen, but the longer it will hold an edge. Blades that are too soft will sharpen easily but then dull just as quickly.

The best indication of steel hardness is the *Rockwell Rating*. It's determined by first lowering a diamond-pointed device with 10 kilograms of pressure onto the blade and then repeating the process with 150 kilograms of pressure. The difference

This selection of Swiss Army knives shows that pocket knives can do more than cut. Available accessories include scissors, corkscrews, tweezers, screwdrivers, can openers and magnifying glasses.

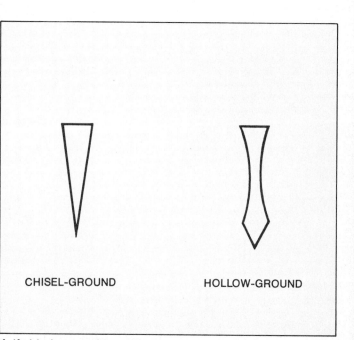

CHISEL-GROUND   HOLLOW-GROUND

Knife blades are either chisel- or hollow-ground. The difference becomes important when you have to sharpen your knife. The chisel blade is drawn across the stone at a flatter angle than the hollow-ground.

It's important to sharpen your knife regularly on a sharpening stone. Here's how: Wet the stone with a drop or two of oil. Set the blade at a slight angle and sharpen in a circular motion. For finishing, draw the edge toward you at a steeper angle. Turn the blade over regularly to keep the edge even.

in the indentations is measured according to a metallurgist's "C" scale. A rating of 56 to 59 is considered acceptable for knife blades.

Sharpening Blades—You sharpen a knife blade by drawing it across a sharpening stone made of novaculite, tiny diamond particles or a synthetic material.

Blades are either *chisel-ground* or *hollow-ground*. Chisel-ground blades, also called *flat-ground,* have an even taper when viewed from the point. Hollow-ground blades curve in just below the top of the blade, then curve out slightly before tapering to the edge.

Look closely to see which kind of blade your knife has because each is sharpened slightly differently. You can draw the chisel-ground across the stone at a flat angle. If the hollow-ground blade is sharpened at too flat an angle, the stone won't make contact with the cutting edge.

CONSTRUCTION

There's more to a pocket knife than the blade. It's an intricate device that may include several blades and accessories, all held together by rivets and side pieces.

Blades and accessories turn on internal springs. On the outside are side panels, called *scales,* and rivets that hold the entire assembly together. Side covers of plastic or other material are usually mounted on the outside of the scales. *Bolsters* of brass, nickel or stainless steel make up the end pieces of the knife.

Be selective when shopping for a knife. Top-quality knives have two

basic things—a good blade and effective movements. Try out each blade and accessory by opening and closing it several times. The blades should be easy to find and open, and should lock securely in place. If there's the slightest wiggle, it's a sign the knife is poorly constructed and may fail when stressed.

Binoculars

Shopping for binoculars can be confusing because of all of the variables you have to consider—magnification, field of view, light-gathering ability, weight and, of course, price. The vast differences in price and quality result more from the quality of workmanship than major differences in materials and design.

Choosing the best pair for your needs requires that you first decide what you intend to use them for. Then make a careful study of the choices available. Answers to the following questions will help:

1) Are you going to be following rapid motion, such as birds in flight?

2) Will you need to do any long-distance viewing over hundreds of yards?

3) Will you ever want to use your binoculars in the dim light of early morning or late evening?

4) Are you planning to take your binoculars along on backpacking trips?

5) Do you wear eyeglasses?

6) How much money are you willing to spend?

SELECTION

Binoculars can be grouped according to prism design—*porro-prism* and *roof-prism* are the most common. To these we add *monoculars,* which technically aren't binoculars at all because they have only one lens. But we include them here because of their applications in outdoor recreation.

Porro-Prism—In this optical system, the eyepieces are usually closer together than the front (objective) lenses. The light enters the objective lens and is reflected four times before it reaches your eyes. A reverse-porro system simply sets the objective lenses closer together than the eyepieces. The reverse system is often used in small binoculars.

The porro system is excellent for producing an image with three-dimensional depth, and it's possible to achieve magnification of up to 20X.

Because light doesn't travel in a straight line to your eyes, porro-prism binoculars are generally larger, bulkier and less expensive than roof-prism models.

Roof-Prism—In a roof prism the prisms are arranged in a line inside the barrel, so the binoculars are slim and more compact. They lack the depth perception and magnification potential of the porro system, but if

Modern roof-prism binoculars are amazingly small, yet powerful. This makes them ideal for backpacking. If you wear eyeglasses, make sure you buy binoculars with rubber eye cups that can be folded back.

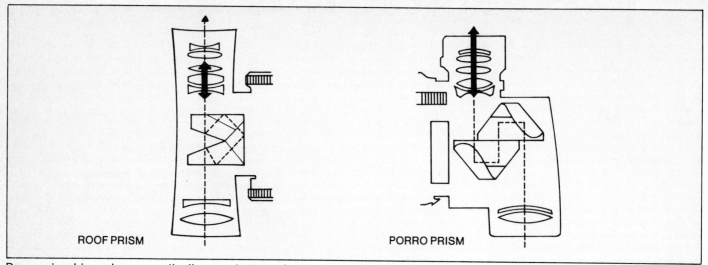

ROOF PRISM   PORRO PRISM

Porro-prism binoculars are optically superior to roof-prism types, but they are larger. The roof-prism design allows for a small, slim binocular. It's the popular choice of many backpackers and mountaineers.

you need a small, compact model, they're a better choice. Magnification is entirely adequate for most handheld purposes. Most small backpacking binoculars are roof-prism types.

Monoculars—As the name suggests, monoculars have only one barrel, not two. They may use either a porro or roof prism. Many people find them uncomfortable to use because you can only look through them with one eye at a time. But, if maximum lightweight compactness is what you're after, they're hard to beat.

VIEWING CHARACTERISTICS

Obviously, the most important feature of any pair of binoculars is the image quality you see. There are several factors to consider—magnification, performance in dim light, the exit pupils and overall image sharpness.

Magnification—This refers to how much larger the image appears through the binoculars than to the naked eye. All binoculars are marked with two numbers separated by an *x*. The first is the magnification factor, usually a number from 6 to 10. For example, 8x20 binoculars magnify an image 8 times (8X), making a deer standing 120 feet away appear as though it were only 15 feet away.

Greater magnification may appear desirable, but there are two drawbacks. The higher the magnification, the smaller the field of view. For example, with an 8X magnification, the binoculars may take in an image 378 feet wide at a distance of 1000 yards. But with 10X binoculars, your

field of view may be reduced to 261 feet. There are slight variations among different models, but the fact remains—the greater the magnification the smaller the field of view.

A second drawback is that as magnification increases, it becomes harder to hold the binoculars still. A magnification of 8X is generally considered maximum for handheld use.

Performance In Dim Light—The number after the magnification rating is the diameter in millimeters of the objective (front) lens. The larger the diameter, the more light it can gather, and the brighter the image you'll see in dim light.

When using a monocular, keep both eyes open.

A large objective-lens diameter means that the binoculars will be bulky. For example, 8x20 binoculars are very compact, but won't take in as much light as their much larger 8x40 cousins.

Exit Pupils—If you hold your binoculars at arm's length and point them at a source of light, you'll see a small circle of light in each eyepiece. These are the exit pupils.

Examining the exit pupil is a reliable way to determine quality. The circles should be perfectly round and evenly lit, with sharp edges. If the pupil is not circular and evenly lit, it could be from misalignment of the lenses inside the barrels.

The size of exit pupils varies, depending on the magnification and objective lens diameter. To determine the diameter of the exit pupils, divide the objective lens diameter (in millimeters) by the magnification. The larger that number, the more light will come through the eyepiece to your eyes, an important figure if you need to use your binoculars in dim or dark places.

A large number also means a larger circle of light is hitting your eye. The binoculars will be easier to use when it's difficult to hold them steady, such as on a boat.

Binoculars For Eyeglass Wearers—If you wear glasses, you won't be able to put your eyes right up against the lens. If not compensated for, this extra distance will cause you to see only a portion of the image coming through the lens. You'll need to find a binocular that has optics to compensate.

In an 8x24 roof-prism model, the *8* indicates degree of magnification, the *24* the diameter of the objective (front) lens in millimeters. The field of view is 8.7°, out of a 360° circle. Greater magnification produces a smaller field of view.

The diameter of the objective lens determines how much light your binoculars can gather and, therefore, their performance in dim light.

The exit pupils are the small circles of light you can see in the eyepieces. The larger the circle you see, the more light will reach your eyes.

Folding rubber eyecups and the letter *B* following the magnification and objective lens diameter indicate that the binoculars are constructed for eyeglass wearers. The cups are folded down for use with glasses and flipped back for those who don't wear glasses. **Overall Image Quality**—There's only one way to get a final idea of how well your binoculars will function— carefully judge the image quality it delivers. A high-quality lens system delivers a top-quality image.

Objects shouldn't be distorted. You can test for this by focusing on something you know to be straight, a flagpole, for example. Even the best binoculars will slightly distort an image at the edges, but it should be minimal.

Similarly, objects should be in focus through almost the entire field of view. It's common to have the extreme edges go out of focus, but everything else should be clear.

Also look for color fringing. A poor-quality, uncoated lens will show a halo of bright colors around objects.

ANOTHER WAY TO RATE LIGHT-GATHERING ABILITY

Performance in dim light is a function of both magnification and objective lens diameter. Here's a way to compare performance in various lighting conditions: Multiply the magnification rating by the objective lens diameter. For example, an 8x40 model gives a product of 320. It will be able to see better in dim light than an 8x24 (=192) model. Use this information as a starting guide to binoculars selection.

0 to 100—Binoculars are usable in full daylight only.
100 to 150—General daylight use.
150 to 200—Dark shade.
200 to 300—Dusk or dawn.
300 to 400—Bright moonlight.
  +400—Night use.

Cameras & Photo Accessories

Photography means different things to different people. For some, photography is the prime reason for heading into the outdoors. For others, it's just a way to record what happens on the trip.

It pays to do some thinking about why you want to take pictures, the kind of pictures you'll be taking, and under what circumstances you'll be clicking the shutter. Since there's no one ideal camera for all photographers, knowing what you need will make it much easier to shop for camera equipment. Do you want to take large-format landscape pictures on sheet film? How about using a 35mm SLR and bringing a few lenses along? Or, perhaps a compact 35mm rangefinder is best?

Photography is a very complex subject. A detailed discussion of camera equipment is beyond the scope of this book. But if you want to learn more, talk to your photo dealer or look at the large selection of HPBooks photobooks at your local camera or book store. Or, take a photography class. Many are offered through schools, community colleges and local camera shops.

PHOTO ACCESSORIES

Outdoor photographers generally buy some accessories to protect their camera, make their job easier, and improve the quality of their pictures. The most commonly purchased accessories are camera cases, bags, straps and tripods.

Large gadget bags such as these meet the needs of outdoor photographers who may need to carry several cameras, lenses and lots of film.

Most outdoor photographers prefer to carry their cameras on their neck. A wide neck strap will be comfortable if you have to carry your camera for a long time.

This special camera strap clips around your back, holding the camera snugly against your body. If you need to take a picture, you can release the camera quickly.

Cases And Bags—You may want a case to protect your camera from the occasional bumps that occur in outdoor activities. Usually, cases fit only a camera fitted with wide-angle or standard lenses. Most photographers keep their telephoto lenses in separate cases. The problem with having a case is that you may need to use your camera quickly. Having it in a case slows you down.

You can put extra lenses in their own cases or in a gadget bag large enough to carry all of your photography equipment. Backpackers may want to purchase a rugged, padded case that lets you pack your lenses without fear of damage. Some bags use shoulder straps. Others attach to your waist like a fanny pack.

Straps—Your camera may come with a shoulder or neck strap, or a small wrist loop. Most serious photographers prefer to carry their cameras on their necks, even when hiking, so it's handy when they want to shoot. Make sure your strap is wide enough to be comfortable when worn for hours. You can buy special straps that clip around your back, holding your camera firm against your chest. This is a handy feature for hikers, climbers and cross-country skiers.

Tripods And Clamps—A tripod is almost a necessity on those occasions when you have trouble holding the camera still, such as when you're using a heavy telephoto lens or shooting long-exposure photos.

Tripods need to be stable, but many of the best models are too heavy to carry in a pack. If you need to carry your tripod on your back, look for a special backpacker's tripod. They are light, compact and stable enough for most 35mm cameras.

Many backpackers have found camera clamps to be a lightweight, compact alternative to a tripod. You can screw the clamp on to an ice axe, pack frame, ski pole, tree limb or any one of many other places. One model even has small legs, so it can function as a small tripod.

A variety of pocket tripods and clamps are available for backpackers who want to take long-exposure photos. This clamp attaches to the end of a ski pole. Others clamp to ice axes, pack frames or stand on small legs.

Altimeters

An altimeter is a route-finding device that indicates elevation by measuring air pressure. Most hiking and backpacking involve elevation gain or loss. As you climb higher, the air pressure decreases and your elevation gain is registered on the altimeter. With an accurate altimeter, a topographic map and a compass, you can precisely determine your location. Even if a thick fog or forest renders the compass useless, you may still be able to find where you are with an altimeter.

An altimeter is actually a barometer with a scale calibrated in feet. In addition, it has an inches-of-mercury scale used in weather forecasting.

Altimeters are *aneroid,* meaning they operate without liquid. Instead of using a column of mercury to measure pressure, most have a hollow metal capsule capable of sensing minute changes in air pressure. As air pressure changes, the capsule contracts or expands. These changes are mechanically magnified and transferred to the needle, which indicates your elevation above sea level.

Air pressure changes as weather changes. Because altimeters respond to those changes too, you can't rely on your altimeter to be a perfect measure of altitude. It is more useful as a gauge of elevation change over a short period of time and distance.

It's possible, however, to compensate somewhat for changing air pressures. If you reach a reference point—a summit, lake or pass—that has its elevation marked on the map or trail marker, you can reset your altimeter to the correct reading.

Obviously, altimeters can be very useful in weather forecasting. If you are located at a fixed elevation and the altimeter registers an altitude gain, you can be sure the air pressure has dropped, a possible indication of approaching bad weather. Similarly, a "drop" in altitude indicates that pressure is rising, usually a sign of improving weather.

An altimeter measures atmospheric pressure, registering your approximate elevation. When used in conjunction with a topographic map, it's possible to get a good approximation of your location.

Water-Purification Kits

Pollution of backcountry water sources is becoming more and more severe. Just a few years ago, hikers could trust any swift-moving stream. Now, caution is required for almost all water sources.

Two purification methods—boiling or treating the water with iodine tablets—are still practical and effective. But some hikers prefer water-purification kits. They're faster than either of the other methods, and because less iodine is used, the water tastes better.

Purification kits consist of a filter that removes large debris and microscopic particles down to a certain size. The water is further purified by a chemically treated element of activated charcoal and iodine crystals. Finally, a "booster" of iodine kills remaining bacteria. Make sure you carefully read the instructions that come with your kit.

Purification kits are light and compact enough to accommodate a backpacker's needs. A pocket purifier is an interesting variation on the standard kit. It has a five-stage purifying element inside a straw-like case. You draw the water through the filter by sucking on the end, just like a straw.

This water-treatment kit filters particles and kills potentially harmful bacteria.

Insect Repellent

A variety of methods—both practical and impractical—have been devised to thwart the onslaught of flying and biting insects. Campfire smoke works, as does a stiff breeze. But lacking either of these, you'll have to take other action. Because it's usually impossible to cover your whole body with clothing, we recommend insect repellent.

The best commercially available repellents use the same chemical—N,N-diethyl-metatoluamide (DEET).

DEET appears in widely differing concentrations, from 100% to 19%, depending on the product. If you are headed into an area with major insect populations, it's a good idea to find a product with a high percentage of DEET. The label will always tell you.

DEET can be harmful to some plastics, so be careful when applying it near your watch crystal, glasses or knife handle.

Insect repellents come in various forms—liquids, cream, roll-on solid, aerosol and foam.

Be sure to check the label on insect repellents to find the percentage of DEET in the solution.

Sunburn Preventive

Sunlight and ultraviolet rays, especially at high altitudes, have the potential to burn human skin badly. The best protection is to cover your skin with clothing. But, for unprotected areas, plan ahead and have some sunburn preventive available.

Most effective sunburn preventives use para-amino benzoic acid (PABA). At concentrations as low as 5%, PABA blocks all ultraviolet rays, and your skin won't burn. This protection is usually rated with a skin-protection factor (SPF), ranging from 2 to 15. The higher the number, the greater the protection offered.

Mountaineers climbing at high altitudes over snow and ice are doubly vulnerable. They must make sure that every square inch of exposed skin is protected, including lips, ears and nostrils. Clown white and zinc-oxide paste block all ultraviolet rays. These are greasy enough to resist perspiration and not wash off.

OUTDOOR-EQUIPMENT CHECKLIST

Photocopy this form and use it when planning and packing for an outdoor excursion. Depending on the activity, you may need more or less than what's shown here. Use the blank spaces to include items important to what you'll be doing.

10 ESSENTIALS
Have these for any trip:
_____ Map of area
_____ Compass
_____ Flashlight with extra batteries & bulbs
_____ Extra food
_____ Matches in waterproof container

_____ Sunglasses
_____ First-aid kit
_____ Pocket knife
_____ Extra clothing
_____ Firestarter

OTHER ESSENTIALS
Useful for most activities:
_____ Sunburn preventive
_____ Toilet paper

_____ Insect repellent
_____ Full water bottle

FOR OVERNIGHT TRIPS
_____ Pack
_____ Ground cloth
_____ Sleeping pad/insulation
_____ Stove, fuel & accessories
_____ Food
_____ General-purpose repair kit
_____ _____
_____ _____
_____ _____
_____ _____

_____ Sleeping bag
_____ Shelter & repair kit
_____ Eating utensils
_____ Pots, pans & accessories
_____ Personal hygiene kit
_____ Change of clothing
_____ _____
_____ _____
_____ _____
_____ _____

CLOTHING
Be sure to prepare for the worst conditions:
_____ Boots
_____ Gaiters
_____ Pants
_____ Sweater, down vest
_____ Parka
_____ Gloves or mittens
_____ Wind pants
_____ _____
_____ _____
_____ _____

_____ Socks (have extras)
_____ Underwear
_____ Shorts
_____ Shirt(s)
_____ Hat
_____ Rain gear
_____ Sneakers
_____ _____
_____ _____
_____ _____

MISCELLANEOUS
_____ Camera & film
_____ Altimeter
_____ Emergency whistle, shelter
_____ Water purifier
_____ _____

_____ Book
_____ Binoculars
_____ Handkerchief
_____ Pad & pencil
_____ _____

SELECTED BIBLIOGRAPHY

General
Fletcher, Colin, *The New Complete Walker.* Alfred Knopf, 1978.
Manning, Harvey, *Backpacking: One Step at a Time.* Vintage, 1980.
Rethmel, R.C. *Backpacking.* Follet, 1979.
Wood, Robert S., *Pleasure Packing For The 80's.* Ten Speed Press, 1980.

Outdoor Food & Cooking
Barker, Harriet, *The One-Burner Gourmet.* Contemporary Books, 1981.
Bunnelle, Hasse, *Food For Knapsackers.* Sierra Club, 1982.
DeLong, Deanna, *How to Dry Foods.* HPBooks, 1979.
Eliason, Harward and Westover, *Make-A-Mix Cookery.* HPBooks, 1977.
Fleming, June, *The Well Fed Backpacker.* Random House, 1976.
Robertson, Laurel, Carol Flinders and Bronwen Godfrey, *Laurel's Kitchen.* Nilgiri Press, 1978.

Cross-Country Skiing & Snowshoeing
Barnett, Steve, *Cross-Country Downhill.* Pacific Search Press, 1979.
Brady, Michael, *Cross-Country Ski Gear.* The Mountaineers, 1979.
Gillette, Ned, *Cross-Country Skiing.* The Mountaineers, 1979.
Prater, Gene, *Snowshoeing.* The Mountaineers, 1980.

Mountaineering
Chouinard, Yvon, *Climbing Ice.* Sierra Club, 1978.
Peters, Ed, Ed., *Mountaineering, The Freedom of the Hills.* The Mountaineers, 1982.
Robbins, Royal, *Basic Rockcraft.* La Siesta Press, 1982.
Robbins, Royal, *Advanced Rockcraft.* La Siesta Press, 1982.

Bicycles & Cycling Accessories
Ballantine, Richard, *Richard's Bicycle Book.* Ballantine Books, 1982.
Cuthbertson, Tom, *The Bike Bag Book.* Ten Speed Press, 1981.
Kolin, Michael J. and Denise M. de la Rosa, *The Custom Bicycle.* Rodale Press, 1979.
Lieb, Thom, *Everybody's Book of Bicycle Riding.* Rodale Press, 1981.
Sanders, William, *Backcountry Bikepacking.* Rodale Press, 1982.
Sloane, Eugene A., *The New Complete Book of Bicycling.* Simon and Schuster, 1980.

Canoes, Kayaks & Inflatable Rafts
Deschner, Whit, *Does The Wet Suit You?.* Eddie Tern Press, 1981.
Harrison, Dave, *Canoeing.* Sports Illustrated, 1981.
Rugge, John and James West Davidson, *The Complete Wilderness Paddler.* Alfred Knopf, 1981.
Tejada-Flores, Lito, *Wildwater.* Sierra Club, 1978.
Watters, Ron, *The White-Water River Book.* Pacific Search Press, 1982.

Map, Compass & Navigation
Bengsston, Hans and George Atkinson, *Orienteering For Sport and Pleasure.* Stephen Greene Press, 1977.
Fleming, June, *Staying Found.* Vintage, 1982.
Kjellstrom, Bjorn, *Be An Expert With Map and Compass.* Charles Scribner's & Sons, 1976.

Outdoor Photography
Krohn, Michael, *Photography For the Hiker and Backpacker.* Signpost Books, 1979.
Maye, Patricia, *Field Book of Nature Photography.* Sierra Club, 1979.

First Aid
Curtis, Lindsay, M.D., *How To Save A Life Using CPR.* HPBooks, 1981.
Darvill, Fred T., *Mountaineering Medicine.* Skagit Mountain Rescue Unit, 1979.
Mitchell, Dick, *Mountaineering First Aid.* The Mountaineers, 1980.
Wilkerson, James A., M.D., *Medicine for Mountaineering.* The Mountaineers, 1982.

INDEX

ACKNOWLEDGEMENTS

This book was a group effort at every step of the way. The staff at REI spent countless hours sharing their knowledge and experience, reviewing the manuscript, and producing the many excellent illustrations.

Heading the REI team was the editorial committee of Dennis Madsen, Sue Brockmann, Ellen Moyer, Kathleen Nichols and Larry Ferguson.

The REI experts who provided valuable information in their specialty and then reviewed the manuscript were Carol Burrell, Dave Chantler, Denise Friend, Cal Magnussen, Ernst Meinhart, Carol Momoda, Mary Peterson, Mike Roberts, Gary Rose, Terry Shively, Suzanne Silletto, Dane Straub, Bill Sumner, Katie Waldrop and Jerry Watt.

Jerry Crick directed photography and graphics, and was assisted by Karin Anderson.

Treva Hoefert typed the final manuscript and attended to the myriad administrative details associated with a book of this scope.

5.738398562843